Learning Ionic

Build real-time and hybrid mobile applications with Ionic

Arvind Ravulavaru

BIRMINGHAM - MUMBAI

Learning Ionic

First published: July 2015

Production reference: 1220715

Published by Packt Publishing Ltd.
Livery Place
35 Livery Street
Birmingham B3 2PB, UK.

ISBN 978-1-78355-260-3

www.packtpub.com

Credits

Author
Arvind Ravulavaru

Reviewers
Bramus Van Damme
Ian Pridham
Indermohan Singh

Commissioning Editor
Dipika Gaonkar

Acquisition Editor
Vivek Anantharaman

Content Development Editor
Merwyn D'souza

Technical Editor
Shashank Desai

Copy Editors
Stephen Copestake
Relin Hedly

Project Coordinator
Nikhil Nair

Proofreader
Safis Editing

Indexer
Monica Ajmera Mehta

Graphics
Disha Haria

Production Coordinator
Arvindkumar Gupta

Cover Work
Arvindkumar Gupta

Foreword

This book is the result of several months of dedicated work by Arvind Ravulavaru, a dedicated developer and writer, with whom I've had the pleasure of collaborating on several occasions. This book provides a great way to get started with Ionic and provides detailed examples from which even experienced developers can learn.

Arvind takes you through the process of installing everything you need to get started with Ionic. He also shows you how to set up native SDKs. Further, Arvind covers the basics of Ionic, such as Ionic's components, navigation using the UI-router, custom styles, and the APIs provided by Ionic. Thus, readers can build two apps: a bookstore app and a real-time chat application.

For experienced developers, the book explains how to enable native device APIs through Cordova's plugins. You'll learn how to use ngCordova (another project by the Ionic team) and Cordova plugins in an AngularJS syntax. In the chat application, you'll see how to connect to external databases, such as Firebase. You will also see how to keep your data in sync with all devices.

Prior to joining Ionic as a core team member and a developer advocate, I worked for another company, where I created many internal hybrid apps. After evaluating other frameworks, I chose Ionic because it offered the only complete solution for hybrid mobile development. Everything I needed to get going was provided by Ionic. Instead of focusing on how to architect my app, I could focus on just building the app.

Ionic offers a complete ecosystem for hybrid mobile app development, saves costs, and offers a high-performance, beautiful alternative to native development. We released the stable version of Ionic in May and then released alpha versions of three of our platform services this summer. We don't have any plans to slow down; our support for the open source Ionic SDK will always remain strong. At Ionic, I worked with experienced and new developers, traveled all over the world to teach newbies, and researched code with Ionic pros. I'm constantly impressed with how much people love the product and with what a dynamic and positive community we have.

You'll find this book to be a great introduction to Ionic. It will give you a chance to learn some more about the SDK. Thank you for being part of the Ionic community.

Enjoy!

Mike Hartington
Core Team Member, Ionic

About the Author

Arvind Ravulavaru is a full-stack consultant with over 6 years of experience in software development. For the last 2 years, he has been working extensively on JavaScript, both on the server side and the client side. Prior to that, Arvind worked on big data analytics, cloud provisioning, and orchestration. He has good exposure to various databases and has also developed and architected an application that was built using Java and ASP.NET.

A year and a half ago, Arvind started a blog titled The Jackal of JavaScript (`http://thejackalofjavascript.com`), where he writes about developing full-stack applications using JavaScript alone as the server-side and client-side programming language. He has written articles on various topics, such as DNA analysis, sentiment analysis with JavaScript, programming Raspberry Pi with JavaScript, and building a node-webkit and a WebRTC-based video chat client, to name a few.

Apart from this, Arvind provides training, empowering companies with the latest and greatest technology available in the market. He also conducts start up workshops, where he teaches rapid prototyping with today's amazing tool stack. Arvind also provides information on how to take ideas to the market in a very short span of time.

He always looks for ways to contribute to the open source community, making this world a better place for developers. As a consultant, Arvind always tries to power amazing business ideas with awesome technology solutions (language-agnostic), moving the human race up the evolution chain.

Arvind recently started his own company in Hyderabad, where he is building products in the Internet of Things space. The aim of the company is to build IoT products for the world at an affordable price so that everyone can enjoy technology that powers lives.

You can reach Arvind on his blog at `http://thejackalofjavascript.com`.

Arvind has also reviewed *Data-oriented Development with AngularJS, Manoj Waikar, Packt Publishing*.

Acknowledgments

First of all, I would like to thank Steve Jobs for being my inspiration and motivation throughout. Selling something that a person does not need at a fancy price is not an easy job. He has done this time and again, right from Mac books to Apple watches. R.I.P, Mr. Jobs.

I don't think a simple thank you would suffice in appreciating what my family has done for me, especially my mother. They have always been there for me through good and bad times, sharing my happiness and encouraging me whenever I was down. I could not have made it so far without their help and support.

I would like to send out a special thank you to Nicholas Gault and Andrew Nuss for all the learning, support, and encouragement that they have provided me so far.

I would like to thank Udaykanth Rapeti for preaching me these golden words: "create a digital presence if you want to really succeed" and for always being there for me. A special thanks to Karthik Naidu, Pavan Musti, and the gang I worked with at Deloitte. The times could not have been better!

I would like to thank Ali Baig, the self-proclaimed yoda, for all the advice and ideas he keeps sharing with me. Keep them coming! A big shout out to the fresher batch at Accenture and the Cactus gang. I cherish each moment I spent with you guys, learning, playing, and rocking! Go Cactus, go!

I would like to take a moment to thank my first love. You have taught me a lot of things and made me a better person. Our breakup was one of the motivations to keep myself busy in technology, which definitely added to where I am today. Thank you so much for everything.

Writing nine chapters and an appendix is a humongous task. Imagine editing and reviewing the same. My sincere thanks to Merwyn D'souza, the content development editor of the book, and the reviewers, Bramus Van Damme, Ian Pridham, and Indermohan Singh. This book is in a lot better shape because of you guys. I am honored to have worked with Shashank Desai, the technical editor of this book. I am very happy that this is his last book before he moves on as a project manager. Congrats! Also, thanks to Nikhil Nair and everyone from the Packt Publishing team for making this possible.

A special shout out to Hemal Desai for finding me and getting me on board to write this book. This book wouldn't have happened without her.

A big thumbs up to my blog readers. You guys rock!

Last but not least, my respect to the Robin Hoods of the developer community, who develop and share free code!

About the Reviewers

Bramus Van Damme is a web enthusiast from Belgium and has been interested in "all things web" ever since he, as a kid, discovered the Internet back in 1997.

Professionally, after having worked as a web developer for several years at several web agencies, he became a lecturer of web technologies at a technical university in Belgium. Apart from teaching basic HTML, CSS, and JavaScript to students, Bramus also taught them how to write proper SQL statements. As a lecturer, he was also responsible for authoring and maintaining the server-side web scripting (PHP) and web and mobile development specialty courses.

Having worked in the education space for 7 years, he moved on to become a part of the team at Small Town Heroes (Ghent, Belgium) to build groundbreaking solutions and make watching TV more interactive than ever.

Bramus also freelances using the 3RDS moniker (`https://www.bram.us/2014/03/26/on-web-development-and-education/`). On a regular basis, he can be found attending and speaking at web meetups and conferences. Seeing a nice piece of optimized and secure code can put a smile on his face.

In his spare time, he likes to goof around with web-related technologies, keep his blog (`https://www.bram.us/`) up to date, and go scuba diving. Being a scout, he has grown to become quite a mapping aficionado. Combined with his technical knowledge, this has led to him to review *Google Maps JavaScript API Cookbook, Packt Publishing*.

He lives in Vinkt (Belgium) with his son, Finn, and his daughter, Tila. He prefers cats over dogs.

Ian Pridham is a freelance full-stack developer with over 15 years of experience. He is based in London. Ian created the electric vehicle charge point API for the Department of Transport (a government client) and developed the site for SB.TV, the UK's leading online youth broadcaster (a consumer client). This site was featured on Google Chrome's television advertisements. Ian provides consultancy and development services to start-ups with AngularJS/Ionic to rapidly bring ideas to the market. He works as a CTO at OpenPlay, an activity marketplace platform.

Indermohan Singh is an Ionic developer and a passionate budding entrepreneur, running a mobile app development studio in the beautiful city of Ludhiana. He is the founder of Ragakosh, the Indian classical music learning app. Indermohan blogs at `http://inders.in` and hosts the AngularJS Ludhiana meetup. He is also the developer of Ionic plugins for Sublime Text and Atom Editor. When he is not in front of his laptop, you can find him singing with his tanpura.

I am thankful to my family—my father, mother, and brother for giving me full support during the reviewing process. I also want to thank God for giving me the strength and education that helped me review this wonderful book.

---

www.PacktPub.com

Support files, eBooks, discount offers, and more

For support files and downloads related to your book, please visit www.PacktPub.com.

Did you know that Packt offers eBook versions of every book published, with PDF and ePub files available? You can upgrade to the eBook version at www.PacktPub.com and as a print book customer, you are entitled to a discount on the eBook copy. Get in touch with us at service@packtpub.com for more details.

At www.PacktPub.com, you can also read a collection of free technical articles, sign up for a range of free newsletters and receive exclusive discounts and offers on Packt books and eBooks.

https://www2.packtpub.com/books/subscription/packtlib

Do you need instant solutions to your IT questions? PacktLib is Packt's online digital book library. Here, you can search, access, and read Packt's entire library of books.

Why Subscribe?

- Fully searchable across every book published by Packt
- Copy and paste, print, and bookmark content
- On demand and accessible via a web browser

Free Access for Packt account holders

If you have an account with Packt at www.PacktPub.com, you can use this to access PacktLib today and view 9 entirely free books. Simply use your login credentials for immediate access.

Thanks to Mike Hartington for taking time from his busy schedule, reviewing the book, and providing valuable insights on Ionic.

Knowing is different and doing is different.

Table of Contents

Preface

Build mobile hybrid applications with ease using Ionic. Be it simple apps that integrate REST API endpoints or complicated apps that involve native features, Ionic provides a simple API to work with them.

With a basic knowledge of HTML, CSS, and a decent knowledge of AngularJS, one can easily convert a million-dollar idea into an app with a few lines of code.

In this book, we will explore how you can do this.

What this book covers

Chapter 1, Ionic – Powered by AngularJS, introduces you to the power of AngularJS. This is why it is considered a good framework for a hybrid framework, such as Ionic.

Chapter 2, Welcome to Ionic, talks about the Mobile Hybrid framework: Cordova. It shows how Ionic fits into the bigger picture. This chapter also shows you how to install the required software for the development of the Ionic framework.

Chapter 3, Ionic CSS Components and Navigation, tells you how to use Ionic as a CSS framework for your mobile web applications. This chapter also talks about how to integrate Ionic CSS only components with AngularJS, apart from routing in Ionic apps.

Chapter 4, Ionic and SCSS, explores how to theme Ionic apps with the help of built-in SCSS support.

Chapter 5, Ionic Directives and Services, provides information on how to use Ionic's built-in directives and services, which helps to quickly bring your application to life.

Chapter 6, Building a Bookstore App, deals with how you can leverage the knowledge you have gained so far in building an Ionic client for a secured REST API. This chapter walks you through the itsy-bitsy pieces that are needed to develop Ionic apps that will simply consume REST API endpoints.

Chapter 7, Cordova and ngCordova, talks about how you can easily integrate device features, such as camera and Bluetooth, with the help of Cordova and ngCordova in your Ionic apps.

Chapter 8, Building a Messaging App, shows you how you can use all the knowledge that you have gained so far to build a messaging app, where users can register, log in, and chat with each other and share pictures and locations.

Chapter 9, Releasing the Ionic App, focuses on how to generate installers for the apps that you have built with Cordova and Ionic using the Ionic CLI and the PhoneGap build.

Appendix, Additional Topics and Tips, discusses how to efficiently use the Ionic CLI and Ionic cloud services to build, deploy, and manage your Ionic applications.

What you need for this book

To start building Ionic apps, you need to have a basic knowledge of HTML, CSS, JavaScript, and AngularJS. A good knowledge of mobile application development, device native features, and Cordova is preferred.

You will need Node.js, Cordova CLI, and Ionic CLI installed to work with Ionic. If you are planning to add theming support and other third-party libraries, you will need Git and Bower. If you want to work with device features, such as camera or Bluetooth, you need to have their mobile OS set up on your machine.

Who this book is for

This book is intended for those who want to learn how to build hybrid mobile applications using Ionic. It is also ideal for people who want to work with theming Ionic apps, integrating with the REST API, and learning more about device features, such as camera or Bluetooth, using ngCordova.

Prior knowledge of AngularJS is essential to complete this book successfully.

Conventions

In this book, you will find a number of text styles that distinguish between different kinds of information. Here are some examples of these styles and an explanation of their meaning.

Code words in text, database table names, folder names, filenames, file extensions, pathnames, dummy URLs, user input, and Twitter handles are shown as follows: "It wraps `setTimeInterval()` and returns a promise when you register this service."

A block of code is set as follows:

```
myApp.controller('logCtrl', ['$log', function($log) {

    $log.log('Log Ctrl Initialized');

    }]);
```

Any command-line input or output is written as follows:

```
# ionic server -l -c
```

New terms and **important words** are shown in bold. Words that you see on the screen, for example, in menus or dialog boxes, appear in the text like this: "In the popup, you will notice that the **Login** button uses the positive class for styling."

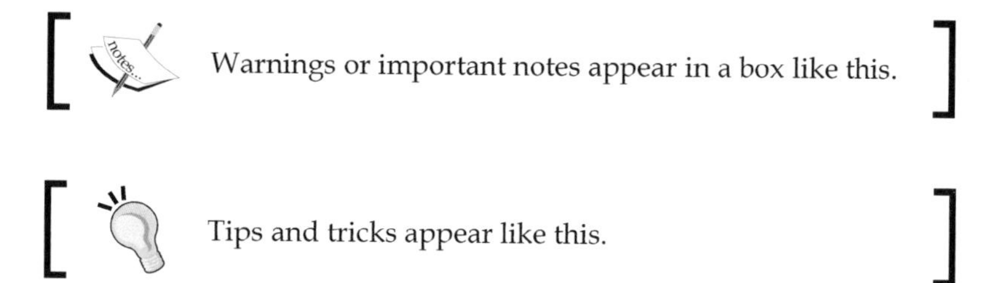

Warnings or important notes appear in a box like this.
Tips and tricks appear like this.

Reader feedback

Feedback from our readers is always welcome. Let us know what you think about this book—what you liked or disliked. Reader feedback is important for us as it helps us develop titles that you will really get the most out of.

To send us general feedback, simply e-mail feedback@packtpub.com, and mention the book's title in the subject of your message.

If there is a topic that you have expertise in and you are interested in either writing or contributing to a book, see our author guide at www.packtpub.com/authors.

Customer support

Now that you are the proud owner of a Packt book, we have a number of things to help you to get the most from your purchase.

Downloading the example code

You can download the example code files from your account at http://www.packtpub.com for all the Packt Publishing books you have purchased. If you purchased this book elsewhere, you can visit http://www.packtpub.com/support and register to have the files e-mailed directly to you. You can access the code, raise issues, chat with the author, and clear your queries at GitHub (https://github.com/learning-ionic).

Downloading the color images of this book

We also provide you with a PDF file that has color images of the screenshots/diagrams used in this book. The color images will help you better understand the changes in the output. You can download this file from: http://www.packtpub.com/sites/default/files/downloads/26030S_ColoredImages.pdf

Errata

Although we have taken every care to ensure the accuracy of our content, mistakes do happen. If you find a mistake in one of our books—maybe a mistake in the text or the code—we would be grateful if you could report this to us. By doing so, you can save other readers from frustration and help us improve subsequent versions of this book. If you find any errata, please report them by visiting http://www.packtpub.com/submit-errata, selecting your book, clicking on the **Errata Submission Form** link, and entering the details of your errata. Once your errata are verified, your submission will be accepted and the errata will be uploaded to our website or added to any list of existing errata under the Errata section of that title.

To view the previously submitted errata, go to https://www.packtpub.com/books/content/support and enter the name of the book in the search field. The required information will appear under the **Errata** section.

Piracy

Piracy of copyrighted material on the Internet is an ongoing problem across all media. At Packt, we take the protection of our copyright and licenses very seriously. If you come across any illegal copies of our works in any form on the Internet, please provide us with the location address or website name immediately so that we can pursue a remedy.

Please contact us at copyright@packtpub.com with a link to the suspected pirated material.

We appreciate your help in protecting our authors and our ability to bring you valuable content.

Questions

If you have a problem with any aspect of this book, you can contact us at questions@packtpub.com, and we will do our best to address the problem.

1
Ionic – Powered by AngularJS

Ionic is one of the most widely used mobile hybrid frameworks. It has more than 17,000 stars and more than 2,700 forks on GitHub at the time of writing this chapter. Ionic is built on top of AngularJS, a super heroic framework for building MVW apps. In this introductory chapter, we will take a look at AngularJS and understand how it powers Ionic. We will take a look at a couple of key AngularJS components, named directives, and services that are widely used when working with Ionic.

This book assumes that you have basic to intermediate knowledge of AngularJS. If not, you can follow the book *AngularJS Essentials, Rodrigo Branas*, or the video *Learning AngularJS, Jack Herrington*, both by *Packt Publishing*, to get yourself acquainted with AngularJS.

In this chapter, I will explain only AngularJS directives and services. For other core AngularJS concepts, refer to the book/video mentioned earlier.

In this chapter, we will cover the following topics:

- What is separation of concerns?
- How does AngularJS solve this problem?
- What are AngularJS built-in directives and custom directives?
- What are AngularJS services and how do custom services work?
- How are directives and services leveraged in Ionic?

Understanding the separation of concerns

Server-side web applications have been around for quite some time now. However, the Web is evolving at such a fast pace that we are driving applications from the client-side rather than the server-side. Gone are those days when the server dictates to the client about what activities to perform and what user interface to display.

With the extensive growth of asynchronous and highly interactive web pages, the user experience can be made better with client-side driven applications than server-side driven applications. As you already know, libraries such as jQuery and Zepto help us in achieving this quite easily.

Let's take a typical use case where a user enters data in a textbox and clicks on a **Submit** button. This data is then posted to the server via AJAX, and the response is rendered in the UI without any page refresh.

If we had to replicate this using jQuery (with a pseudo syntax), it would look something like this:

```
// Assuming that jQuery is loaded and we have a textbox, a button and
a container to display the results

var textBox = $('#textbox');
var subBtn = $('#submitBtn');

subBtn.on('click', function(e) {
  e.preventDefault();
  var value = textbox.val().trim();
  if (!value) {
    alert('Please enter a value');
   return;
  }

  // Make an AJAX call to get the data
  var html2Render = '';

  $.post('/getResults', {
      query: value
    })
    .done(function(data) {
      // process the results
      var results = data.results;
      for (var i = 0; i < results.length; i++) {
```

```
            // Get each result and build a markup
            var res = results[i];
            html2Render += ' < div class = "result" > ';
            html2Render += ' < h2 > ' + res.heading + ' < /h2>';
            html2Render += ' < span > ' + res.summary + ' < /span>';
            html2Render += ' < a href = "' + res.link + '" > ' + res.
linkText + ' < /a>';
            html2Render += ' < /div>'
          }
          // Append the results HTML to the results container
          $('#resultsContainer').html(html2Render);
        });

    });
```

The preceding code is not for execution. It is just an example for reference.

When you click on the button, the textbox value is posted to the server. Then, an HTML markup is generated with results (JSON object) from the server and injected into the results container.

But, how maintainable is the preceding code?

How can you test individual pieces? For example, we want to test whether the validations work fine or whether the response is coming correctly.

Let's assume that we want to make modifications (such as adding a favicon of the resultant web page next to each search result as an inline icon) to the results template that we are building on the fly. How easy would it be to introduce this change in the preceding code?

This is a concern with separations. These separations are between validations, making AJAX requests and building markups. The concern is that they are tightly coupled with each other, and if one breaks, all would break and none of the preceding code can be reused.

If we were to separate the preceding code into various components, we would end up with a **Model View Controller** (**MVC**) architecture. In a typical MVC architecture, a model is an entity where you save the data, and a controller is where you massage the data before you display it on a view.

Unlike the server-side MVC, the client-side MVC has an extra component named the router. A router is typically a URL of the web page that dictates which model/view/controller should be loaded.

This is the basic idea behind AngularJS, and how it achieves separation of concerns and at the same time provides a single-page application architecture.

Referring to the preceding example, the server interaction layer (AJAX) would be separated from the main code and will interact with a controller on an on-demand basis.

Knowing this, we will now take a quick look at few key AngularJS components.

AngularJS components

AngularJS is driven from HTML, unlike most client-side JavaScript frameworks. In a typical web page, AngularJS takes care of wiring key pieces of code for you. So, if you add a bunch of AngularJS directives to your HTML page and include the AngularJS source file, you could easily build a simple app without writing a single line of JavaScript code.

To illustrate the preceding statement, we can build a login form with validations, without writing a single line of JavaScript.

It would look something like this:

```
<html ng-app="">
<head>
   <script src="angular.min.js" type="text/JavaScript"></script>
</head>
<body>
   <h1>Login Form</h1>
   <form name="form" method="POST" action="/authenticate">
         <label>Email Address</label>
         <input type="email" name="email" ng-model="email"
required>


         <label>Password</label>
         <input type="password" name="password" ng-
model="password" required>

         <input type="submit" ng-disabled="!email || !password"
value="Login">
   </form>
</body>
</html>
```

In the preceding code snippet, the attributes that start with `ng-` are called as AngularJS directives.

Here, the `ng-disabled` directive takes care of adding the disabled attribute to the **Submit** button when the e-mail or password is not valid.

Also, it is safe to say that the scope of the directive is limited to the element and its children on which the directive is declared. This solves another key issue with the JavaScript language where, if a variable were not declared properly, it would end up in the Global Object, that is, the Window Object.

> If you are new to scope, I recommend that you go through `https://docs.angularJS.org/guide/scope`. Without proper knowledge of scope and root scope, this book would be very difficult to follow.

Now, we will go to the next component of AngularJS named **Dependency Injection (DI)**. DI takes care of injecting units of code where required. It is one of the key enablers that help us achieve separation of concerns.

You can inject various AngularJS components, as you require. For instance, you can inject a service in a controller.

> DI is another core component of AngularJS that you need to be aware of. You can find more information at `https://docs.angularJS.org/guide/di`.

To understand services and controllers, we need to take a step back. In a typical client-side MVC framework, we know that the model stores the data, the view displays the data, and the controller massages the data present in the model before it gets displayed to the view.

In AngularJS, you can relate with the preceding line as follows:

- HTML—Views
- AngularJS controllers—Controllers
- Scope objects—Model

In AngularJS, HTML acts as the templating medium. An AngularJS controller would take the data from scope objects or the response from a service and then fuse them to form the final view that gets displayed on the web page. This is analogous to the task we did in the search example where we iterated over the results, built the HTML string, and then injected the HTML into the DOM.

Here, as you can see, we are separating the functionality into different components.

To reiterate, the HTML page acts as a template, and the factory component is responsible for making an AJAX request. Finally, the controller takes care of passing on the response from factory to the view, where the actual UI is generated.

The AngularJS version of the search engine example would be as shown here.

The `index.html` or the main page of the app would look like this:

```
<html ng-app="searchApp">
<head>
   <script src="angular.min.js" type="text/JavaScript">
   <script src="app.js" type="text/JavaScript">
</head>
<body ng-controller="AppCtrl">
   <h1>Search Page</h1>
   <form>
         <label>Search : </label>
          <input type="text" name="query" ng-model="query"
required>
          <input type="button" ng-disabled="!query" value="Search"
ng-click="search()">
   </form>

   <div ng-repeat="res in results">
         <h2>{{res.heading}}</h2>
         <span>{{res.summary}}</span>
         <a ng-href="{{res.link}}">{{res.linkText}}</a>
   </div>

</body>
</html>
```

The `app.js` would look like this:

```
var searchApp = angular.module('searchApp', []);

searchApp.factory('ResultsFactory', ['$http', function($http) {

return {

   getResults : function(query){
```

```
            return $http.post('/getResults', query);
        }

};


}]);


searchApp.controller('AppCtrl', ['$scope','ResultsFactory',function($s
cope, ResultsFactory) {

    $scope.query = '';
    $scope.results = [];

    $scope.search = function(){
            var q = {
                query : $scope.query
                };
            ResultsFactory.getResults(q)
                    .then(function(response){

                    $scope.results = response.data.results;

                    });
        }


}]);
```

In AngularJS, the factory component and the service component are interchangeably used. If you would like to know more about them, refer to the discussion on stack overflow at `http://stackoverflow.com/questions/15666048/service-vs-provider-vs-factory`.

The `index.html` file consists of the HTML template. This template is hidden by default when the page is loaded. When the results array is populated with data, the markup is generated from the template using the `ng-repeat` directive.

In `app.js`, we started off by creating a new AngularJS module with the name as `searchApp`. Then, we created a factory named `ResultsFactory`, whose sole purpose is to make an AJAX call and return a promise. Finally, we created the controller, named `AppCtrl`, to coordinate with the factory and update the view.

If you are new to promises, refer to `http://www.dwmkerr.com/promises-in-angularJS-the-definitive-guide/`.

The `search` function declared on the button's `ng-click` directive is set up in the `AppCtrl`. This button would only be enabled if valid data is entered in the search box. When the **Search** button is clicked, the listener registered in the controller is invoked. Here, we will build the `query` object needed for the server to process and call `getResults` method in `ResultsFactory`. The `getResults` method returns a promise, which gets resolved when the response from the server is back. Assuming a success scenario, we will set `$scope.results` to the search results from the server.

This modification to the `$scope` object triggers an update on all instances of the results array. This, in turn, triggers the `ng-repeat` directive on the HTML template, which parses the new `results` array and generates the markup. And voila! The UI is updated with the search results.

Downloading the example code

You can download the example code files from your account at `http://www.packtpub.com` for all the Packt Publishing books you have purchased. If you purchased this book elsewhere, you can visit `http://www.packtpub.com/support` and register to have the files e-mailed directly to you. For this chapter, you can chat with the author and clear your queries at GitHub (`https://github.com/learning-ionic/Chapter-1`).

The preceding example shows how you can structure your code in an orderly fashion that can be maintainable and testable. Now, adding an extra image next to each search result is very easy, and any developer with basic knowledge of the Web can update the application.

AngularJS directives

Quoting from the AngularJS documentation.

> *"At a high level, directives are markers on a DOM element (such as an attribute, element name, comment or CSS class) that tell AngularJS's HTML compiler ($compile) to attach a specified behavior to that DOM element or even transform the DOM element and its children."*

This is a very useful feature when you want to abstract out the common functionality on your web page. This is similar to what AngularJS has done with its directives, such as the following ones:

- `ng-app`: This initializes a new default AngularJS module when no value is passed to it; otherwise, it initializes the named module
- `ng-model`: This maps the input element's value to the current scope
- `ng-show`: This shows the DOM element when the expression passed to `ng-show` is true
- `ng-hide`: This hides the DOM element when the expression passed to `ng-hide` is true
- `ng-repeat`: This iterates the current tag and all its children based on the expression passed to `ng-repeat`

Referring to the Search App, which we built earlier, imagine that there are multiple pages in your web application that need this search form. The expected end result is pretty much the same across all pages.

So, instead of replicating the controller and the HTML template where needed, we would abstract this functionality into a custom directive.

You can initialize a new directive on a DOM element by referring to it using an attribute notation, such as `<div my-search></div>`, or you can create your own tag/element, such as `<my-search></my-search>`.

This would enable us to write the search functionality only once but use it many times. AngularJS takes care of initializing the directive when it comes into view and destroying the directive when it goes away from the view. Pretty nifty, right?

We will update our Search App by creating a new custom directive called `my-search`. The sole functionality of this directive would be to render a textbox and a button. When the user clicks on the **Search** button, we will fetch the results and display them below the search form.

So, let's get started.

As with any AngularJS component, the directives are also bound to a module. In our case, we already have a `searchApp` module. We will bind a new directive to this module:

```
searchApp.directive('mySearch', [function () {
    return {
            template : 'This is Search template',
            restrict: 'E',
```

```
        link: function (scope, iElement, iAttrs) {

        }
    };
}]);
```

The directive is named `mySearch` in camel case. AngularJS will take care of matching this directive with `my-search` when used in HTML. We will set a sample text to the `template` property. We will restrict the directive to be used as an element (`E`).

> Other values that you can restrict in an AngularJS directive are `A` (attribute), `C` (class), and `M` (comment). You can also allow the directive to use all four (ACEM) formats.

We have created a link method. This method is invoked whenever the directive comes into view. This method has three arguments injected to it, which are as follows:

- `scope`: This refers to the scope in which this tag prevails in the DOM. For example, it could be inside `AppCtrl` or even directly inside `rootScope` (`ng-app`).
- `iElement`: This is the DOM node object of the element on which the directive is present.
- `iAttrs`: These are the attributes present on the current element.

In our directive, we would not be using `iAttrs`, as we do not have any attributes on our `my-search` tag.

In complex directives, it is a best practice to abstract your directive template to another file and then refer it in the directive using the `templateUrl` property. We will do the same in our directive too.

You can create a new file named `directive.html` in the same folder as `index.html` and add the following content:

```
<form>
    <label>Search : </label>
    <input type="text" name="query" ng-model="query" required>
    <input type="button" ng-disabled="!query" value="Search" ng-
click="search()">
</form>

<div ng-repeat="res in results">
    <h2>{{res.heading}}</h2>
    <span>{{res.summary}}</span>
    <a ng-href="{{res.link}}">{{res.linkText}}</a>
</div>
```

In simple terms, we have removed all the markup in the `index.html` related to the search and placed it here.

Now, we will register a listener for the `click` event on the button inside the directive. The updated directive will look like this:

```
searchApp.directive('mySearch', [function() {
        return {
            templateUrl: './directive.html',
            restrict: 'E',
            link: function postLink(scope, iElement, iAttrs) {
                scope.search = function() {
                      var q = {
                          query : scope.query
                      };

                    // Interact with the factory (next step)
                }
            }
        };
    }])
```

As you can see from the preceding lines of code, the `scope.search` method is executed when the `click` event on the button is fired and `scope.query` returns the value of the textbox. This is quite similar to what we did in the controller.

Now, when a user clicks on the **Search** button after entering some text, we will call `getResults` method from `ResultsFactory`. Then, once the results are back, we will bind them to the `results` property on scope.

The completed directive will look like this:

```
searchApp.directive('mySearch', ['ResultsFactory',
function(ResultsFactory) {
        return {
            templateUrl: './directive.html',
            restrict: 'E',
            link: function postLink(scope, iElement, iAttrs) {
                scope.search = function() {
                      var q = {
                          query : scope.query
                      };

                    ResultsFactory.getResults(q).
then(function(response){
```

```
                        scope.results = response.data.results;
                    });
                }
            }
        };
    }])
```

With this, we can update our `index.html` to this:

```
<html ng-app="searchApp">
<head>
   <script src="angular.min.js" type="text/JavaScript"></script>
   <script src="app.js" type="text/JavaScript"></script>
</head>
<body>
   <my-search></my-search>
</body>
</html>
```

We can update our `app.js` to this:

```
var searchApp = angular.module('searchApp', []);

searchApp.factory('ResultsFactory', ['$http', function($http){

return {

   getResults : function(query){
          return $http.post('/getResults', query);
       }

};


}]);


searchApp.directive('mySearch', ['ResultsFactory',
function(ResultsFactory) {
        return {
            templateUrl: './directive.html',
            restrict: 'E',
            link: function postLink(scope, iElement, iAttrs) {
                scope.search = function() {
                    var q = {
                        query : scope.query
```

```
                        };

                    ResultsFactory.getResults(q).
then(function(response){
                        scope.results = response.data.results;
                    });
                }
            }
        };
    }]);
```

Quite simple, yet powerful!

Now, you can start sprinkling the `<my-search></my-search>` tag wherever you need a search bar.

You can take this directive to another level, where you can pass in an attribute named `results-target` to it. This would essentially be an ID of an element on the page. So, instead of showing the results below the search bar always, you can show the results inside the target provided.

AngularJS comes with a lightweight version of jQuery named jqLite. jqLite does not support selector lookup. You need to add jQuery before AngularJS for AngularJS to use jQuery instead of jqLite. You can read more about jqLite at `https://docs.angularJS.org/api/ng/function/angular.element`.

This very feature makes AngularJS directives a perfect solution for reusable components when dealing with DOM.

So, if you want to add a new navigation bar to your Ionic app, all you need to do is throw in an `ion-nav-bar` tag, such as the following one, one your page:

```
<ion-nav-bar class="bar-positive">
  <ion-nav-back-button>
  </ion-nav-back-button>
</ion-nav-bar>
```

Then, things will fall in place.

We went through the pain of understanding a custom directive so that you could easily relate to Ionic components that are built using AngularJS directives.

AngularJS services

AngularJS services are substitutable objects that can be injected into directives and controllers via Dependency Injection. These objects consist of simple pieces of business logic that can be used across the app.

AngularJS services are lazily initialized only when a component depends on them. Also, all services are singletons, that is, they get initialized once per app. This makes services perfect for sharing data between controllers and keeping them in memory if needed.

The `$interval` is another service that is available in AngularJS. The `$interval` is the same as `setTimeInterval()`. It wraps `setTimeInterval()` and returns a promise when you register this service. This promise then can be used to destroy `$interval` later on.

Another simple service is `$log`. This service logs messages to the browser console. A quick example of this would be as follows:

```
myApp.controller('logCtrl', ['$log', function($log) {

    $log.log('Log Ctrl Initialized');

    }]);
```

So, you can see the power of services and understand how simple pieces of business logic can be made reusable across the app.

You can write your own custom services that can be reused across the app. Let's say that you are building a calculator. Here, methods such as `add`, `subtract`, `multiply`, `divide`, `square`, and so on, can be part of the service.

Coming back to our Search App, we used a factory that is responsible for server-side communications. Now, we will add our own service.

Service and factory components can be used interchangeably. Refer to `http://stackoverflow.com/questions/15666048/service-vs-provider-vs-factory` for more information.

For instance, when the user searches for a given keyword(s) and posts displaying the results, we would like to save the results in the local storage. This will ensure that, next time, if the user searches with the same keyword(s), we will display the same results rather than making another AJAX call (like in offline mode).

So, this is how we will design our service. Our service will have the following three methods:

- `isLocalStorageAvailable()`: This method checks whether the current browser supports any storage API
- `saveSearchResult(keyword, searchResult)`: This method saves a keyword and search result in the local storage
- `isResultPresent(keyword)`: This method retrieves the search result for a given keyword

Our service will look as follows:

```
searchApp.service('LocalStorageAPI', [function() {
    this.isLocalStorageAvailable = function() {
         return (typeof(localStorage) !== "undefined");
    };

    this.saveSearchResult = function(keyword, searchResult) {
        return localStorage.setItem(keyword,
JSON.stringify(searchResult));
    };

    this.isResultPresent = function(keyword) {
        return JSON.parse(localStorage.getItem(keyword));
    };
}]);
```

Local storage cannot store an object. Hence, we are stringifying the object before saving and parsing the object after retrieving it.

Now, our directive will use this service while processing the search. The updated `mySearch` directive will look like this:

```
searchApp.directive('mySearch', ['ResultsFactory', 'LocalStorageAPI',
function(ResultsFactory, LocalStorageAPI) {
        return {
            templateUrl: './directive.html',
            restrict: 'E',
            link: function postLink(scope, iElement, iAttrs) {

                var lsAvailable =
LocalStorageAPI.isLocalStorageAvailable();
                scope.search = function() {
                    if (lsAvailable) {
                        var results = LocalStorageAPI.
isResultPresent(scope.query);
                        if (results) {
                            scope.results = results;
                            return;
                        }
                    }
                    var q = {
                        query: scope.query
                    };

                    ResultsFactory.getResults(q).
then(function(response) {
                        scope.results = response.data.results;
                        if (lsAvailable) {

   LocalStorageAPI.saveSearchResult(scope.query,
data.data.results);
                        }
                    });
                }
            }
        };
    }]);
```

As mentioned earlier, we will check whether local storage is available and then save and fetch the results using the `LocalStorageAPI` service.

Similarly, Ionic also provides custom services that we are going to consume. We will take a look at them in detail in *Chapter 5, Ionic Directives and Services*.

An example of an Ionic service would be the loading service. This service shows a loading bar with the text you have provided. It looks something like this:

```
$ionicLoading.show({
  template: 'Loading...'
});
```

Then, you will see an overlay that is generally used to indicate background activity and block the user from interaction.

AngularJS resources

I would like to point out a few GitHub repositories that consist of valuable AngularJS resources. You can refer to these repositories to know what is the greatest and latest in the AngularJS world. Some of the repositories are as follows:

- `jmcunningham/AngularJS-Learning` at `https://github.com/jmcunningham/AngularJS-Learning`
- `gianarb/awesome-angularjs` at `https://github.com/gianarb/awesome-angularjs`
- `aruzmeister/awesome-angular` at `https://github.com/aruzmeister/awesome-angular`

Note that the Ionic 1.0.0 that we will use throughout the book uses the AngularJS 1.3.13 version.

Summary

In this chapter, we saw what separation of concerns is and how AngularJS is designed to solve this problem. We quickly went through some of the key AngularJS components that we would use while working with Ionic. You also saw how to create custom directives and custom services, and learned about their usage. The rule of thumb while creating reusable pieces of code when working with AngularJS is to use directives when dealing with HTML elements (DOM), and services/factories otherwise.

You also understood that Ionic uses these AngularJS components to expose an easy-to-use API while building mobile hybrid apps.

In the next chapter, you will be introduced to Ionic. You will learn how to set it up, scaffold a basic app, and understand the project structure. You will also take a look at the bigger picture of developing a mobile hybrid application.

2
Welcome to Ionic

In the previous chapter, we saw a couple of key AngularJS features, namely the directives and services. In this chapter, we will understand the big picture of mobile hybrid apps, set up the required software to develop Ionic apps, and finally scaffold a few apps.

The topics covered in this chapter are as follows:

- Mobile Hybrid Architecture
- What is Apache Cordova?
- What is Ionic?
- Setting up the tools needed to develop and run Ionic apps
- Working with Ionic templates
- The Yeoman Ionic Generator

Mobile Hybrid Architecture

Before we start working with Ionic, we need to understand the bigger picture of the Mobile Hybrid platform.

The concept is pretty simple. Almost every mobile operating system (also called Platform when working with Cordova) has an API to develop apps. This API consists of a component named Web View. A Web View is typically a browser that runs inside the scope of a mobile application. This browser runs the HTML, CSS, and JS codes. This means that you can build a web page using the preceding technologies and then execute it inside your app.

You can use the same knowledge of web development to build native-hybrid mobile apps (here, native refers to installing the platform-specific format file on the device after it has been packaged along with the assets), for instance:

- Android uses Android Application Package (`.apk`)
- iOS uses iPhone Application Archive (`.ipa`)
- Windows Phone uses Application Package (`.xap`)

The package/installer consists of a piece of native code that initializes the web page and a bunch of assets needed to show the web page content.

This setup of showing a web page inside the mobile app container that consists of your application business logic is called as a Hybrid App.

What is Apache Cordova?

In simple terms, Cordova is the piece of software that stitches the web application and the native application together. The Apache Cordova website states that:

> "*Apache Cordova is a platform for building native mobile applications using HTML, CSS and JavaScript.*"

Apache Cordova does not just stitch the web app with the native app, but it also provides a set of APIs written in JavaScript to interact with the native features of the device. Yes, you can use JavaScript to access your camera, take a picture, and send it in an e-mail. Sounds exciting, right?

To get a better understanding of what is happening, let's take a look at the following image:

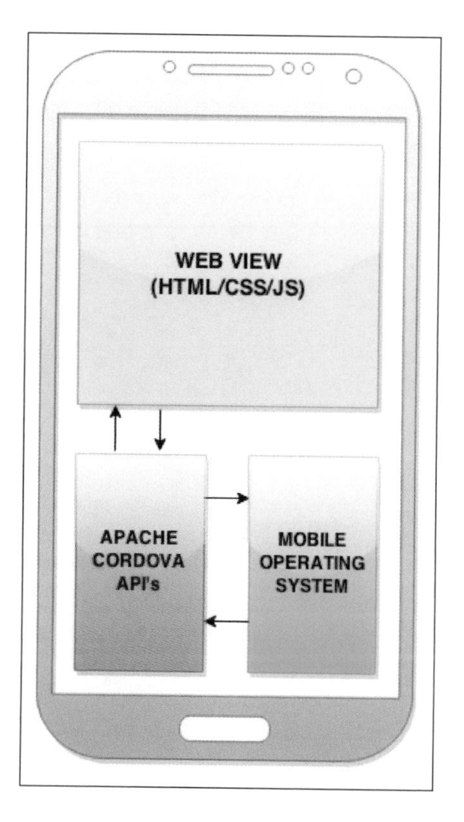

As you can see, we have a web view where the HTML/CSS/JS code gets executed. This code can be a simple standalone piece of user interface; at best you are making an AJAX request to get some data from a remote server. Or, this code can do much more, like talking to the Bluetooth of the device and getting the list of devices in the vicinity.

For this chapter, you can also access the code, raise issues, and chat with the author at GitHub (`https://github.com/learning-ionic/Chapter-2`).

In the latter case, Cordova has a bunch of APIs that interface with the web view using JavaScript and then talk to the device in its native language (for example, Java for Android), thus providing a bridge between them. For instance, if you would like to know more from the JavaScript about the device in which your app is running, all you need to do is write the following code inside the JS file:

```
var platform = device.platform;
```

After installing the device plugin, you can also access the UUID, model, OS version, and the Cordova version of the device from inside the web view using JavaScript as follows:

```
var uuid = device.uuid;
var model = device.model;
var version = device.version;
var Cordova = device.Cordova;
```

We will deal more with Cordova plugins in *Chapter 7, Cordova and ngCordova.*

The preceding explanation was to give you an idea of how Mobile Hybrid apps are structured and how you can use device features from the web view using JavaScript.

Cordova does not convert the HTML, CSS, and JS code to an OS-specific binary code. All it does is wrap the HTML, CSS, and JS code and execute it inside a web view.

So, you must have guessed by now that Ionic is the framework with which we build the HTML/CSS/JS code that runs in the web view and talks with Cordova to access device specific APIs.

What is Ionic?

Ionic is a beautiful, open source, front-end SDK for developing hybrid mobile apps with HTML5. Ionic provides mobile-optimized HTML, CSS, and JS components, as well as gestures and tools for building highly interactive apps.

Ionic is performance efficient with its minimal DOM manipulation and hardware-accelerated transitions as compared to other frameworks in this league. Ionic uses AngularJS as its JavaScript framework.

With the power of AngularJS inside a framework like Ionic, the possibilities are unlimited (you can use any AngularJS component inside Ionic as long as it makes sense in a mobile app). Ionic has a very good integration with Cordova's device API. This means that you can access device APIs using a library like ngCordova and integrate it with the beautiful user interface components of Ionic.

Ionic has its own **Command Line Interface** (**CLI**) to scaffold, develop, and deploy Ionic apps. Before we start working with the Ionic CLI, we need to set up a few pieces of software.

Software setup

Now we are going to set up all the required software needed to develop and run an Ionic app smoothly.

Install Node.js

Since Ionic uses Node.js for its CLI as well as for the build tasks, we will first install the same as follows:

1. Navigate to `https://nodejs.org/`.
2. Click on the **Install** button on the homepage and an installer for your OS will automatically be downloaded. Or you can navigate to `https://nodejs.org/download/` and download a specific copy.
3. Install Node.js by executing the downloaded installer.

To verify that Node.js has been successfully installed, open a new Terminal (`*nix` systems) or Prompt (Windows systems) and run the following command:

```
node -v
```

Now you should see the version of Node.js. Now execute the following command:

```
npm -v
```

You should see the npm version:

```
→ ~ node -v
v0.12.2
→ ~ npm -v
2.10.0
```

npm is a Node Package Manager that we will be using to download various dependencies for our Ionic Project.

> You need Node.js only during the development. The version specified in the preceding image is only for illustration. You may have the same version or the latest version of the software. This applies to all the images that show the software version in this chapter.

Install Git

Git is a free and open source distributed version control system designed to handle everything from small to very large projects with speed and efficiency. In our case, we will be using a package manager named Bower, which uses Git to download the required libraries. Also, the Ionic CLI uses Git to download the project templates.

To install Git, navigate to `http://git-scm.com/downloads` and download the installer for your platform. Once you have successfully installed it, you can navigate to your terminal/prompt and run the following command:

```
git --version
```

You should see the following output:

```
→ ~ git --version
git version 2.3.2 (Apple Git-55)
```

Install Bower

We are going to use Bower (`http://bower.io/`) to manage our application library dependencies. Bower is a package manager similar to npm but a linear/flat version of it. This kind of package manager is more suitable for downloading the assets needed for web development.

Bower is built on top of Node.js. To install Bower globally from the terminal/prompt you need to run the following command:

```
npm install bower -g
```

We are installing a node module named Bower globally. Hence, the `-g` flag. On `*nix` systems, you may need to use `sudo` to run this command:

```
sudo npm install bower -g
```

If you need `sudo` for running the preceding command, please recheck your npm installation. Refer to `http://competa.com/blog/2014/12/how-to-run-npm-without-sudo/` for more information on `sudo` less npm global installs.

Once Bower is successfully installed, you can verify the same by running the following command:

```
bower -v
```

```
→ ~ bower -v
1.4.1
```

Install Gulp

Next, we are going to install Gulp (`http://gulpjs.com/`), which is a build system that is developed on top of Node.js. Automating a lot of monotonous, tedious tasks can be taken care of by Gulp.

For instance, when your web project is ready to go live, you would want to minify the CSS, JS, and HTML, optimize the images for the Web, and push the code to your production environment; in that case, Gulp would be your go-to tool.

There are a lot of plugins in Gulp that automate most of your monotonous tasks, and it is heavily driven by the open source community. In Ionic, we will be using Gulp primarily to convert SCSS code to CSS. We use the SCSS code to customize the Ionic visual elements. We will talk more about that in *Chapter 4, Ionic and SCSS*.

To install gulp globally run the following command:

```
npm install gulp -g
```

For *nix systems, run this:

```
sudo npm install gulp -g
```

Once Gulp is successfully installed, you can verify the same by running this command:

```
gulp -v
```

```
→ ~ gulp -v
[22:17:58] CLI version 3.8.11
```

Install Sublime Text

This is a totally optional installation. Everyone has their own preferred text editor. After running around many text editors, I fell in love with Sublime Text, purely for its simplicity and the number of Plug and Play packages.

If you would like to give this editor a try, you can navigate to `http://www.sublimetext.com/3` to download Sublime Text 3.

Install Cordova and Ionic CLI

Finally, to complete the Ionic setup, we will install the Ionic CLI. Ionic CLI is a wrapper around the Cordova CLI with some additional features.

All the code examples in this book use Cordova version 5.0.0, Ionic CLI version 1.5.0, and Ionic version 1.0.0 (uranium-unicorn).

To install the Ionic CLI run the following command:

```
npm install cordova@5.0.0 ionic@1.5.0  -g
```

To verify the install run the following command:

```
cordova -v
```

You can also run this:

```
ionic -v
```

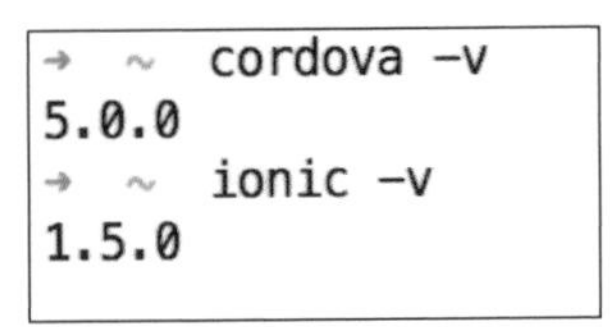

To get a feel of what Ionic CLI is packed with, run:

```
ionic
```

You should see a list of tasks as seen in the following screenshot:

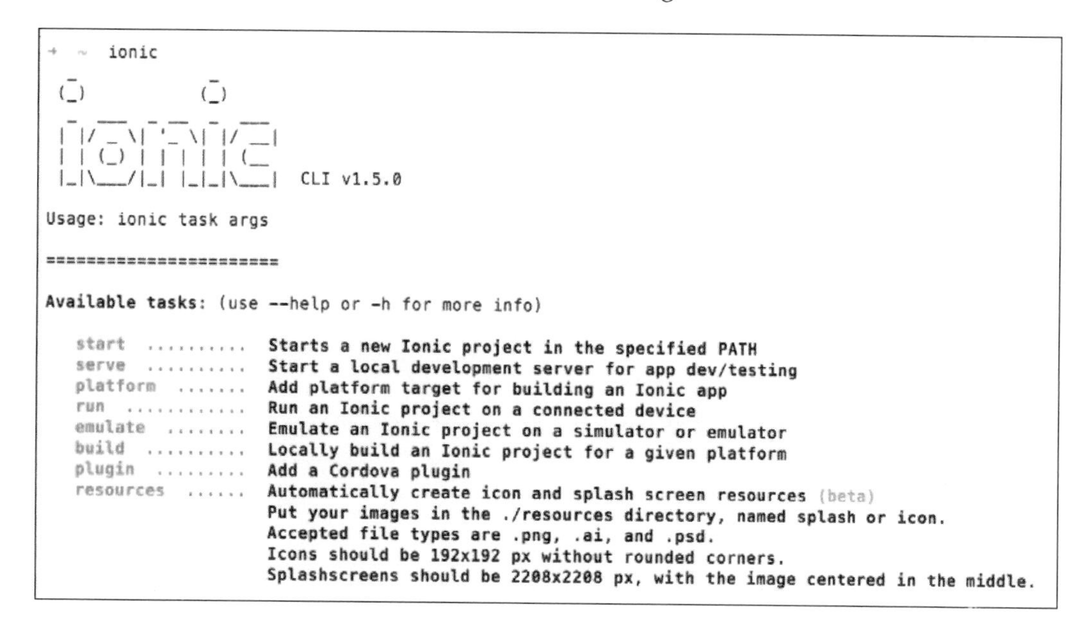

ionic
CLI v1.5.0
Usage: ionic task args
=======================
Available tasks: (use --help or -h for more info)
start .... Starts a new Ionic project in the specified PATH
serve .... Start a local development server for app dev/testing
platform .... Add platform target for building an Ionic app
run .... Run an Ionic project on a connected device
emulate .... Emulate an Ionic project on a simulator or emulator
build .... Locally build an Ionic project for a given platform
plugin .... Add a Cordova plugin
resources ...... Automatically create icon and splash screen resources (beta)
Put your images in the ./resources directory, named splash or icon.
Accepted file types are .png, .ai, and .psd.
Icons should be 192x192 px without rounded corners.
Splashscreens should be 2208x2208 px, with the image centered in the middle.

There are a few more tasks apart from the ones seen in the preceding screenshot.

You can read through the tasks and explanations to get an idea about what they do. Also, note that some of the tasks are still in beta as of today.

With this, we have completed the installation of all the software needed to develop apps with Ionic.

The platform guide

By the end of this book, we will be building apps that are ready to be deployed on to the device. Since Cordova takes HTML, CSS, and JS code as input and generates a platform-specific installer, you need to have the build environments available on your machine.

Android users can follow the instructions on the Android Platform Guide at http://cordova.apache.org/docs/en/edge/guide_platforms_android_index.md.html#Android%20Platform%20Guide to set up SDK on your local machine.

iOS users can follow the instructions from the iOS Platform Guide at http://cordova.apache.org/docs/en/edge/guide_platforms_ios_index.md.html#iOS%20Platform%20Guide to set up SDK on your local machine.

You would need an OSX environment to develop iOS apps.

As of today, Ionic supports only Android 4.0+ (although, it works on 2.3 as well) and iOS 6+ mobile platforms. But Cordova supports a few more.

You can check out the other supported platforms here: http://cordova.apache.org/docs/en/edge/guide_platforms_index.md.html#Platform%20Guides.

Hello Ionic

Now that we are done with the software setup, we will scaffold a few Ionic apps.

Ionic has three main/go-to templates using which we can quickly start developing apps:

- **Blank**: This is a blank Ionic project with one page
- **Tabs**: This is a sample app that is built using Ionic tabs
- **Side menu**: This is a sample app that is built to consume side menu driven navigation

To understand the basics of scaffolding, we will start with the blank template.

To keep our learning process clean, we will create a folder structure to work with Ionic projects. Create a folder named `ionicApps`, and then create a folder inside it called `chapter2`.

Next, open a new terminal/prompt and change the directory (`cd`) to the `ionicApps` folder and from there to `chapter2` folder. Now run the following command:

```
ionic start -a "Example 1" -i app.example.one example1 blank
```

In the preceding command:

- `-a "Example 1"`: This is the human-readable name of the app
- `-i app.example.one`: This is the app ID/reverse domain name
- `example1`: This is the name of the folder
- `blank`: This is the name of the template

Refer to the *Appendix, Additional Topics and Tips*, to know more about the Ionic start task.

The Ionic CLI is very verbose when it comes to performing tasks. As you can see from the terminal/prompt, while the project is getting created a lot of information is printed.

To start off, a new blank project is downloaded and saved to the `example1` folder. Next, the `ionic-app-base` is downloaded from the `ionic-app-base` GitHub repo, `https://github.com/driftyco/ionic-app-base`. Post that, `ionic-starter-template` is downloaded from the `ionic-starter-template` GitHub repo at `https://github.com/driftyco/ionic-starter-blank`.

After that, the config file is updated with the app name and ID. Next, a script runs and five Cordova plugins are downloaded:

- `org.apache.cordova.device` (`https://gitHub.com/apache/cordova-plugin-device`): This is used to get device information, as we have seen earlier in this chapter
- `org.apache.cordova.console` (`https://gitHub.com/apache/cordova-plugin-console`): This plugin is meant to ensure that `console.log()` is as useful as it can be
- `cordova-plugin-whitelist` (`https://github.com/apache/cordova-plugin-whitelist`): This plugin implements a whitelist policy for navigating the application web view on Cordova 4.0
- `cordova-plugin-splashscreen` (`https://github.com/apache/cordova-plugin-splashscreen`): This plugin shows and hides a splash screen during the application launch
- `com.ionic.keyboard` (`https://gitHub.com/driftyco/ionic-plugins-keyboard`): This is the keyboard plugin providing functions to make interaction with the keyboard easier, and fires events to indicate whether the keyboard will hide/show

All this information is then added to the `package.json` file and a new `ionic.project` file is created.

Once the project has been successfully created, you will see a bunch of instructions on how to proceed further. Your output should look something like the following screenshot:

```
Your Ionic project is ready to go! Some quick tips:

 * cd into your project: $ cd example1

 * Setup this project to use Sass: ionic setup sass

 * Develop in the browser with live reload: ionic serve

 * Add a platform (ios or Android): ionic platform add ios [android]
   Note: iOS development requires OS X currently
   See the Android Platform Guide for full Android installation instructions:
   https://cordova.apache.org/docs/en/edge/guide_platforms_android_index.md.html

 * Build your app: ionic build <PLATFORM>

 * Simulate your app: ionic emulate <PLATFORM>

 * Run your app on a device: ionic run <PLATFORM>

 * Package an app using Ionic package service: ionic package <MODE> <PLATFORM>

For more help use ionic --help or ionic docs

Visit the Ionic docs: http://ionicframework.com/docs


New! Add push notifications to your Ionic app with Ionic Push (alpha)!
https://apps.ionic.io/signup
+---------------------------------------------------------+
+ New Ionic Updates for June 2015
+
+ The View App just landed. Preview your apps on any device
+ http://view.ionic.io
+
+ Invite anyone to preview and test your app
+ ionic share EMAIL
+
+ Generate splash screens and icons with ionic resource
+ http://ionicframework.com/blog/automating-icons-and-splash-screens/
+
+---------------------------------------------------------+
```

To proceed further, we will use the `cd` command to go to the `example1` folder. We will not follow the instructions provided in the terminal/prompt, as we still understand the project setup. Once we have a fair idea on the various components in Ionic, we can start using the commands from the terminal/prompt output after we scaffold a new Ionic App.

Once we have changed directory to `example1` folder, we will serve the app by giving the following command:

```
ionic serve
```

This will start a new `dev` server on port `8100`, and then launch the app in your default browser. I highly recommend setting Google Chrome or Mozilla Firefox as your default browser while working with Ionic.

When the browser launches, you should see the blank template.

If you run this:

```
ionic serve
```

You will see an error as shown here:

```
→ example1  ionic serve
The port 35729 was taken on the host localhost - using port 35730 instead
Running live reload server: http://localhost:35730
Watching : [ 'www/**/*', '!www/lib/**/*' ]
Running dev server: http://localhost:8100
Ionic server commands, enter:
  restart or r to restart the client app from the root
  goto or g and a url to have the app navigate to the given url
  consolelogs or c to enable/disable console log output
  serverlogs or s to enable/disable server log output
  quit or q to shutdown the server and exit

ionic $ An uncaught exception occured and has been reported to Ionic



listen EADDRINUSE (CLI v1.5.0)

Your system information:

Cordova CLI: 5.0.0
Gulp version:  CLI version 3.8.11
Gulp local:
Ionic Version: 1.0.0
Ionic CLI Version: 1.5.0
Ionic App Lib Version: 0.1.0
ios-deploy version: 1.7.0
ios-sim version: 3.1.1
OS: Mac OS X Yosemite
Node Version: v0.12.2
Xcode version: Xcode 6.3.2 Build version 6D2105
```

This means that some other application on your machine is running on the port `8100`. To fix this, you can use any other port like `8200` while running Ionic serve:

```
ionic serve -p 8200
```

Once the application is successfully launched and we have seen the output in the browser, we will navigate back to the terminal/prompt and we should see something like the following screenshot:

```
→  example1  ionic serve
Running live reload server: http://localhost:35729
Watching : [ 'www/**/*', '!www/lib/**/*' ]
Running dev server: http://localhost:8100
Ionic server commands, enter:
  restart or r to restart the client app from the root
  goto or g and a url to have the app navigate to the given url
  consolelogs or c to enable/disable console log output
  serverlogs or s to enable/disable server log output
  quit or q to shutdown the server and exit

ionic $
```

As mentioned earlier, Ionic CLI tasks are pretty verbose. They will not leave you hanging. You can see that while the Ionic server command is running, you can type *R* and hit *Enter* and the application restarts. Similarly, you can press *C* to enable or disable printing browser JavaScript logs to the terminal/prompt.

Once you are done running the application, press *Q* and hit *Enter* to stop the server. You can do the same by pressing *Ctrl* + *C* from the keyboard.

The browser developer tools setup

Before we proceed further, I would recommend setting up the developer tools in your browser in the following format.

Google Chrome

Once the Ionic app is launched, open the developer tools by pressing *Cmd* + *Opt* + *I* on Mac and *Ctrl* + *Shift* + *I* on Windows/Linux. Then click on the last but one icon in the top row, next to the close button as seen in the following screenshot:

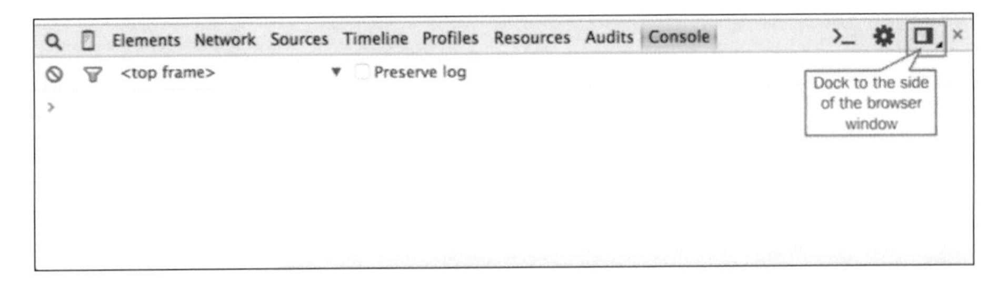

This will dock developer tools to the side of the current page. Drag the demarcation line between the browser and the developer tools till you see the view becoming similar to a mobile.

If you click on the **Elements** tab in the developer tools, you can easily inspect the page and see the output in one go, as shown in the following screenshot:

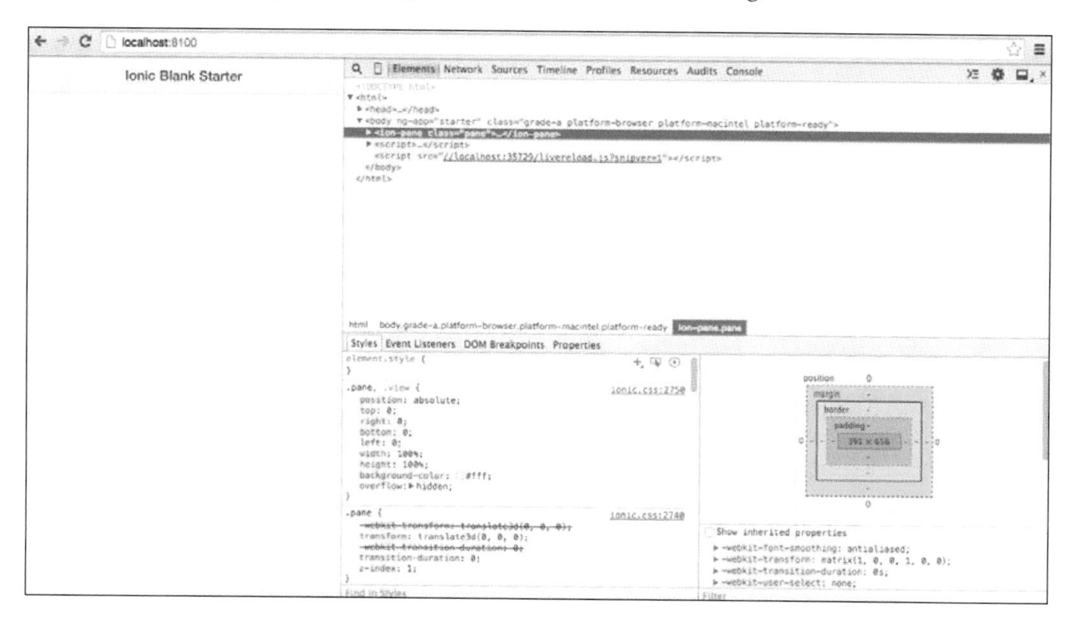

This view is very helpful for fixing errors and debugging issues.

Mozilla Firefox

If you are a Mozilla Firefox fan, you can achieve the same result as above as well. Once the Ionic app is launched, open developer tools (not Firebug, Firefox's native development tools) by pressing *Cmd* + *Opt* + *I* on Mac and *Ctrl* + *Shift* + *I* on Windows/Linux. Then click on the **Dock** to side of browser window icon, as shown in the following screenshot:

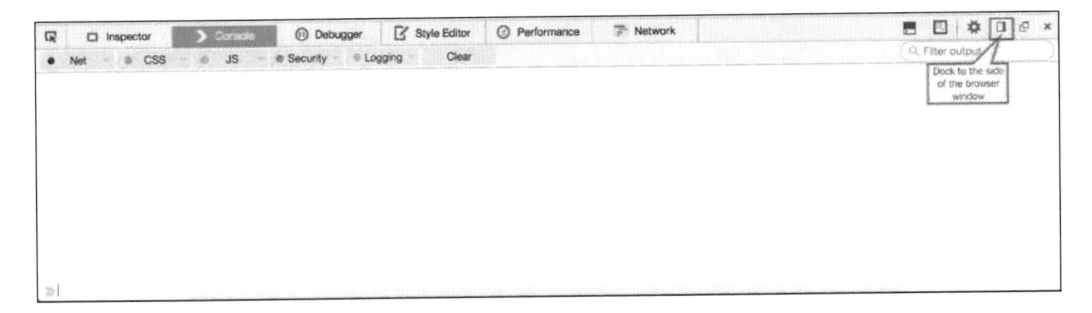

Now, you can drag the demarcation line to achieve the same result as we have seen in Chrome:

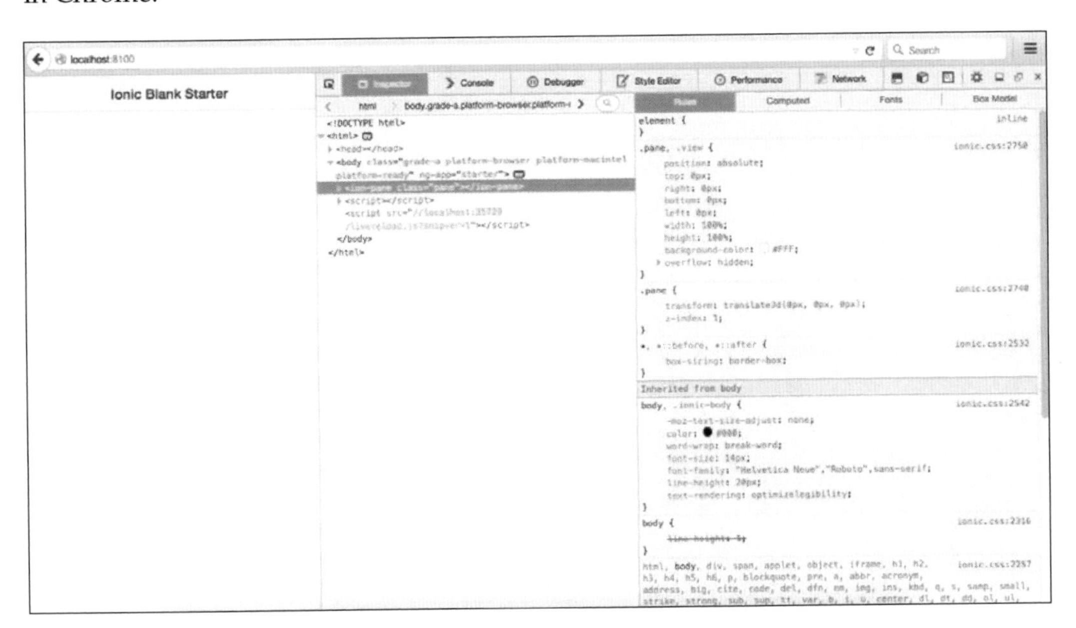

The Ionic project structure

So far, we have scaffolded a blank Ionic app and launched it in a browser. Now, we will walk through the scaffolded project structure.

To quickly remind you, we know that the Ionic sits inside the Cordova application. So before we go to the Ionic code, we will talk about the Cordova wrapper.

If you open the `chapter2 example1` folder in your text editor, you should see the following folder structure at the root of the project:

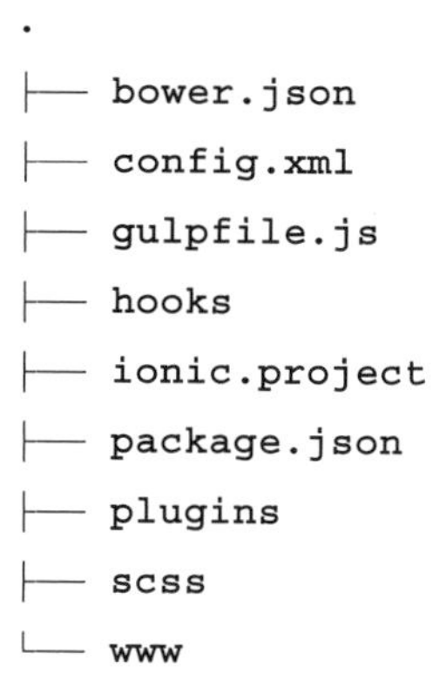

```
.
├── bower.json
├── config.xml
├── gulpfile.js
├── hooks
├── ionic.project
├── package.json
├── plugins
├── scss
└── www
```

Here is a quick explanation of each of the items:

- `bower.json`: This consists of the dependencies loaded via Bower. In future, we will install other Bower packages to be used along with our app. All the information regarding the same will be available here.
- `config.xml`: This file consists of all the meta information needed by Cordova while converting your Ionic app to a platform-specific installer. If you open config.xml, you will see a bunch of XML tags that describes your project. We will take a look at this file in detail again.
- `gulpfile.js`: This file consists of the build tasks that we would be using while developing the Ionic app.
- `ionic.project`: This file consists of the information regarding the Ionic app.

- `hooks`: This folder consists of scripts that get executed when a particular Cordova task is performed. A Cordova task can be any of the following: `after_platform_add` (after a new platform is added), `after_plugin_add` (after a new plugin is added), `before_emulate` (before emulation begins), `after_run` (before the app run), and so on. Each task is placed inside a folder named after the Cordova task. If you open the `hooks` folder, you will see an `after_prepare` folder and a `README.md` file. Inside the `after_prepare` folder, you will find a script file named `010_add_platform_class.js`. This will get executed after the prepare task of Cordova is executed. All that this task does is add a class to the `<body>` tag, which is the same name as the platform on which the app is running. This would help us in styling the app better, based on the platform. You can find a list of tasks that you can hook into from the `README.md` file present inside the `hooks` folder.
- `plugins`: This folder consists of all the plugins added to the project. We will be adding a few more plugins later on, and you can see them reflected here.
- `scss`: This folder consists of the base `scss` file which we will be overwriting to customize the styles of the Ionic components. More on this in *Chapter 4, Ionic and SCSS*.
- `www`: This folder consists of the Ionic code. Anything you write inside this folder is intended to land inside the web view. This is where we will be spending most of our time.

The config.xml file

The `config.xml` file is a platform agnostic configuration file. As mentioned earlier, this file consists of all the information needed by Cordova to convert the code in the `www` folder to the platform-specific installer.

Setting up of the `config.xml` file is based on the W3C's Packaged Web Apps (Widgets) specification (`http://www.w3.org/TR/widgets/`) and extended to specify core Cordova API features, plugins, and platform-specific settings. There are two types of configurations that you can add to this file. One is global, that is, common to all devices, and the other is specific to the platform.

If you open `config.xml` in your text editor, the first tag you encounter is the XML root tag. Next, you can see the widget tag:

```
<widget id="app.example.one" version="0.0.1" xmlns="http://www.w3.org/ns/
widgets" xmlns:cdv="http://cordova.apache.org/ns/1.0">
```

The id specified above is the reverse domain name of your app, which we provided while scaffolding. Other specifications are defined inside the widget tag as its children. The children tags include the app name (that gets displayed below the app icon when installed on the device), app description, and author details.

It also consists of the configuration that needs to be adhered to while converting code in the www folder to a native installer.

The content tag defines the starting page of the application. The access tag defines the URLs that are allowed to load in the app. By default, it loads all the URLs. The preference tag sets the various options as name value pairs. For instance, DisallowOverscroll describes if there should be any visual feedback when the user scrolls past the beginning or end of the document.

You can read more about platform-specific configurations at the following links:

- Android: http://docs.phonegap.com/en/4.0.0/guide_platforms_android_config.md.html#Android%20Configuration
- iOS: http://docs.phonegap.com/en/4.0.0/guide_platforms_ios_config.md.html#iOS%20Configuration

The importance for the platform-specific configurations and global configuration is same. You can read more about global configuration at http://docs.phonegap.com/en/4.0.0/config_ref_index.md.html#The%20config.xml%20File

The www folder

As mentioned earlier, this folder consists of our Ionic app, the HTML, CSS, and JS codes. If you open the www folder, you will find the following file structure:

```
.
├── css
│   └── style.css
├── img
│   └── ionic.png
├── index.html
├── js
│   └── app.js
└── lib
    └── ionic
```

```
├── css
├── fonts
├── js
├── scss
└── version.json
```

Let's look at each of these in detail:

- `index.html`: This is the application startup file. If you remember, in `config.xml`, we pointed the `src` on the content tag to this file. Since we are using AngularJS as our JavaScript framework, this file would ideally act as the base/first page for the **Single Page Application** (**SPA**). If you open `index.html`, you can see that the body tag has the `ng-app` attribute which points to the starter module defined inside the `js/app.js` file.
- `css`: This folder consists of styles that are specific to our app.
- `img`: This folder consists of images that are specific to our app.
- `js`: This folder consists of the JavaScript code specific to our app. This is where we write the AngularJS code. If you open the `app.js` file present inside this folder, you can see that an AngularJS module is set up, passing in Ionic as a dependency.
- `lib`: This folder is where all the packages would be placed when we run bower install. When we scaffold the app, this folder comes along with it, loaded with Ionic files. If you want to download the assets again along with its dependencies, you can use the `cd` command to go to the `example1` folder from your terminal/prompt and run the following command:

  ```
  bower install
  ```

  You will see that four more folders get downloaded. These are a part of the dependencies listed in the `ionic-bower` package, present in `bower.json` file, located at the root of the project.

  Ideally, we would not be using these libraries explicitly in our app. Rather, we would use the Ionic bundle which is built on top of these libraries.

This completes our tour of the blank template. Before we scaffold the next template, let us take a quick peek at the `www/js/app.js` file.

As you can see, we are creating a new AngularJS module with the name `starter`, and then we are injecting `ionic` as a dependency.

The `$ionicPlatform` service is injected as a dependency to the `run` method. This service is used to detect the current platform, as well as handle the hardware buttons on (Android) devices. In the current context, we are using the `$ionicPlatform.ready` method to be notified when the device is ready for us to perform operations on it.

It is a good practice, or rather a necessity in some cases, to include all your code inside the `$ionicPlatform.ready` method. This way, your code executes only when the entire app is initialized.

So far you must have worked on AngularJS code related to the Web. But when you are dealing with Ionic, you would be working with scripts related to device features as well, inside the AngularJS code. Ionic provides us services to make these things happen in a more organized fashion. Hence, we went through the concept of custom services in *Chapter 1, Ionic – Powered by AngularJS*, and we will be going through Ionic Services in depth in *Chapter 5, Ionic Directives and Services*.

Scaffolding the tabs template

To get a good feel of the Ionic CLI and the project structure, we will scaffold the other two starter templates as well. First we will scaffold the tabs template.

Using the `cd` command go back to the `chapter2` folder and run the following command:

```
ionic start -a "Example 2" -i app.example.two example2 tabs
```

As you can see, the tabs project is scaffolded inside the `example2` folder. Using the `cd` command go to the `example2` folder and execute the following command:

```
ionic serve
```

You should see the tabbed interface app built using Ionic as seen in the following screenshot:

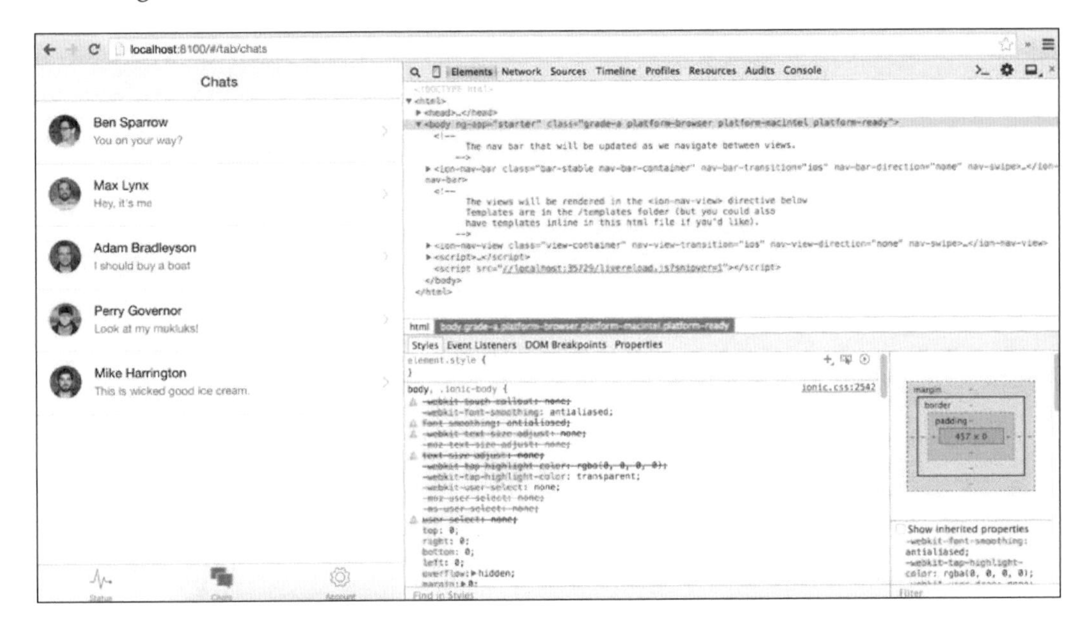

The tabs are located at the bottom of the page. We will talk more about customizations in *Chapter 3, Ionic CSS Components and Navigation* and *Chapter 5, Ionic Directives and Services*.

If you go back to the `example2` folder and analyze the project structure, everything would be the same except for the contents of the `www` folder.

This time, you will see a new folder named `templates`. This folder will consist of partial pages associated with each AngularJS route. And if you open the `js` folder, you will find two new files:

- `controller.js`: This consists of the AngularJS controller code
- `services.js`: This consists of the AngularJS service code

Now you can get a good idea of how Ionic is integrated with AngularJS, and how all the components go hand-in-hand. When we deal with a few more pieces of Ionic, this structure will make a lot of sense.

Scaffolding the side menu template

Now, we will scaffold the final template. Using the `cd` command go back to the `chapter2` folder and run the following command:

```
ionic start -a "Example 3" -i app.example.three example3 sidemenu
```

To execute the scaffolded project, using the `cd` command go to the `example3` folder and give the following command:

```
ionic serve
```

And the output should be similar to the following screenshot:

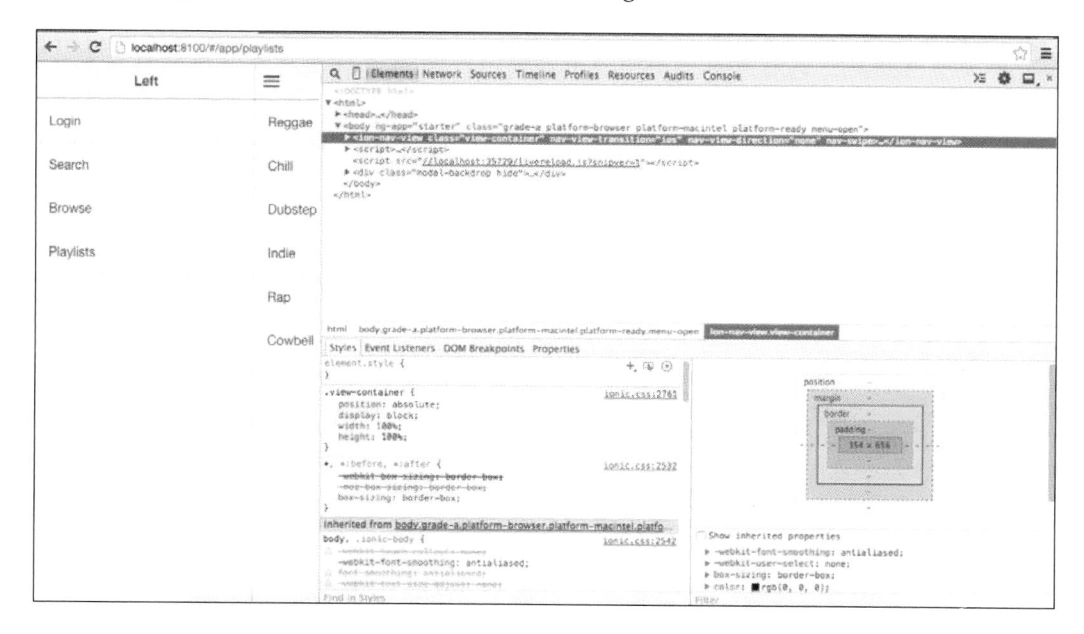

You can analyze the project structure yourself and see the difference.

> You can run `Ionic start -l` or `ionic templates` to view the list of available templates. You can also use the ionic start task with the template name from the list to scaffold the app.

generator-ionic

I feel that the Ionic CLI is pretty good, but it does not have a workflow associated with it. When I say workflow, I mean a demarcation between the development code and production code. In the project scaffolded by the Ionic CLI, the `www` folder hosts both the development code and production code. This will become an issue very fast when your app starts growing.

This is where generator-ionic proves to be invaluable. The generator-ionic is a Yeoman generator that is used to scaffold Ionic projects. If you did not already know this, Yeoman is a scaffolding tool that uses Grunt, Bower, and Yo to scaffold apps. Of late, they've started supporting gulp as well.

Why Yeoman?

Unlike the IDEs for other languages, JavaScript or web development does not have a unified development environment, where a user would navigate to **File** | **New** | **AngularJS project** or **File** | **New** | **HTML5 project**. This is where Yeoman fits in.

Ionic has its own CLI to scaffold apps. But for other frameworks, which do not have a generator, Yeoman provides base generators.

You can know more about Yeoman at `http://yeoman.io/` and to search for a Yeoman generator, you can navigate to `http://yeoman.io/generators/`.

There are other generators available for Ionic, but I prefer `generator-ionic` (`https://gitHub.com/diegonetto/generator-ionic`) for its workflow and features.

Installing generator-ionic

Before we install generator-ionic, we need to install `yo`, `grunt`, and `grunt-cli` globally. To do this, run the following command:

```
npm install yo grunt grunt-cli -g
```

Grunt is another build tool similar to Gulp. The main difference between Grunt and Gulp is that, Grunt is a configuration-over-code build tool, whereas gulp is a code-over-configuration build tool.

You can read more about Grunt at http://gruntjs.com/.

You can find the presentation from my talk on Gulp versus Grunt at http://arvindr21.github.io/building-n-Scaffolding for some more insights into them.

Next, we will install generator-ionic globally:

```
npm install generator-ionic -g
```

Packages which are installed with a `-g` flag need to be installed only once. You need not install them again and again for each usage.

Now, we can scaffold a new Ionic project using generator-ionic. Using the `cd` command go back to the `chapter2` folder and create a new folder inside it named `example4`. Run the following command:

```
yo ionic example
```

Unlike the Ionic CLI, you need to answer a few questions on how you would like to scaffold your app. You can answer the questions as shown below:

```
? Would you like to use Sass with Compass (requires Ruby)?
  N
? Which Cordova plugins would you like to include?
  org.apache.cordova.device
  org.apache.cordova.console
  com.ionic.keyboard
? Which starter template would you like to use?
  Tabs
```

Yeoman will go ahead and download all the stuff needed for the project to run. Once the Yeoman scaffolding is complete, you can navigate to the `example4` folder. As you can see, there are a lot more files and folders present in this folder.

You can read more about the complete project structure at https://gitHub.com/diegonetto/generator-ionic#project-structure.

The key differences between the Ionic CLI scaffolded app and the generator-ionic scaffolded app are as follows:

- `app`: unlike the Ionic CLI scaffolded app, we will carry out the development not inside the `www` folder but inside the `app` folder. This was the code demarcation that I was referring to. We develop inside the `app` folder and run a build script that takes care of cleaning up the files and putting them inside the `www` folder, ready for production use.
- `hooks`: If you open the `hooks` folder, you can find four more scripts.
- `Gruntfile.js`: Unlike the Ionic CLI, generator-ionic uses Grunt to manage tasks. If you feel that there are too many things to learn, I recommend you follow the Ionic CLI scaffolded app over generator-ionic and Gulp over Grunt.

If you are using generator-ionic to scaffold your app, do not work inside the `www` folder. When you run the `build` command, the contents of this folder will be deleted and recreated from the `app` folder.

You can check out the workflow commands that you can use to run the app from `https://gitHub.com/diegonetto/generator-ionic#workflow-commands`.

All the Ionic CLI methods are wrapped with the `grunt` command. So, for instance, when you want to execute Ionic serve, you will run `grunt serve` when using generator-ionic.

So, let's serve the scaffolded app by running the following command:

```
grunt serve
```

You should see the same output that you have seen for the tabs app when we scaffolded it with the Ionic CLI.

Three more reasons that made me choose generator-ionic over Ionic CLI is the out-of-the-box support for:

- Code hinting (`https://github.com/diegonetto/generator-ionic#grunt-jshint`)
- Testing with Karma (testing framework) and code coverage using Istanbul (`https://github.com/diegonetto/generator-ionic#grunt-karma`)
- Ripple emulator (`https://github.com/diegonetto/generator-ionic#grunt-ripple`)

The main reason I am demonstrating generator-ionic is to introduce you to the workflow so that you can adapt to it when your app becomes bigger. Again, this is a personal preference and you may like to work with the Ionic CLI itself.

You can play around with other Ionic generators as well and see which you are comfortable with.

Summary

In this chapter, you gained some knowledge on mobile hybrid architecture. You also learned how a Hybrid app works. We saw how Cordova stitches the HTML, CSS, and JS code to be executed inside the web view of the app. Then, we installed the required software to develop Ionic apps locally. We scaffolded a blank template using the Ionic CLI and analyzed the project structure. Later on, we scaffolded the other two templates and observed the difference. We also installed generator-ionic and scaffolded a sample app, and observed the difference between a generator-ionic and Ionic CLI scaffolded app.

You can also refer to Ionic slides at `http://ionicframework.com/present-ionic/slides` for some more information.

In the next chapter, we will understand Ionic CSS components and the router. This will help us in building interesting user interfaces and multipage applications using the Ionic API.

3
Ionic CSS Components and Navigation

So far we have seen what Ionic is, where it fits in the big picture of mobile hybrid application development. We have also seen two ways of scaffolding an Ionic app: one using the Ionic CLI, and the other using generator-ionic. In this chapter, we will work with Ionic CSS components, the Ionic grid system, and the Ionic state router. We will look at the various components of Ionic, using which you can build apps that provide a good user experience.

In this chapter, we will cover the following topics:

- Ionic grid system
- Various CSS components
- Integrating Ionic CSS components with AngularJS
- Ionic state router

For this chapter, you can also access the code, raise issues, and chat with the author at GitHub (`https://github.com/learning-ionic/Chapter-3`).

Ionic CSS components

Ionic is a combination of a powerful mobile CSS framework and a bunch of awesome AngularJS directives and services. With these, the time taken to market any idea is quite minimal. The Ionic CSS framework consists of most of the components you need to build an app.

To test-drive the available CSS components, we will scaffold a blank starter template and then add the visual components of Ionic.

Before we start scaffolding, we will create a new folder named `chapter3`, and scaffold all the examples from this chapter in that folder.

In this chapter, we will be scaffolding one app per component to understand it better. If you want, you can use one app for all the examples.

To scaffold a blank app, run this:

```
ionic start -a "Example 5" -i app.example.five example5 blank
```

The Ionic grid system

To get a fine grain control of your layout in terms of positioning the components on the page or aligning elements next to each other with consistency, you need a grid system, and Ionic provides one.

The beauty of the Ionic grid system is that it is FlexBox-based. FlexBox—or the CSS Flexible Box Layout Module—provides a box model for optimized user interface design.

You can read more about FlexBox at `http://www.w3.org/TR/css3-flexBox/` and you can find an amazing tutorial about FlexBox at `https://css-tricks.com/snippets/css/a-guide-to-flexbox/`.

The advantage of a FlexBox-based grid system is that you need not have a fixed-column grid system. You can define as many columns as you want inside a row and they will be automatically assigned with equal width. This way, unlike any other CSS-based grid systems, you need not worry about the sum of class names adding up to the total columns in the grid system.

To get a feel for the grid system, open the `index.html` file present inside the `example5/www` folder. Inside the `ion-content` directive, add the following code:

```
<div class="row">
   <div class="col">col-20%-auto</div>
   <div class="col">col-20%-auto</div>
   <div class="col">col-20%-auto</div>
   <div class="col">col-20%-auto</div>
   <div class="col">col-20%-auto</div>
</div>
```

And, to visually see the difference, we will add the following style in the `<head>` tag:

```
<style>
.col {
    border: 1px solid red;
}
</style>
```

[The preceding style is not needed to use the grid system; it is merely to show the visual demarcation of each column in the layout.]

Save the `index.html` file and, using the `cd` command, go to the `example5` folder and run this:

```
ionic serve
```

Then you should see:

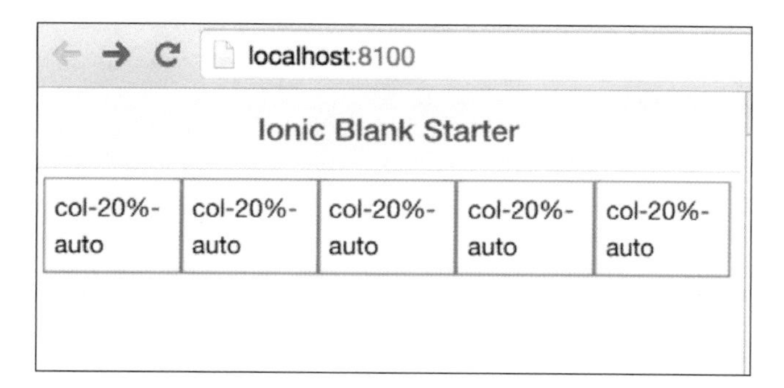

To check whether the width varies automatically, we will reduce the number of child `divs` to `3`, as shown here:

```
<div class="row">
    <div class="col">col-33%-auto</div>
    <div class="col">col-33%-auto</div>
    <div class="col">col-33%-auto</div>
</div>
```

Then you should see:

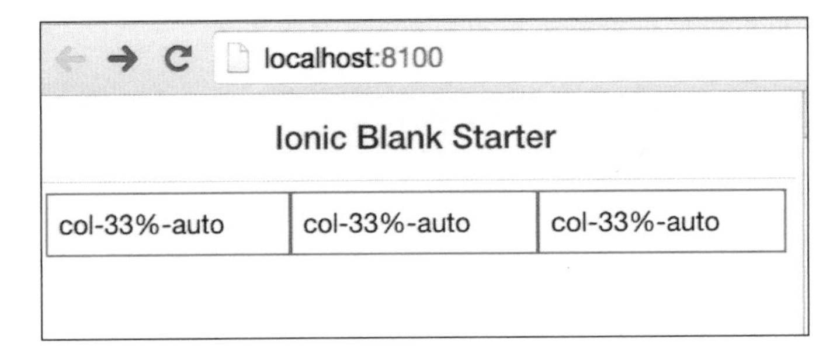

No hassle, no counting; all you need to do is add the `cols` that you want to use, and they are automatically allocated with equal width.

But this does mean that you cannot apply custom widths. You can do that easily with the classes provided by Ionic.

For instance, let's say that, in the preceding 3 columns, you want the first column to span 50 percent and the remaining 2 columns to take the remaining width; all you need to do is add a class named `col-50` to the first `div`, as shown here:

```
<div class="row">
   <div class="col col-50">col-50%-set</div>
   <div class="col">col-25%-auto</div>
   <div class="col">col-25%-auto</div>
</div>
```

Then you should see:

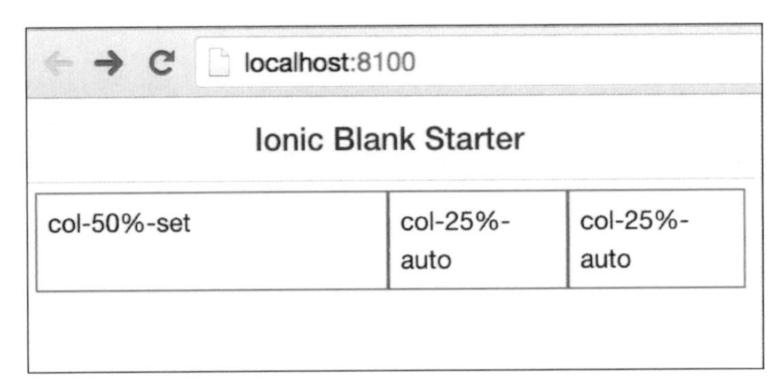

You can refer to the following table for a list of predefined classes and their implied width:

Class name	Percentage width
.col-10	10 percent
.col-20	20 percent
.col-25	25 percent
.col-33	33.3333 percent
.col-50	50 percent
.col-67	66.6666 percent
.col-75	75 percent
.col-80	80 percent
.col-90	90 percent

Along with the class `col`, you can add any one of the classes mentioned in the preceding table to get the specified width.

You can also offset a column by a certain percentage. For instance, append the following markup to our current example:

```
<div class="row">
   <div class="col col-offset-33">col-33%-offset</div>
   <div class="col">col-25%-auto</div>
</div>
```

Then you should see:

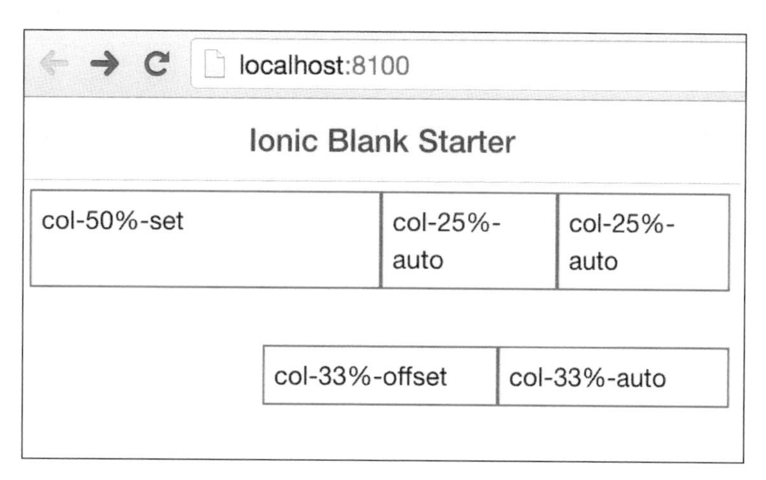

The first `div` is offset by 33 percent, and the remaining ~66 percent will be split between the 2 `divs`. All the `offset` class does is add a padding of the specified percentage to the left of the `div`.

You can refer to the following table for a list of predefined classes and their implied offset width:

Class name	Percentage width
`.col-offset-10`	10 percent
`.col-offset-20`	20 percent
`.col-offset-25`	25 percent
`.col-offset-33`	33.3333 percent
`.col-offset-50`	50 percent
`.col-offset-67`	66.6666 percent
`.col-offset-75`	75 percent
`.col-offset-80`	80 percent
`.col-offset-90`	90 percent

You can also align the columns in the grid vertically. This is another advantage of using FlexBox for a grid system.

Append the following markup after the "offset" grid row we added earlier:

```
<div class="row">
   <div class="col col-top">.col-top</div>
   <div class="col col-center">.col-center</div>
   <div class="col col-bottom">.col-bottom</div>
   <div class="col">1
          <br>2
          <br>3
          <br>4
   </div>
</div>
```

Then you should see:

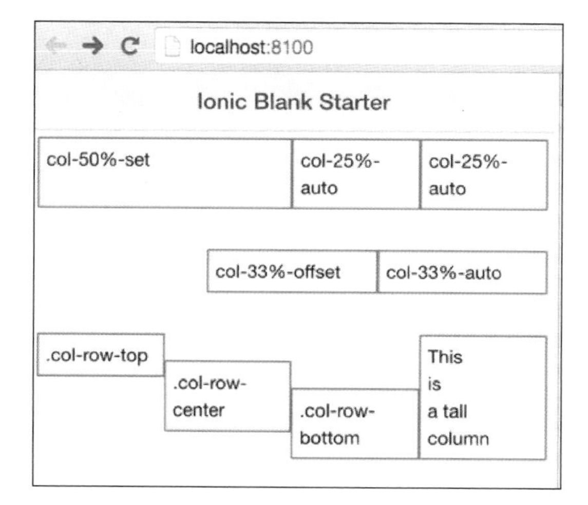

If one of the columns in your row is taller than the others, you can add a class `col-top` to position the contents of that column at the top of the row, as shown above. Or you can add a class named `col-center` to position the contents of that column at the center of the row, or `col-bottom` to position the contents of that column at the bottom of the row.

With such a simple and powerful grid system, the layout possibilities are unlimited.

> We will look at responsive grids and building a dynamic grid using `ng-repeat` in *Chapter 6, Building a Book Store App*.
>
> You can read more about Ionic grid system at `http://ionicframework.com/docs/components/#grid`.

The page structure

Next we will understand the page structure needed for working with single-page Ionic apps. We will scaffold a new blank project to work within the next section.

To scaffold a blank app, run this:

```
ionic start -a "Example 6" -i app.example.six example6 blank
```

Using the `cd` command, go to the `example6` folder and run this:

```
ionic serve
```

You should see the blank app launch in the default browser.

Open the `example6/www/index.html` file in your favorite editor. Inside the `body` tag, you should see a structure like this:

```
<ion-pane>
    <ion-header-bar class="bar-stable">
      <h1 class="title">Ionic Blank Starter</h1>
    </ion-header-bar>
    <ion-content>
    </ion-content>
</ion-pane>
```

The entire page is wrapped inside an `ion-pane` directive.

The `ion-pane` (`http://ionicframework.com/docs/api/directive/ionPane/`) is a simple container that fits content in the viewport.

Next, you can see an `ion-header-bar` directive (`http://ionicframework.com/docs/api/directive/ionHeaderBar/`). This directive adds a fixed header to the page. Do note the class attribute added to the `ion-header-bar` directive.

Out-of-the-box, Ionic ships with a color swatch with nine "moods". These are as shown here:

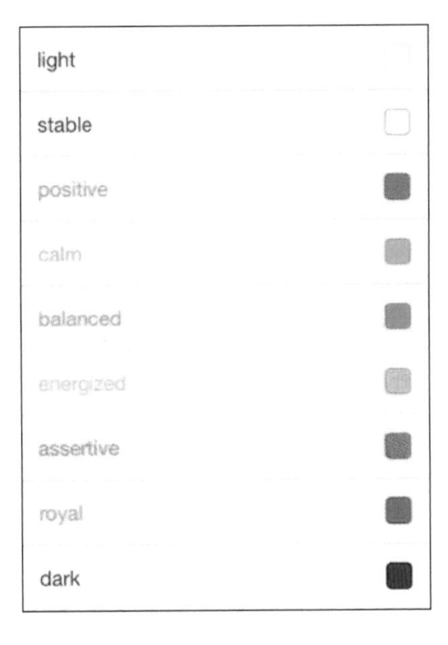

You can see the `bar-stable` class was applied to the `ion-header-bar` directive. You can change the header to any of the preceding by simply replacing the stable part of the class with any of the earlier names.

For instance, if you replace the class from `bar-stable` to `bar-assertive`, the header background will look something like this:

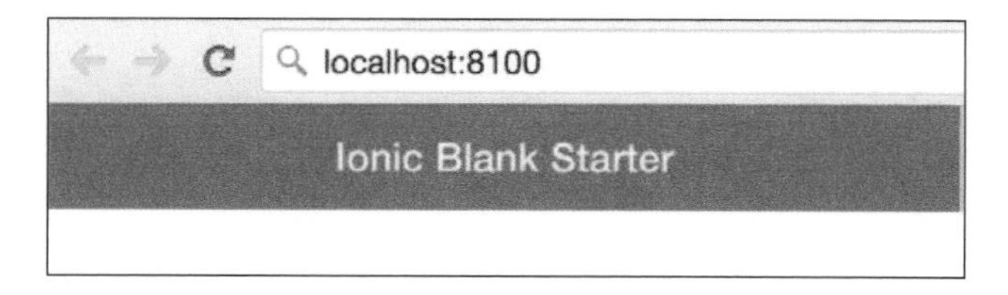

Simple and easy, right? In the next chapter, we will take a look at overwriting the default color swatch using SCSS.

The next directive on the page after the `ion-header-bar` is `ion-content` directive. The `ion-content` (`http://ionicframework.com/docs/api/directive/ionContent/`) directive enables building content areas, which overflow the screen real estate and need scrolling. You can also control these view better with `$ionicScrollDelegate`. More on that in *Chapter 5, Ionic Directives and Services*.

To give a complete structure to the page, we will add a `footer` too. Before the end of `ion-pane` directive, add this:

```
<ion-footer-bar class="bar-assertive">
   <div class="title">Footer</div>
</ion-footer-bar>
```

Now, save the file; in the browser, you should see the following screenshot:

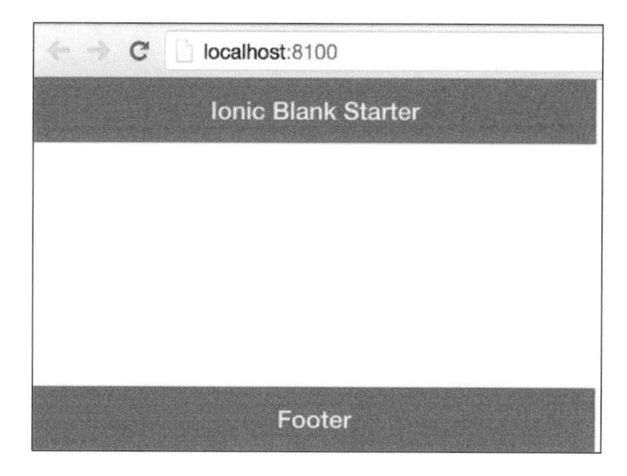

So, you can see that, if you are building a single page app with Ionic, you can structure your app like this:

```
<body ng-app="starter">
    <ion-pane>
        <ion-header-bar class="bar-assertive">
            ...
        </ion-header-bar>
        <ion-content>
          ...
        </ion-content>
        <ion-footer-bar class="bar-assertive">
          ...
        </ion-footer-bar>
    </ion-pane>
</body>
```

The non-directive version of the preceding structure would be:

```
<div class="pane">
      <div class="bar bar-header bar-assertive">
          ...
      </div>
      <div class="content has-header has-footer padding">
          ...
      </div>
      <div class="bar bar-footer bar-assertive">
          ...
      </div>
  </div>
```

Also, you can add buttons to either the header or footer easily. The structure for adding buttons inside the header would look like:

```
<ion-header-bar class="bar-assertive">
    <div class="buttons">
        <button class="button">Left</button>
    </div>
    <h1 class="title">Ionic Blank Starter</h1>
    <div class="buttons">
        <button class="button">Right</button>
    </div>
</ion-header-bar>
```

The button placed before the `h1` tag inside the `ion-header-bar` directive will appear on the left and the button placed after the `h1` tag will appear to the right of the header bar:

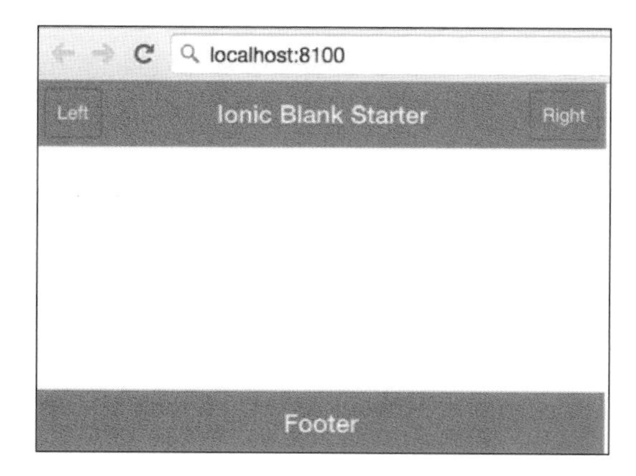

You can use the same markup inside the footer as well to generate buttons.

The `ion-header-bar` directive is one way of generating a header. The `ion-header-bar` directive is perfect for static headers. But things get complex very fast when we introduce the Ionic state router. When you are dealing with a multi-page application, and you want Ionic to take care of showing the back button automatically based on the navigation, we use the `ion-nav-bar` directive instead of the `ion-header-bar` directive. We will work with `ion-nav-bar` a bit later when we look at the Ionic state router.

For more information about the header component, refer to `http://ionicframework.com/docs/components/#header`.

For the content component, refer to `http://ionicframework.com/docs/components/#content`.

For the footer component, refer to `http://ionicframework.com/docs/components/#footer`.

Buttons

Ionic provides different variations on the buttons, by size or style.

Update the `ion-content` directive inside the `www/index.html` with the following code, and you should see different button variations:

```
<ion-content class="padding">
    <button class="button">
```

```
            Default
        </button>
        <button class="button button-full button-positive">
            Full Width Block Button
        </button>
        <button class="button button-small button-assertive">
            Small Button
        </button>
        <button class="button button-large button-calm">
            Large Button
        </button>
        <button class="button button-outline button-dark">
            Outlined Button
        </button>
        <button class="button button-clear button-energized">
            Clear Button
        </button>
        <button class="button icon-left ion-star button-balanced">
    Icon Button
        </button>
    </ion-content>
```

Do notice the class on the `ion-content` directive. This will add 10px padding to the `ion-content` directive. If you save the file, you should see this:

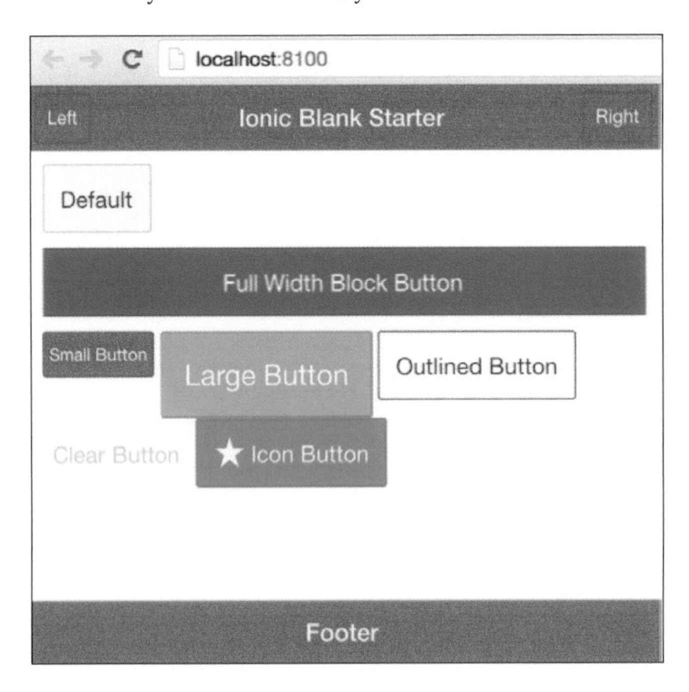

The preceding screenshot speaks for all your button needs based on the default Ionic color swatch.

For more information about the buttons component, refer to http://ionicframework.com/docs/components/#buttons.

Lists

The most essential component for any app that involves displaying a list of items is a list component. List structure is pretty simple and, as with any Ionic CSS component, lists are driven by CSS classes and HTML structure. In Ionic, if you have a parent element with a class-named list and any number of children inside it with the class-named item, the items align themselves in the form of an Ionic-styled list. For instance:

```
<ul class="list">
    <li class="item">
        Item 1
    </li>
    <li class="item">
        Item 2
    </li>
    <li class="item">
        Item 3
    </li>
</ul>
```

You can also use this:

```
<div class="list">
    <div class="item">
        Item 1
    </div>
    <div class="item">
        Item 2
    </div>
    <div class="item">
        Item 3
    </div>
</div>
```

It leads to the same layout and looks like this:

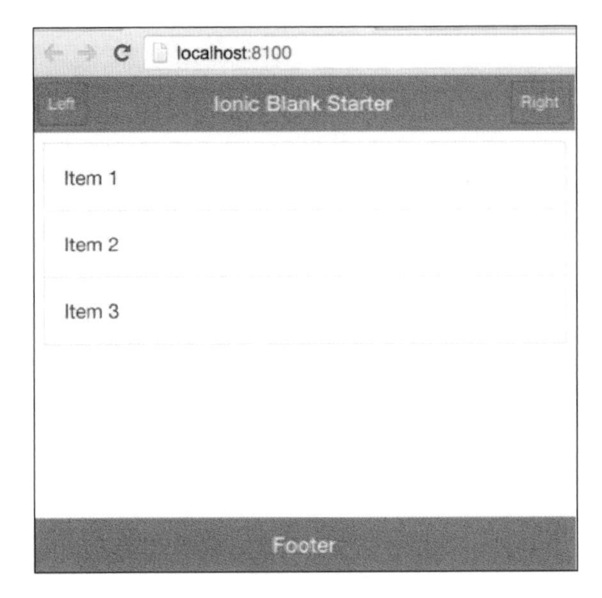

Based on my experience with Ionic so far, if the list consists of more than 250 items, is built using ng-repeat with an array of objects, and if each object has around 10 properties, the app becomes less responsive. Having said that, you can work around this limitation to improve the performance based on your needs.

The versatility of Ionic components lies in its CSS classes. Most layouts you intend to build are already achievable with the classes provided.

For instance, if you want to add an icon to the left of each list item, all you need to do is add a class named `item-icon-left` to the item. This will add enough space on the left of the list item to add an icon.

> An example can be found at `http://ionicframework.com/docs/components/#item-icons`.

Similarly, you can add a thumbnail to the left of your list item. All you need is a class named `item-thumbnail-left`.

> An example can be found at `http://ionicframework.com/docs/components/#item-thumbnails`.
>
> You can read more about lists at `http://ionicframework.com/docs/components/#list`.

Cards

Cards are one of the best design patterns for showcasing content on a mobile device. For any page or app that displays users' personalized content, cards are the way to go. The world is moving towards cards to display content on mobiles, and in some cases, on desktops too. Examples include Twitter (`https://dev.twitter.com/cards/overview`) and Google Now (`http://www.google.com/landing/now/#cards`).

So, you can simply port that design pattern to your app as well. All you need to do is design the personalized content that fits into a card and then add a class named card to the container. If you want to display a series of cards as a list, all you need to do is add the class card to the list container.

A simple card that shows weather information will be structured as shown here:

```
<ion-content class="padding">
            <div class="list card">
                <div class="item text-center">
                    <h1>Today's Weather</h1>
                </div>
                <div class="item item-body">
                    <p>
                        <div class="text-center">
                            <i class="icon ion-ios-partlysunny"
style="font-size:128px"></i>
                        </div>
                        <div class="text-center">
                            <h2>Partly Sunny</h2>
                        </div>
                    </p>
                </div>
                <div class="item tabs tabs-secondary tabs-icon-left">
                    <a class="tab-item" href="#">
                        <i class="icon ion-thumbsup"></i> Like
                    </a>
                    <a class="tab-item" href="#">
                        <i class="icon ion-chatbox"></i> Comment
                    </a>
                    <a class="tab-item" href="#">
                        <i class="icon ion-share"></i> Share
                    </a>
                </div>
            </div>
</ion-content>
```

Your page will look like this:

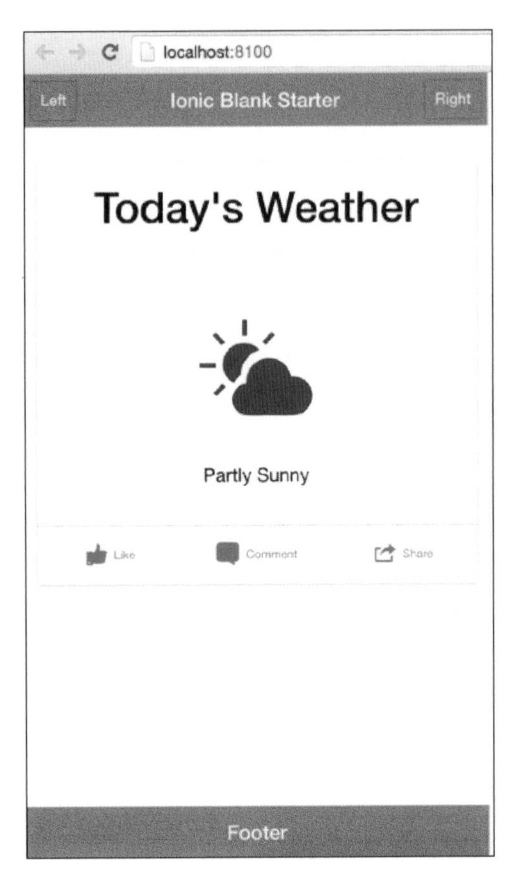

This design looks elegant at the same time as it displays all the essential information in one glance. Next time you are designing a layout where you want the users to get an impression of personalization, do consider the card layout.

> You can read more about the Ionic cards component at `http://ionicframework.com/docs/components/#cards`.

Ionicons

Ionic comes out of box with a bunch of font icons. The weather icon you see in the preceding example uses Ionic's font icons. You can navigate to `http://ionicons.com/`, and you should be able to find font icons that you can start to use immediately.

For your convenience, there is a **Search** bar, where you can search for a type of icon. For instance, if you type `sunny` into the **Search** bar, you should see the icon shown in the preceding screenshot.

A very important caveat here is to ensure your Ionicons version on the website matches the Ionicons version in your Ionic CSS file. The Ionic team keeps adding more icons and upgrading the version. The sunny icon used here ships with Ionicons version 2.0.1.

Note you can find more information on Ionicons and their usage at `http://ionicframework.com/docs/components/#icons`.

Form elements

Ionic comes with its share of form elements and layouts. Right from a textbox to a toggle switch, you name it and you got it.

A simple login form would be structured as shown here:

```
<ion-content class="padding">
<div class="list">
    <label class="item item-input">
        <span class="input-label">Username</span>
        <input type="text">
    </label>
    <label class="item item-input">
        <span class="input-label">Password</span>
        <input type="password">
    </label>
</div>
</ion-content>
```

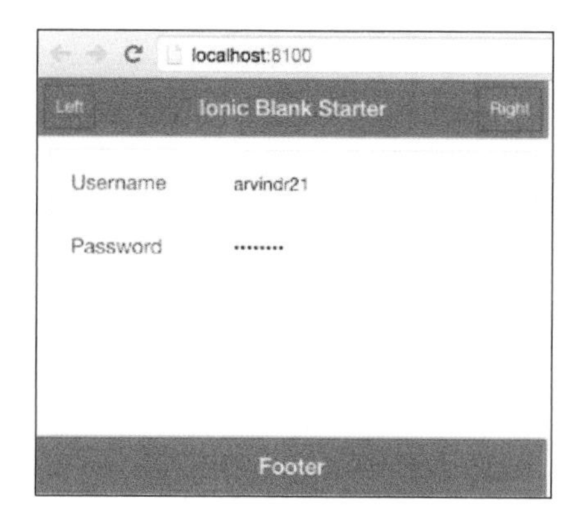

You can also build a fancy form with a floating label. All you need to do is add the class `item-floating-label` to the label:

```
<ion-content class="padding">
<div class="list">
    <label class="item item-input item-floating-label">
        <span class="input-label">Username</span>
        <input type="text" placeholder="Username">
     </label>
     <label class="item item-input item-floating-label">
         <span class="input-label">Password</span>
         <input type="password" placeholder="Password">
     </label>
 </div>
</ion-content>
```

The output looks like this:

You can also add icons to these form elements. You need to add an `i` tag, with a class named `placeholder-icon` inside the label for the icon to appear:

```
<ion-content class="padding">
<div class="list list-inset">
    <label class="item item-input">
        <i class="icon ion-search placeholder-icon"></i>
        <input type="text" placeholder="Search...">
    </label>
</div>
</ion-content>
```

It should look like this:

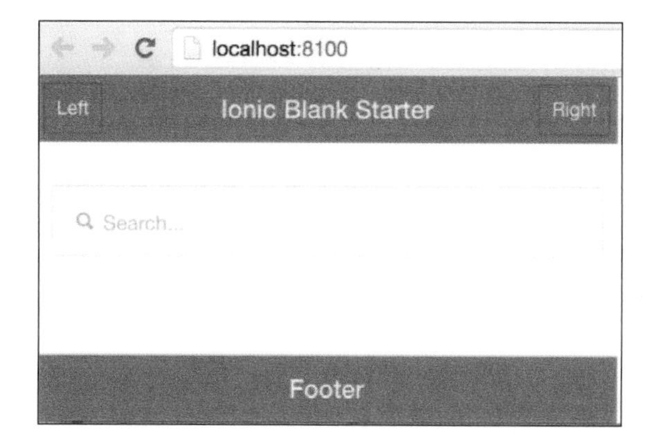

You can also add other form elements, such as a text area or a select; they come up as expected and will be pretty neatly blended with the remaining form elements in terms of look and feel:

```
<ion-content class="padding">
<div class="list">
      <label class="item item-input">
            <textarea placeholder="This is a &lt;textarea&gt;
&lt;/textarea&gt;"></textarea>
           </label>
           <label class="item item-input item-select">
           <div class="input-label">
                 Gender
                  </div>
                      <select>
                             <option>Male</option>
                             <option>Female</option>
                      </select>
```

```
            </label>
    </div>
    </ion-content>
```

There are two ways you can represent a checkbox. You can either show it as a checkbox, or as a toggle switch.

The following markup shows a list of selectable fruits:

```
<ion-content class="padding">
  <ul class="list">
    <li class="item item-checkbox">
            <label class="checkbox checkbox-assertive">
                  <input type="checkbox">
        </label>
        Apples
    </li>
    <li class="item item-checkbox">
        <label class="checkbox">
              <input type="checkbox">
        </label>
        Oranges
    </li>
    <li class="item item-checkbox checkbox-energized">
        <label class="checkbox">
               <input type="checkbox">
        </label>
        Lemons
    </li>
</ul>
</ion-content>
```

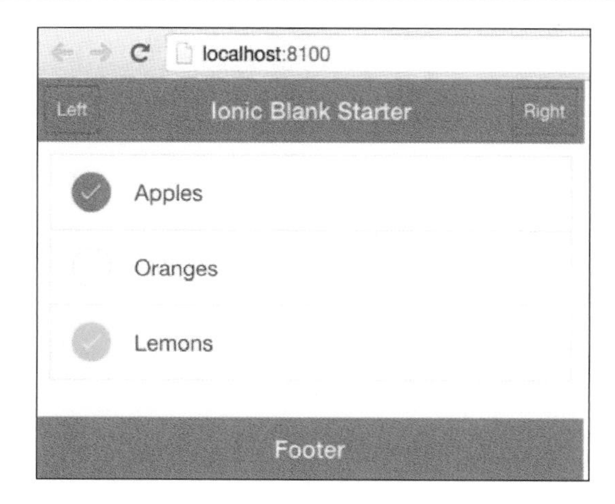

Ionic themes apps with iOS styles by default; hence you can see the circled checkbox. We will take a look at modifying this in *Chapter 5, Ionic Directives and Services*.

The following markup shows toggle-able switches:

```
<ion-content class="padding">
<ul class="list">
          <li class="item item-toggle">
                Wifi
                <label class="toggle toggle-assertive">
                      <input type="checkbox">
                        <div class="track">
                            <div class="handle"></div>
                        </div>
                  </label>
            </li>
            <li class="item item-toggle">
                    Bluetooth
                    <label class="toggle toggle-positive">
                        <input type="checkbox">
                        <div class="track">
                            <div class="handle"></div>
                        </div>
                    </label>
            </li>
            <li class="item item-toggle">
                    Aeroplane Mode
                    <label class="toggle toggle-calm">
                        <input type="checkbox">
```

```
                    <div class="track">
                        <div class="handle"></div>
                    </div>
                </label>
            </li>
    </ul>
    </ion-content>
```

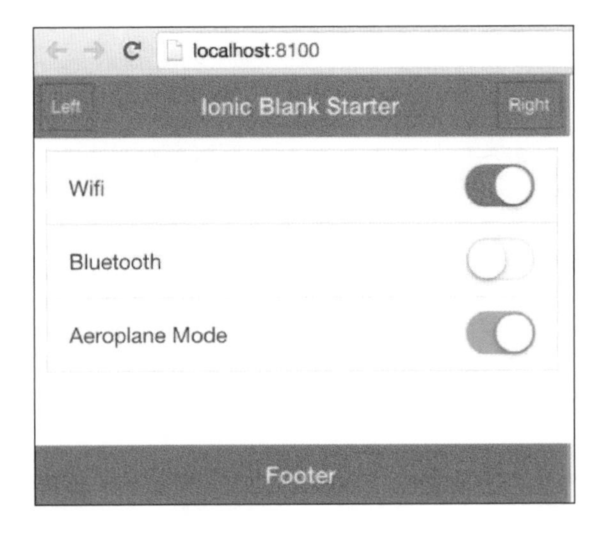

Finally, we will wrap up Ionic CSS-based components with a range input. This is a very handy and powerful component when dealing with variable inputs from the user. The best use case for this component is a brightness slider, which would look something like this:

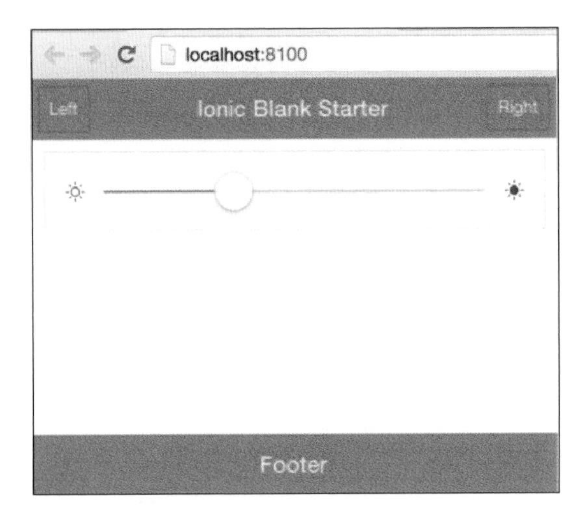

The markup you will need is as follows:

```
<ion-content class="padding">
<div class="list">
      <div class="item range range-positive">
            <i class="icon ion-ios-sunny-outline"></i>
            <input type="range" name="volume" min="0" max="100"
value="33">
                  <i class="icon ion-ios-sunny"></i>
            </div>
      </div>
</ion-content>
```

Integrating Ionic CSS components with AngularJS

What is the point if you have beautiful-looking pages with cool-looking components, and none of them do anything in real time? So, in this subtopic, we are going to take a look at integrating the beautiful looking Ionic components with AngularJS to make the page more functional.

The first example we are going to deal with is disabling the form submit button till the form fields are valid. We are going to create a login form with an e-mail address and password. Till the user enters a valid e-mail and a password with length greater than 3, we keep the login button disabled.

To build this, we will scaffold a blank app, and run the following command:

```
ionic start -a "Example 7" -i app.example.seven example7 blank
```

Next, we will update the `index.html` file with a form and add an AngularJS directive named `ng-disabled` to the button. The `ng-disabled` is evaluated to `true` if the e-mail model value and password model value are `false` (or falsy).

To get an idea on truthy and falsy in JavaScript refer to `http://adripofjavascript.com/blog/drips/truthy-and-falsy-values-in-javascript.html`.

The `www/index.html` will look like this:

```
<div class="list">
  <label class="item item-input">
      <span class="input-label">Email</span>
            <input type="email" ng-model="email">
```

```
        </label>
        <label class="item item-input">

                <span class="input-label">Password</span>
                <input type="password" ng-model="password"
ng-minlength="3">
        </label>
        <div class="padding">
                <button ng-disabled="!email || !password"
class="button button-block button-positive">Sign In</button>
        </div>
</div>
```

Save the file, and run the following command:

```
ionic serve
```

If nothing or invalid data was entered in the form, the button will be disabled and will look like this:

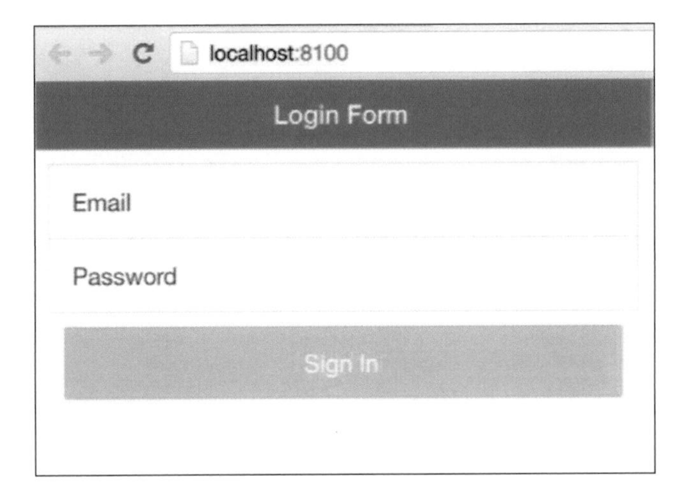

If the form is valid, the button will be enabled:

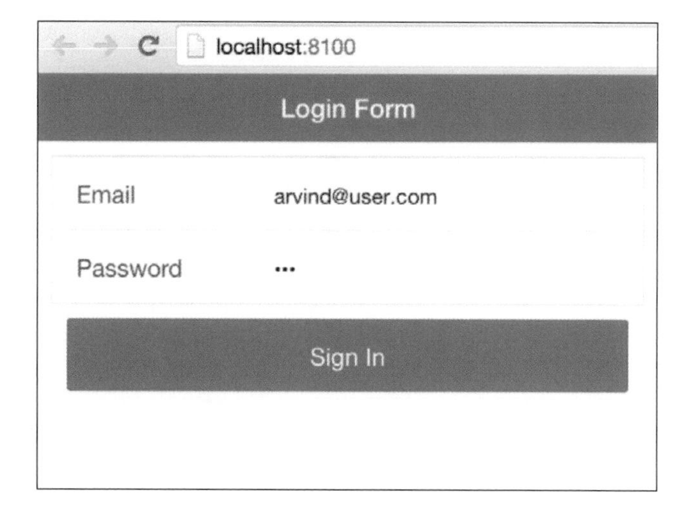

This is a simple example that shows how AngularJS and Ionic work together to create a great experience for the users. The preceding example can be extended to show the validation message.

In the next example, we will deal with a slightly more complex integration between Ionic and AngularJS. We will be implementing a simple rating widget. The widget will consist of five stars shown as outlines. When a user clicks on any of the five stars to indicate his/her rating, we will fill all the stars from the beginning up to the star the user has clicked.

To scaffold a blank app, run this:

```
ionic start -a "Example 8" -i app.example.eight example8 blank
```

Next, we will update the `www/js/app.js` by adding the following controller:

```
.controller('MainCtrl', ['$scope', function($scope) {

    $scope.ratingArr = [{
        value: 1,
        icon: 'ion-ios-star-outline'
    }, {
        value: 2,
        icon: 'ion-ios-star-outline'
    }, {
        value: 3,
        icon: 'ion-ios-star-outline'
    }, {
```

```
            value: 4,
            icon: 'ion-ios-star-outline'
        }, {
            value: 5,
            icon: 'ion-ios-star-outline'
        }];

        $scope.setRating = function(val) {
            var rtgs = $scope.ratingArr;
            for (var i = 0; i < rtgs.length; i++) {
                if (i < val) {
                    rtgs[i].icon = 'ion-ios-star';
                } else {
                    rtgs[i].icon = 'ion-ios-star-outline';
                }
            };
        }

    }])
```

As you can see from the preceding code, we have created an array named `ratingArr`. This array consists of two properties: one, the value of a star, and two, the class that needs to be applied to the star. And we have created another method named `setRating()` that will be invoked when the user clicks on a star. This method takes the value of the star that was clicked as the argument. Then, we iterate through all the rating objects and, from the start to the selected star value, we set the icon as a filled star, and the others as just an outline.

The body section of `www/index.html` will be:

```
<body ng-app="starter" ng-controller="MainCtrl">
    <ion-pane>
        <ion-header-bar class="bar-positive">
            <h1 class="title">Ionic Blank Starter</h1>
        </ion-header-bar>
        <ion-content class="padding">
            <div class="padding text-center">
                <h3>Rate the App</h3>
                <div>
                    <a href="javascript:" ng-repeat="r in
ratingArr" class="padding" style="text-decoration:none;">
                        <i class="icon {{r.icon}}"
ng-click="setRating(r.value)"></i>
                    </a>
                </div>
```

```
            </div>
        </ion-content>
</ion-pane>
</body>
```

We have added the `ng-controller` directive to the `body` tag and, inside the `ion-content` directive, we have added the `div` that will iterate the `ratingArr` and render the stars.

If you save all the files and run this:

```
ionic serve
```

You should see the following screenshot:

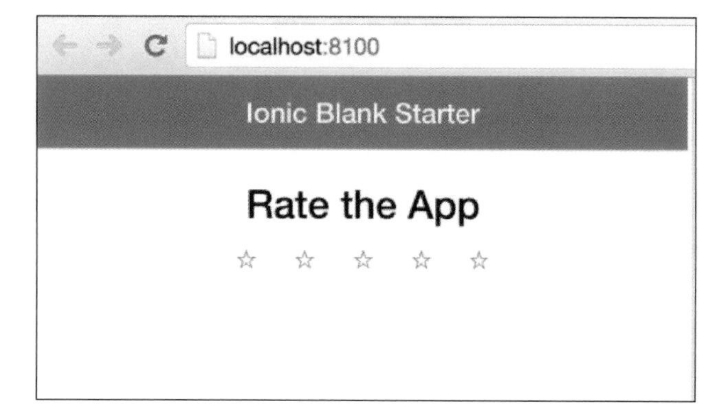

If you select the third star, you should see this:

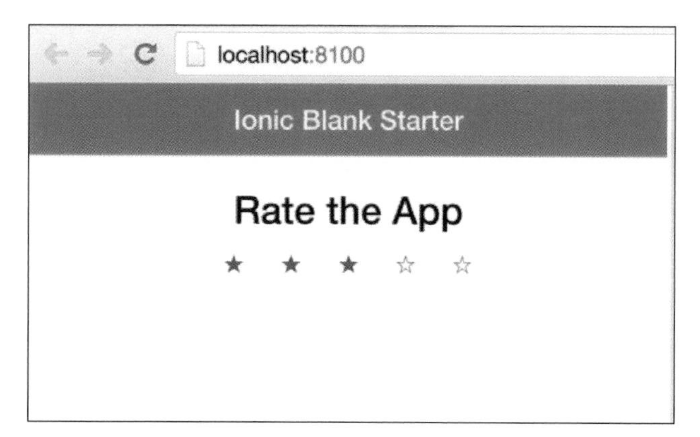

This is another example of how you can integrate the Ionic CSS components with AngularJS.

With this, we wrap up this simple introduction on integrating Ionic components with AngularJS. In the next topic, we are going to take a look at the AngularUI router.

The Ionic router

As long as the application is small and has only a few pages, it is easy to maintain its state and manage the data. But as the application becomes more and more complex, it gets difficult to deal with templates, template data, data associated with a route, and so on.

So, to make managing complex multi-page Ionic applications easy, we use the Ionic router. The Ionic router is the same as the AngularUI router. For more information, refer to `https://github.com/angular-ui/ui-router`.

From the AngularUI router documentation:

> *"AngularUI Router is a routing framework for AngularJS, which allows you to organize the parts of your interface into a state machine. Unlike the $route service in the Angular ngRoute module, which is organized around URL routes, UI-Router is organized around states, which may optionally have routes, as well as other behavior, attached."*

> You can read more about AngularUI router from `https://github.com/angular-ui/ui-router/wiki`.

A simple two-page app

The Ionic source bundles the AngularUI router with it. So, we can directly inject `$stateProvider` and `$urlRouterProvider` in our `config` method to create routes, after we add Ionic as one of the dependencies. You will learn about the router via a few examples.

In the first example, we are going to build a two-page application, and a navigation button to navigate between them. The aim of this example is to understand the syntax and setup of the router so that we can apply the same logic in other examples.

We are going to create a blank template and then add routes to it, making it a multi-page application.

You can scaffold a new blank template with the following command:

```
ionic start -a "Example 9" -i app.example.nine example9 blank
```

Once the app is scaffolded, open `www/js/app.js`. We are going to create a `config` method and add the routes to our app. We will add the following `config` method after the `run` method in `www/js/app.js`, as shown here:

```
.config(function ($stateProvider, $urlRouterProvider) {

  $stateProvider
  .state('view1', {
    url: '/view1',
    template: '<div class="padding"><h2>View 1</h2><button
class="button button-positive" ui-sref="view2">To View
2</button></div>'
  })
  .state('view2', {
    url: '/view2',
    template: '<div class="padding"><h2>View 2</h2><button
class="button button-assertive" ui-sref="view1">To View
1</button></div>'
  })

  $urlRouterProvider.otherwise('/view1');

})
```

As you can see, `$stateProvider` and `$urlRouterProvider` are injected as dependencies to the `config` method. These services are shipped along with the Ionic bundle reference on the homepage.

Next, we used the `$stateProvider` to define states of our application. In this case, states are the same as views. The `state` method on `$stateProvider` is used to declare the routes. The first argument to this method is the readable name of the state. The second argument is an object that consists of the route configuration. As part of the route configuration, we provide a URL and a template that needs to be rendered when this URL is triggered.

For our preceding config, we have created two states: one named `view1`, which will be activated when we navigate to `http://localhost:8100/#/view1`, and a second state named `view2`, which will be activated when we navigate to `http://localhost:8100/#/view2`.

If you observe the URL, there is a `#` (hash) before the view name. This hash tells the browser not to fire a request to the server to get the resources; rather, these resources are present on the client side, and the JavaScript framework will take care of rendering them.

In simple terms, when anything after the hash changes in the URL, a `hashchange` event is fired. The router has a listener, which gets activated when this event is fired. This listener will take care of managing the UI based on the hash value (that is, `view1` or `view2`) and its state config. (In simple terms, when the hash changes, the router invokes the corresponding controller and template for the changed hash.)

Do notice that we have written the template that we want to render for this view, inline. We will look at using external files for this in the next example. Also, the button has a directive named `ui-sref` (`http://angular-ui.github.io/ui-router/site/#/api/ui.router.state.directive:ui-sref`). The `ui-sref` is a directive that binds the link to a state. If the state has a URL associated with it, this directive will automatically generate and update the `href`.

So, in our scenario, when we click on the button present in the template for `view1`, the app will navigate to `view2`—and vice versa.

Finally, we complete the `config` method by providing a default URL:

```
$urlRouterProvider.otherwise('/view1');
```

In the preceding line, we specify that, if the current URL does not match any of the configured state URLs, the user is redirected to the `view1` state.

With this, we have successfully set up the states. But we still are left with one key part of the setup. We need to tell the router which portion of the page should be updated with the contents of the state. This is done by adding the `ion-nav-view` directive in our `index.html`.

`ion-nav-view` is the same as the `ui-view` of the state router. The `ion-nav-view` extends `ui-view` and adds features such as animations and history.

In our `index.html`, replace the `ion-content` directive with the following code:

```
<ion-nav-view class="has-header"></ion-nav-view>
```

The class `has-header` adds a padding to the top of the container. This will make sure the contents of the template do not start from behind the header bar.

The complete body of the `index.html` looks like this:

```
<body ng-app="starter">
 <ion-pane>
     <ion-header-bar class="bar-stable">
       <h1 class="title">Two Page Application</h1>
     </ion-header-bar>
```

```
        <ion-nav-view class="has-header"></ion-nav-view>
    </ion-pane>
  </body>
```

Save all the files and run the following command:

```
ionic serve
```

You will see the following screenshot:

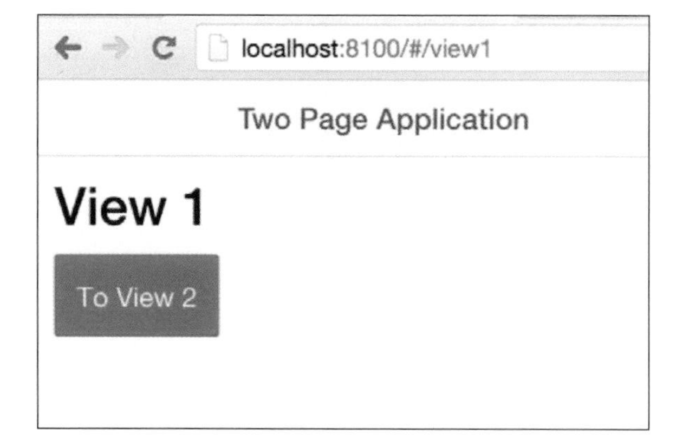

When you click on the **To View 2** button, it will take you to **View 2**, as shown here:

Do observe the URLs, post-navigation.

In the next example, we are going to create templates in separate HTML files and then configure them in our router. We will also be introducing a new property named controller to our route `config` object.

The app we are going to build is a two-page app; page 1 is a login form, which we developed earlier, and page 2 is the rating page.

The purpose of this example is to understand external templates and binding controllers to views. We will start off by scaffolding a blank template:

```
ionic start -a "Example 10" -i app.example.ten example10 blank
```

Next, we will set up our routes. Add a `config` method to `www/js/app.js`, which will look like this:

```
.config(function($stateProvider, $urlRouterProvider) {

  $stateProvider
    .state('login', {
            url: '/login',
            templateUrl: 'templates/login.html',
            controller: 'LoginCtrl'
        })

    .state('app', {
        url: '/app',
        templateUrl: 'templates/app.html',
        controller: 'AppCtrl'
    })

    $urlRouterProvider.otherwise('/login');

})
```

We have two states: `login` and `app`. We used a new property named `templateUrl` instead of template. `templateUrl` takes the location of the template file. A template file can be a separate file located on the hard disk, or it can be part of the `index.html` as a `script` tag. We will look at both the approaches.

We also added a new property named `controller`. This property tells the router the controller to be invoked when navigating to a route. As you can see, we will create two controllers, one for each view.

To get started off with the `script` tag-based templating, we will be creating two empty controllers first. Add the following code to your `www/js/app.js` after the `run` method, as shown here:

```
.controller('LoginCtrl', function ($scope) {

})

.controller('AppCtrl', function ($scope) {

})
```

Since we declared the controllers on the `route` config, AngularJS is going to look for the controller when it navigates to that view. For this reason, we created two dummy controllers. We will add the functionality a bit later.

Next, in our `www/index.html`, we will replace the `ion-content` directive with the following code:

```
<ion-nav-view class="has-header"></ion-nav-view>
```

Anywhere inside the `body` tag, you can add the templates. The `body` section of `www/index.html` will look like this:

```
<body ng-app="starter">

<ion-pane>
  <ion-header-bar class="bar-stable">
    <h1 class="title">My Awesome App</h1>
  </ion-header-bar>
  <ion-nav-view class="has-header"></ion-nav-view>
</ion-pane>

<script type="text/ng-template" id="templates/login.html">
  <h1>Login Template</h1>
  <button class="button button-calm" ui-sref="app">To App</button>
</script>

<script type="text/ng-template" id="templates/app.html">
  <h1>App Template</h1>
  <button class="button button-royal" ui-sref="login">To
Login</button>
</script>

</body>
```

Do observe the `id` attribute on the `script` tags. These are exactly same as the `templateUrl`. This is the hook, which links a script `tag/ng-template` to a route's `templateUrl`.

Save all the files and run this command:

```
ionic serve
```

You will see the contents of following screenshot:

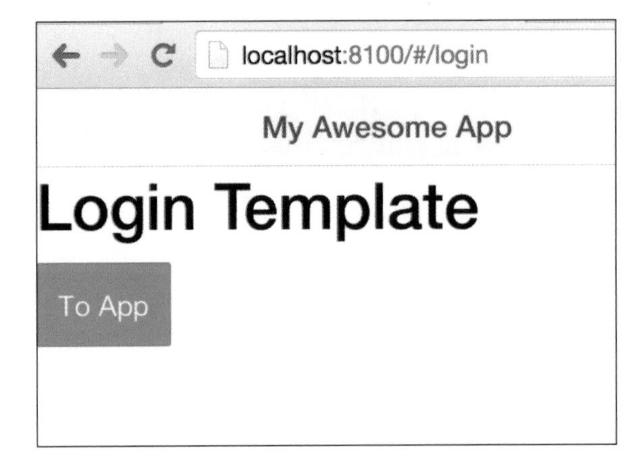

When you click on the **To App** button, you will see the app view:

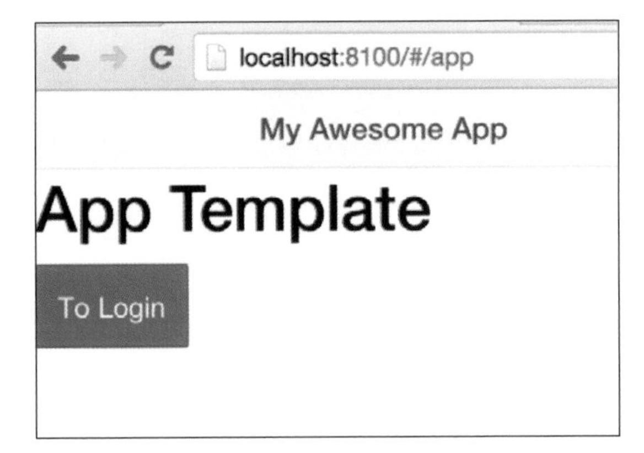

The preceding example shows how you can use `script` tags to write templates inside HTML files.

Before moving on to our actual example, remove the inline templates we created in `www/index.html`.

We will create a folder named `templates` inside the `www` folder—not at the root of the project but inside the `www` folder.

Inside the `templates` folder, create a file named `login.html`. The content of `login.html` will be the same as we have used in `example7`. The contents of the `login.html` will be:

```
<div class="list">
    <label class="item item-input">
        <span class="input-label">Email</span>
        <input type="email" ng-model="email">
    </label>
    <label class="item item-input">
        <span class="input-label">Password</span>
        <input type="password" ng-model="password"
ng-minlength="3">
    </label>
    <div class="padding">
        <button ui-sref="app" ng-disabled="!email || !password"
class="button button-block button-positive">Sign In</button>
    </div>
</div>
```

Do notice that we have added `ui-sref` to the button. As long as the button is disabled, clicking on the button will not redirect to the app view.

Next, create another file inside the `templates` folder and name it `app.html`. The contents of this file are the same as `example8` earlier:

```
<div class="padding text-center">
    <h3>Rate the App</h3>
    <div>
        <a href="javascript:" ng-repeat="r in ratingArr"
class="padding" style="text-decoration:none;">
            <i class="icon {{r.icon}}"
ng-click="setRating(r.value)"></i>
        </a>
    </div>
     <button ui-sref="login" class="button button-block
button-clam">Sign Out</button>
</div>
```

If you save all the files and go back to page, you should see the login page. When you enter a valid e-mail address and a password greater than three characters, the sign-in button will be enabled. You can click on the **Sign in** button and it should take you to the app view.

> If you do not see the updated UI, it means that you have not deleted the script-based templates from `www/index.html`. Templates written in `script` tags take preference over the one on the disk, which needs to be requested by AJAX. You can learn more about AngularJS template caching from `https://docs.angularjs.org/api/ng/service/$templateCache`.

If you checked out the app view, you will see that the stars are not appearing. This is because our stars are based on a scope variable named `ratingArr`. We will update our `AppCtrl` like we did in `example8`:

```
.controller('AppCtrl', function($scope) {
    $scope.ratingArr = [{
        value: 1,
        icon: 'ion-ios-star-outline'
    }, {
        value: 2,
        icon: 'ion-ios-star-outline'
    }, {
        value: 3,
        icon: 'ion-ios-star-outline'
    }, {
        value: 4,
        icon: 'ion-ios-star-outline'
    }, {
        value: 5,
        icon: 'ion-ios-star-outline'
    }];

    $scope.setRating = function(val) {
        var rtgs = $scope.ratingArr;
        for (var i = 0; i < rtgs.length; i++) {
            if (i < val) {
                rtgs[i].icon = 'ion-ios-star';
            } else {
                rtgs[i].icon = 'ion-ios-star-outline';
            }
        };
    }
})
```

Now if you go back to the view, you should see the stars and, when you click on them, they work as expected:

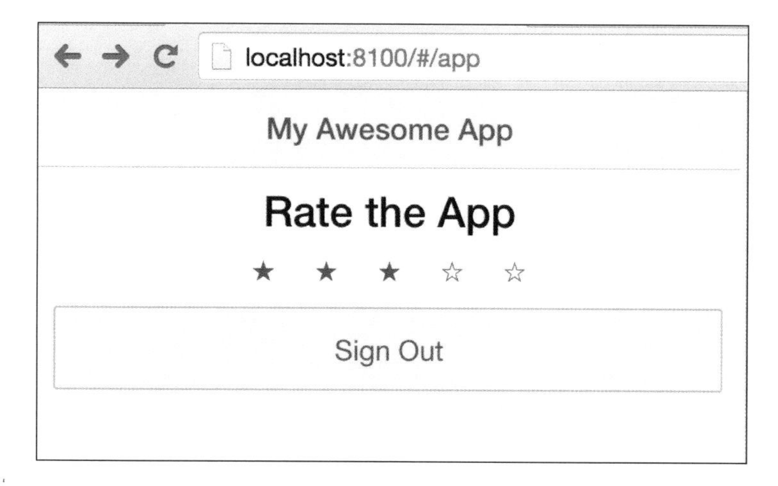

Also, we left our `LoginCtrl` empty. If you want, you can bind an `ng-click` to the **Submit** button and call a function in the controller to do your validations. You can remove the `ui-sref` attribute from the button tag and use the `$state` service inside the controller to navigate to the app view. The button tag in `www/templates/login.html` can be replaced with the following code:

```
<button ng-click="validate()" ng-disabled="!email || !password"
class="button button-block button-positive">Sign In</button>
```

The `LoginCtrl` in `www/js/app.js` is shown here:

```
.controller('LoginCtrl', function($scope, $state) {

    $scope.validate = function() {
        // some other validations...
        $state.go('app');
    }

})
```

In the next example, we are going to build a slightly more complex UI using the state router. We are going to build a tabbed component. But first, we are going to take a look at named views in the AngularUI router.

Let's say that we have three places on our page that need to be updated when a route changes. Using the AngularJS `ngRoute` router, we cannot do this, as the `ngRoute` router lets us have only one `ng-view` per app. But the AngularUI router provides something called "named views", whereby you can have many `ui-views` on the page and name them. So, based on the view state, different templates will be loaded in each of those.

Consider the following HTML, where we have three partial views in one page:

```
<body>
  <div ui-view="partialview1"></div>
  <div ui-view="partialview2"></div>
  <div ui-view="partialview3"></div>
</body>
```

So, while configuring our routes, we will introduce a new property in our route config object named `views`. And then we will mention which controllers and templates need to be invoked when that state is changed. For instance:

```
$stateProvider
  .state('page1',{
    views: {
      'partialview1': {
        templateUrl: 'page1-partialview1.html',
        controller: 'Page1Partialview1Ctrl'
      },
      'partialview2': {
        templateUrl: 'page1-partialview2.html',
        controller: 'Page1Partialview2Ctrl'
      },
      'partialview3': {
        templateUrl: 'page1-partialview3.html',
        controller: 'Page1Partialview3Ctrl'
      }
    }
  })
  .state('page2',{
    views: {
      'partialview1': {
        templateUrl: 'page2-partialview1.html',
        controller: 'Page2Partialview1Ctrl'
      },
      'partialview2': {
        templateUrl: 'page2-partialview2.html',
        controller: 'Page2Partialview2Ctrl'
```

```
      },
      'partialview3': {
        templateUrl: 'page2-partialview3.html',
        controller: 'Page2Partialview3Ctrl'
      }
    }
  })
```

As you can see, if you are in the `page1` state, appropriate views and controllers will be called for each of the three named views—and similarly for `page2`.

Taking the same concept to Ionic, we are going to work with named views using the `ion-nav-view` directive, and adding a `name` attribute to it. We will be building one page with two states or rather two tabs.

We will start off by scaffolding a blank template:

```
ionic start -a "Example 11" -i app.example.eleven example11 blank
```

Our tabbed interface is going to have two tabs - `login` and `register`. We are going to configure these two states in our `www/js/app.js` file after the module is instantiated:

```
.config(function($stateProvider, $urlRouterProvider) {

    $stateProvider
        .state('login', {
            url: '/login',
            views: {
                login: {
                    templateUrl: 'templates/login.html'
                }
            }
        })

    .state('register', {
        url: '/register',
        views: {
            register: {
                templateUrl: 'templates/register.html'
            }
        }
    })

    $urlRouterProvider.otherwise('/login');

})
```

Do notice the `view` property and the name of the subproperty (`login` and `register`). This is how we declare the `views` object.

Next, we are going to work with the Ionic tabs directive (`http://ionicframework.com/docs/api/directive/ionTabs/`). This is a pretty simple directive that wraps the `ion-tab` directives with the `ion-tabs` directive to create a tabbed interface.

So, in our `www/index.html`, we replace the `body` tag with the following command:

```
<body ng-app="starter">
    <ion-nav-bar class="bar-royal">
    </ion-nav-bar>
    <ion-tabs class="tabs-royal">
        <ion-tab icon="ion-power" ui-sref="login">
            <ion-nav-view name="login"></ion-nav-view>
        </ion-tab>
        <ion-tab icon="ion-person-add" ui-sref="register">
            <ion-nav-view name="register"></ion-nav-view>
        </ion-tab>
    </ion-tabs>
</body>
```

As you can see, the `ion-tabs` directive consists of two `ion-tab` directives and `ion-tab` consists of `ion-nav-view` as the content for each view. Each `ion-nav-view` has a `name` attribute set to the view that it needs to load.

Now all we need to do is create the two templates. Create a folder named `templates` inside the `www` folder, and create a file named `login.html` inside the `templates` folder. The contents of `www/templates/login.html` will be:

```
<ion-view view-title="Login">
    <ion-content class="padding">
        <div class="list">
            <label class="item item-input">
                <span class="input-label">Email</span>
                <input type="email" ng-model="email">
            </label>
            <label class="item item-input">
                <span class="input-label">Password</span>
                <input type="password" ng-model="password"
ng-minlength="3">
            </label>
            <div class="padding">
                <button ng-disabled="!email || !password"
class="button button-block button-royal">Sign In</button>
            </div>
```

```
        </div>
    </ion-content>
</ion-view>
```

Do notice how we have wrapped the template inside an `ion-view` directive and then the `ion-content` directive. Next, create another file named `register.html` inside the `www/templates` folder and update it as shown here:

```
<ion-view view-title="Register">
    <ion-content class="padding">
        <div class="list">
            <label class="item item-input">
                <span class="input-label">Email</span>
                <input type="email" ng-model="email">
            </label>
            <label class="item item-input">
                <span class="input-label">Password</span>
                <input type="password" ng-model="password"
ng-minlength="3">
            </label>
            <label class="item item-input">
                <span class="input-label">Re-Enter Password</span>
                <input type="password" ng-model="password2"
ng-minlength="3">
            </label>
            <div class="padding">
                <button ng-disabled="(!email || !password) ||
(password != password2)" class="button button-block button-
royal">Sign In</button>
            </div>
        </div>
    </ion-content>
</ion-view>
```

Save all the files and run the following command:

```
ionic serve
```

You will see the following screenshot:

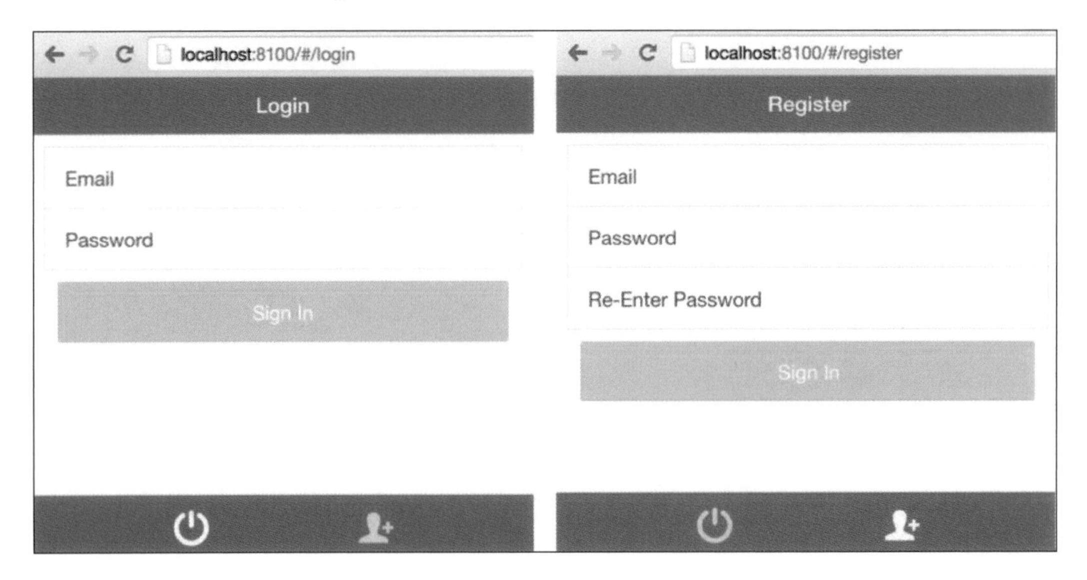

In the preceding example, we have built a tabbed component from the ground up, using just the starter template. We need not do this every time. There is a template available to scaffold tabbed interface apps. We are going to use that to scaffold an app and quickly walkthrough it.

Scaffold a `tabs` template as follows:

```
ionic start -a "Example 12" -i app.example.twelve example12 tabs
```

Once the scaffolding is done, open `www/js/app.js` and scroll to the `config` method. You should see the routes configured for this app. They should look like this:

```
.config(function($stateProvider, $urlRouterProvider) {
  $stateProvider
    .state('tab', {
    url: "/tab",
    abstract: true,
    templateUrl: "templates/tabs.html"
  })

  .state('tab.dash', {
    url: '/dash',
    views: {
      'tab-dash': {
        templateUrl: 'templates/tab-dash.html',
        controller: 'DashCtrl'
```

```
        }
      }
    })

    .state('tab.chats', {
        url: '/chats',
        views: {
          'tab-chats': {
            templateUrl: 'templates/tab-chats.html',
            controller: 'ChatsCtrl'
          }
        }
      })
      .state('tab.chat-detail', {
        url: '/chats/:chatId',
        views: {
          'tab-chats': {
            templateUrl: 'templates/chat-detail.html',
            controller: 'ChatDetailCtrl'
          }
        }
      })

    .state('tab.account', {
      url: '/account',
      views: {
        'tab-account': {
          templateUrl: 'templates/tab-account.html',
          controller: 'AccountCtrl'
        }
      }
    });

    $urlRouterProvider.otherwise('/tab/dash');

  });
```

If you notice, the `tab` state property has a new property called `abstract` and it is set to `true`. An abstract state is simply a state that can't be transitioned to. It is activated implicitly when one of its descendants is activated.

In our scenario, the `tab` holder will be an abstract state and, when any of the child tabs is activated, this `tab` state will be activated automatically.

You can read more about abstract states at https://github.com/angular-ui/ui-router/wiki/Nested-States-%26-Nested-Views#abstract-states.

If you open `templates/tabs.html`, you can see the `ion-tabs` directive set up in a template file and not in the `index.html` file like our previous example. This template will behave like an abstract state for the `tabs` component. Also, you can see that `tab-dash.html`, `tab-chats.html`, and `tab-account.html` are structured in the same way as our last example.

You can test the app by running the following command:

```
ionic serve
```

As you may have noticed, the `chats` tab has a list of chats shown and, when you click on a chat item, it takes you to another view showing the details of the selected chat. This kind of setup is called a master detail view, the "master" being list of chats and the "detail" being chat details. Also, do notice that the URLs for different chats are different, such as `http://localhost:8100/#/tab/chats/0` or `http://localhost:8100/#/tab/chats/1` and so on.

If you go back to the state configuration in `www/js/app.js` for `tab.chat-detail`, you should see the following code:

```
.state('tab.chat-detail', {
    url: '/chats/:chatId',
    views: {
        'tab-chats': {
            templateUrl: 'templates/chat-detail.html',
            controller: 'ChatDetailCtrl'
        }
    }
})
```

The `url` property has a value `'/chats/:chatId'`. Do notice the colon before the `chatId`. This tells the router that the value of `chatId` is a dynamic value; when you encounter this route, validate the route till the chats part, and then store the value after the chats part of the URL in a variable named `chatId`.

So, when we are dealing with our application in real-time, this value will be available on `$stateParams`. You can check it out in `www/js/controllers.js` - `ChatDetailCtrl`:

```
.controller('ChatDetailCtrl', function($scope, $stateParams, Chats) {
  $scope.chat = Chats.get($stateParams.chatId);
})
```

The preceding example shows how you can mix-and-match tabbed views with a master detail view.

You can also scaffold a `sidemenu` template and see how the side menu is configured in the routes.

Summary

In this chapter, we have taken a look at most of the Ionic CSS components. We also went through the color swatch available out of the box. Next, we integrated the Ionic CSS components with AngularJS to add in some functionality. We worked with the Ionic state router from the ground up, building a simple two-page app. Finally, we explored the tabbed interfaces and master detail views.

In the next chapter, we will be looking at customizing the Ionic CSS with the power of SCSS.

4

Ionic and SCSS

In this chapter, we are going to take a look at the styling aspects of an Ionic app. By default we have seen that Ionic has 7 shades, or a swatch with predefined colors. In this chapter, we are going to edit those colors, and modify the look and feel of Ionic components. This chapter sets out to give you an understanding of how to work with Ionic SCSS in general, rather than focusing on certain components.

In this chapter, we are going to cover the following topics:

- SASS versus SCSS
- Setting up SCSS
- Working with SCSS variables
- Working with SCSS mixins
- Theming a side menu app

For this chapter, you can also access the code, raise issues, and chat with the author at GitHub (`https://github.com/learning-ionic/Chapter-4`).

What is Sass?

According to the Sass documentation at `http://sass-lang.com/documentation/`:

> *"Sass is an extension of CSS that adds power and elegance to the basic language. It allows you to use variables, nested rules, mixins, inline imports, and more, all with a fully CSS-compatible syntax. Sass helps keep large stylesheets well organized, and get small stylesheets up and running quickly."*

In simpler terms, Sass makes CSS programmable. You may wonder why, if the chapter is called SCSS, we are talking about Saas. Well, Sass and SCSS are pretty much the same CSS pre-processor, with each having its own way of writing the pre-CSS syntax.

Sass was developed as part of another pre-processor named HAML (`http://haml.info/`) by Ruby developers. So, it inherited a lot of syntax style from Ruby, such as indentation, no braces, no semi-colons, and so on.

A sample Sass file looks like this:

```
// app.sass

brand-primary= blue

.container
    color= !brand-primary
    margin= 0px auto
    padding= 20px

=border-radius(!radius)
    -webkit-border-radius= !radius
    -moz-border-radius= !radius
    border-radius= !radius

*
    +border-radius(0px)
```

When you run the preceding Sass code through a Sass compiler, it returns good-old CSS. The generated CSS looks like this:

```
.container {
  color: blue;
  margin: 0px auto;
  padding: 20px;
}

* {
  -webkit-border-radius: 0px;
  -moz-border-radius: 0px;
  border-radius: 0px;
}
```

But did you notice that `brand-primary` in the Sass code acted as a variable, substituting its value inside the `container` class, or that the `border-radius` acted as a function (also called a mixin), generating the required CSS rules when called with an argument? This was missing in CSS.

People who are used to the bracket-based coding languages found this way of writing code a bit difficult. So, enter SCSS.

Sass stands for Syntactically Awesome Style Sheets and SCSS stands for Sassy CSS. SCSS is pretty much same as Sass, except for the CSS-like syntax. The preceding Sass code when written in SCSS looks like this:

```
// app.scss
$brand-primary: blue;

.container{
    color: !brand-primary;
    margin: 0px auto;
    padding: 20px;
}

@mixin border-radius($radius) {
    -webkit-border-radius: $radius;
    -moz-border-radius: $radius;
    border-radius: $radius;
}

* {
    @include border-radius(5px);
}
```

This looks a lot closer to CSS itself, right? And it is expressive. The best part, Ionic uses SCSS to style its components.

If you want to know more about SCSS versus Sass, you can go through this post at http://thesassway.com/editorial/sass-vs-scss-which-syntax-is-better.

Now that we have a basic understanding of what SCSS and Sass are, we will leverage them in our Ionic app to theme our components.

Setting up SCSS in our Ionic project

Now we will see how to set up SCSS in an existing Ionic project. We will start off by scaffolding a new tabs project. Create a folder named chapter4 and inside that open a new terminal/prompt and run:

```
ionic start -a "Example 13" -i app.example.thirteen example13 tabs
```

We can set up SCSS in our project in two ways:

- Manual setup
- Ionic CLI task

The manual setup

To set up SCSS manually, we will follow these steps:

1. Using the `cd` command, step into the `example13` folder:

   ```
   cd example13
   ```

2. Install the required dependencies. The Ionic project that we scaffold from templates comes with a `package.json` file. This file already has all the dependencies needed to set up SCSS. Also, the project ships with a `gulpFile.js`, with the SCSS task defined, that watches for the changes in your SCSS files and builds the CSS file on-the-fly.
3. To set up these dependencies, run this:

   ```
   npm install
   ```

4. Also, if you did not install Gulp globally earlier, you can do so by running the following command:

   ```
   npm install gulp --global
   ```

5. Next, open `www/index.html`, and you should find a commented line inside the `head` tag that looks like:

   ```
   <!-- IF using Sass (run gulp sass first), then uncomment below
   and remove the CSS includes above
       <link href="css/ionic.app.css" rel="stylesheet">
       -->
   ```

   Remove the comments and you should be left with only the `link` tag. Next, remove the reference to `ionic.css` from above this reference. We do not need that any more.

6. Back in the terminal/prompt, run this command:

   ```
   gulp sass
   ```

   And this generates `ionic.app.css` and `ionic.app.min.css` files inside the `www/css` folder.

That is all you need to set up SCSS inside your Ionic project. We will take a look at customizing the SCSS a bit later.

The Ionic CLI task

Next, we will take a look at setting up SCSS using Ionic CLI's setup task. Since we already set up SCSS in `example13`, we will scaffold another project and implement using the CLI task.

To scaffold a new project, run this command:

```
ionic start -a "Example 14" -i app.example.fourteen example14 tabs
```

Next, change directory inside the `example14` folder, and run this command:

```
ionic setup sass
```

This will take care of downloading the dependencies, removing the comments in `index.html`, and creating the `ionic.app.css` and `ionic.app.min.css` files inside the `www/css` folder. Pretty sweet, right!

Working with Ionic SCSS

This section covers how you can customize Ionic's SCSS variables and mixins.

The code we are going to write will assume that you have the basics needed to work with SCSS.

If you are new to SCSS, I recommend following this guide `http://sass-lang.com/guide`.

Basic swatch

Earlier, we have seen the basic color swatch provided by Ionic: Positive, Assertive, Calm, and so on. They are all pre-defined and set up by the Ionic team. What if you want to change the color for components using the class positive? Let's take a look at how this is done.

Referring to the `example14` folder, open `www/index.html` and update the class on the `ion-nav-bar` directive from `bar-stable` to `bar-positive`. Next, open `www/templates/tabs.html` and remove the class named `tabs-color-active-positive` on the `ion-tabs` directive, and add `tabs-positive`.

At the time of writing, the `tabs` template is shipped with the stable style for the `ion-nav-bar` directive.

To see the output, run this command:

```
ionic serve
```

The tabbed interface looks like this:

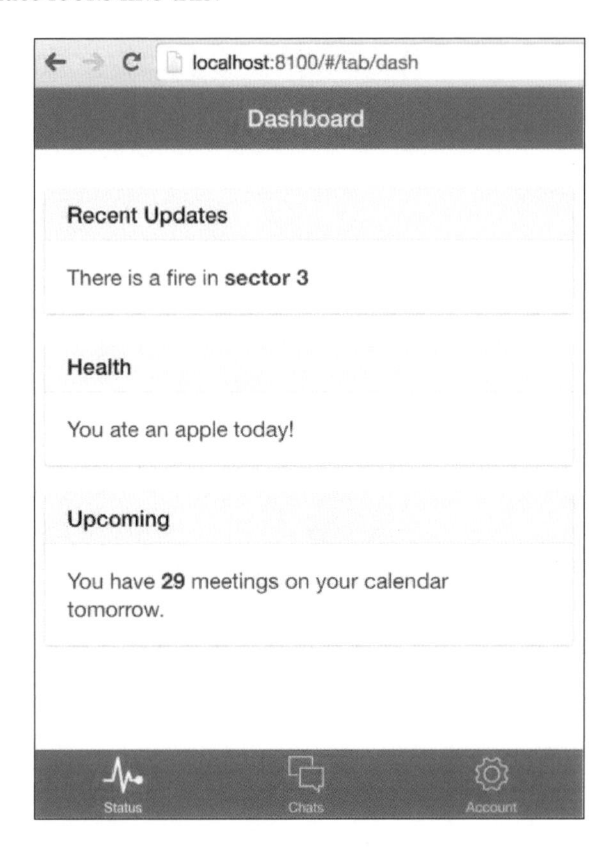

Let's assume that this is our final app. Now we want to build a theme for this layout and the theme is pretty simple. All the blue needs to be replaced with teal.

To achieve this, we will open the `scss/ionic.app.scss` file, and copy the following line from the comments at the top of the file:

```
$positive:                          #387ef5 !default;
```

Then add it after the block comments (after `*/`). Next, we update the value of the `$positive` variable to `teal`:

```
$positive:                          teal;
```

Save the file and the Sass task runs in the background, automatically generating the new `ionic.app.css` and `ionic.app.min.css` files. Then the page is automatically refreshed. You should see the teal-themed page:

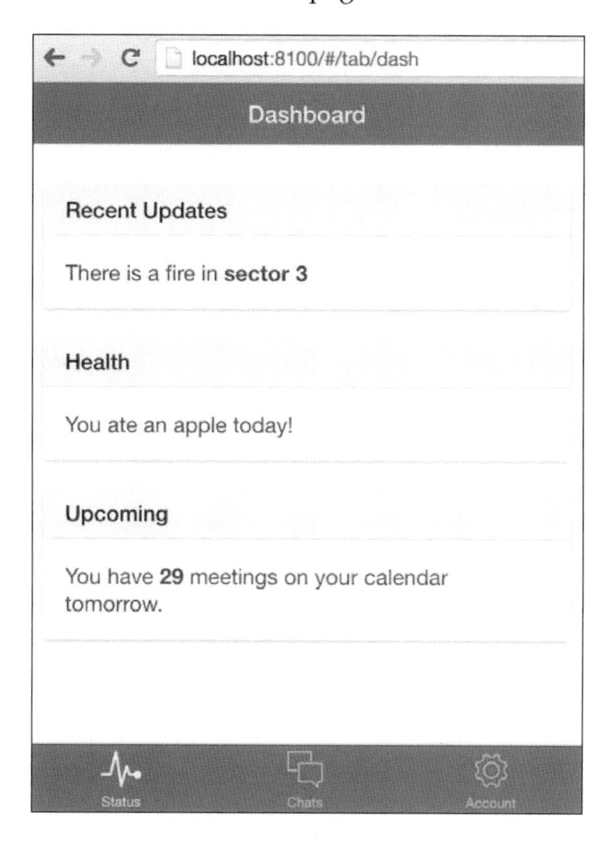

Do notice how all the references of the positive class are updated to teal. Isn't this awesome! Managing themes for your mobile apps isn't rocket science anymore!

Understanding the Ionic SCSS setup

In this section, we will take a look at how Ionic SCSS is set up.

If you look at the scaffolded project structure, you will see an `scss` folder, which consists of the `ionic.app.scss` file. For customizing the default Ionic theme, you should override the variable here, and here only. If you are planning to have multiple themes, I recommend using `theme1.scss`, `theme2.scss`, and so on files inside the `scss` folder.

Do remember that any of the theme files should have the following two lines:

```
// The path for our ionicons font files, relative to the built CSS
in www/css
$ionicons-font-path: "../lib/ionic/fonts" !default;

// Include all of Ionic
@import "www/lib/ionic/scss/ionic";
```

In a typical theme file, the first section overrides SCSS variables. The second section loads Ionic core SCSS files; finally we override the generated classes.

The Ionic core SCSS files refer to the following two statements:

`$ionicons-font-path: "../lib/ionic/fonts" !default;`

`@import "www/lib/ionic/scss/ionic";`

If you have worked with SCSS before, you will understand that any variable declared with `!default` will not be reassigned a new value if a value is already assigned, just like the preceding example.

To get a better understating of what is happening, we will first navigate to the path of the `$ionicons-font-path` variable—that is, `www/lib/ionic/fonts`. This folder will contain four font files, dispatched according to browser compatibility.

Next, we will navigate to the path of the Ionic SCSS framework. This will be `www/lib/ionic/scss/ionic`. As you may have noticed, there is no folder named `ionic` inside the `scss` folder. This refers to the `ionic.scss` file inside the `www/lib/ionic/scss/` folder. Also do notice that other SCSS files inside the `scss` folder start with an underscore (_).

If you open the `ionic.scss` file, you will notice that all this file does is import other SCSS files present inside the current folder:

```
@charset "UTF-8";

@import
  // Ionicons
  "ionicons/ionicons.scss",

  // Variables
  "mixins",
  "variables",

  // Base
  "reset",
```

```
"scaffolding",
"type",

// Components
"action-sheet",
"backdrop",
"bar",
"tabs",
"menu",
"modal",
"popover",
"popup",
"loading",
"items",
"list",
"badge",
"slide-box",
"refresher",
"spinner",

// Forms
"form",
"checkbox",
"toggle",
"radio",
"range",
"select",
"progress",

// Buttons
"button",
"button-bar",

// Util
"grid",
"util",
"platform",

// Animations
"animations",
"transitions";
```

If you want to make any changes to Ionicons, you will refer to `ionicons/ionicons.scss`; or, if you have to make changes to the modal component, you will refer to `_modal.scss`. Also, if you want to make changes to the animations, you will refer to `_animations.scss`.

There are two important files that you need to be aware of pretty well if you want to modify the default look and feel of the Ionic components. They are as follows:

- `_variables.scss`
- `_mixins.scss`

As the names suggest, they store all the variables that can be overridden and mixins that can be reused, respectively. If you open `_variables.scss`, you will notice the variables for colors, fonts, paddings, margins, borders, and so on.

For instance, you can search for the text - `button`, and you will find an entire section that has the configuration of how each button is set up. Taking an excerpt from this section:

```
$button-positive-bg:              $positive !default;
$button-positive-text:            #fff !default;
$button-positive-border:          darken($positive, 10%) !default;
$button-positive-active-bg:       darken($positive, 10%) !default;
$button-positive-active-border:   darken($positive, 10%) !default;
```

You can see how buttons themed with positive class are set up. With one change to the `$positive` variable, you can see how the button look and feel update.

Another example is the `Grids` section, as follows:

```
// Grids
// -------------------------------

$grid-padding-width:              10px !default;
$grid-responsive-sm-break:        567px !default;  // smaller than
landscape phone
$grid-responsive-md-break:        767px !default;  // smaller than
portrait tablet
$grid-responsive-lg-break:        1023px !default; // smaller than
landscape tablet
```

If you want to change the way your grids behave, this is the place to come to. Also, you can set your media query break points for small, medium, and large devices looking up variable names from here.

You can spend some time with this file and get an idea of what variables you can override. As of today, there is no official documentation on the SCSS variables and what they do. But commented sections inside the `_variables.scss` seem to help at times.

Next, open up `_mixins.scss`. This file consists of mixins used by the Ionic components. For instance, the `button-style` mixin:

```
@mixin button-style($bg-color, $border-color, $active-bg-color,
$active-border-color, $color) {
  border-color: $border-color;
  background-color: $bg-color;
  color: $color;

  // Give desktop users something to play with
  &:hover {
    color: $color;
    text-decoration: none;
  }
  &.active,
  &.activated {
    border-color: $active-border-color;
    background-color: $active-bg-color;
    box-shadow: inset 0 1px 4px rgba(0,0,0,0.1);
  }
}
```

This mixin takes a background color, a border color, and an active state color and then generates the `border-color`, `background-color`, `color`, `.hover`, `.active`, and `.activated` rules.

Another commonly used mixin is `clearfix`:

```
@mixin clearfix {
  *zoom: 1;
  &:before,
  &:after {
    display: table;
    content: "";
    line-height: 0;
```

```
    }
    &:after {
      clear: both;
    }
}
```

All it does is clear the row, and this class is used in multiple places for managing the layouts.

Again, there is no official documentation and you can spend some time with this file to understand the mixins that are available.

Using variables and mixins

Now that we have seen the two core parts of the Ionic SCSS framework, we will see how they are used.

Open _button.scss. If you remember, earlier when we were working with the button components, for every button style or button type we added the button class followed by the style or type. For instance:

```
<button class="button button-positive button-block">Click Me</button>
```

The button class provides the default styling for the button. The other classes provide the style or type modifications. Quite a decoupled way of handling the CSS, isn't it?

Back to our file, and you should see how the button class is set up. Inside the button class definition, you will find various variables and mixins, whose use we saw earlier.

An excerpt from the button class definition is as follows:

```
&.button-positive {
    @include button-style($button-positive-bg, $button-positive-border,
$button-positive-active-bg, $button-positive-active-border, $button-
positive-text);
    @include button-clear($button-positive-bg);
    @include button-outline($button-positive-bg);
  }
```

Here three mixins are used to generate the styles for a button-positive class. The style will be applied only when both classes are applied to the element.

Another file to check out is _util.scss. All the utility classes such as hide, show, padding, and so on are generated here.

If you want to make any changes to the animations and transitions, you can checkout `_animations.scss` and `_transitions.scss`.

The filename helps a lot while searching for SCSS code for a component.

The SCSS workflow

Now that we are aware of where and how the Ionic SCSS framework is set up, we will come up with a workflow that we can use while working with SCSS in an Ionic project.

The steps are as follows:

1. Set up Ionic SCSS.
2. Open the `scss/ionic.app.scss` file.
3. Add/update the variables you want to override before you import the Ionic SCSS framework.
4. Add the required fonts before you import the Ionic SCSS framework.
5. Add/override pre-defined classes or create new classes after the Ionic SCSS framework is imported.

So, a typical customized `ionic.app.scss` looks like this:

```
// Override or add variables
$positive: teal;
$custom: #aaa;

// add custom button variables
$button-custom-bg: $custom !default;
$button-custom-text: #eee !default;
$button-custom-border: darken($custom, 10%) !default;
$button-custom-active-bg: darken($custom, 10%) !default;
$button-custom-active-border: darken($custom, 10%) !default;

// define the ionic fonts path
$ionicons-font-path: "../lib/ionic/fonts" !default;

// import Ionic SCSS Framework
```

```
@import "www/lib/ionic/scss/ionic";

// build a custom button class that is specific to our app
.button-custom {
    /*
        Usage : <button class="button button-custom">
                Custom Styled Button
                </button>
        */

    @include button-style($button-custom-bg, $button-custom-border,
$button-custom-active-bg, $button-custom-active-border, $button-custom-
text);
    @include button-clear($button-custom-bg);
    @include button-outline($button-custom-bg);
}
```

If you want to change the complete look and feel of the Ionic app, you can start by overriding the default swatch:

```
$light:                              #fff !default;
$stable:                             #f8f8f8 !default;
$positive:                           #387ef5 !default;
$calm:                               #11c1f3 !default;
$balanced:                           #33cd5f !default;
$energized:                          #ffc900 !default;
$assertive:                          #ef473a !default;
$royal:                              #886aea !default;
$dark:                               #444 !default;
```

Then you can identify what components you are trying to modify. Navigate to the appropriate SCSS file and look for variables that are affecting the class. Head back to `ionic.app.scss` and override them.

Building a swatch

In order to understand the preceding process a bit better, we will build a theme of our own, overriding variables and classes. We will scaffold a side menu app, and then change its default look and feel.

To scaffold a new side menu app run this:

```
ionic start -a "Example 15" -i app.example.fifteen example15 sidemenu
```

Next, using the `cd` command, go to the `example15` folder and run this:

```
ionic setup sass
```

This will download and set up the SCSS dependencies for your project. Open `ionic.app.scss`. The idea here is not to change any markup or add new classes, but rather to modify the appropriate variables to reflect our new theme.

This is not the only way in which you can theme your application. You can modify your markup, add appropriate classes that reflect your brand (for example, `button-mybrand` or `bar-mybrand`), and then create variables and classes appropriately in SCSS.

We will be theming the side menu app in shades of teal. The first thing we will do is modify the `$stable` variable:

```
$stable: #009688;
```

If you serve the app after adding the preceding style, you will notice that the header bar has turned teal, as shown here:

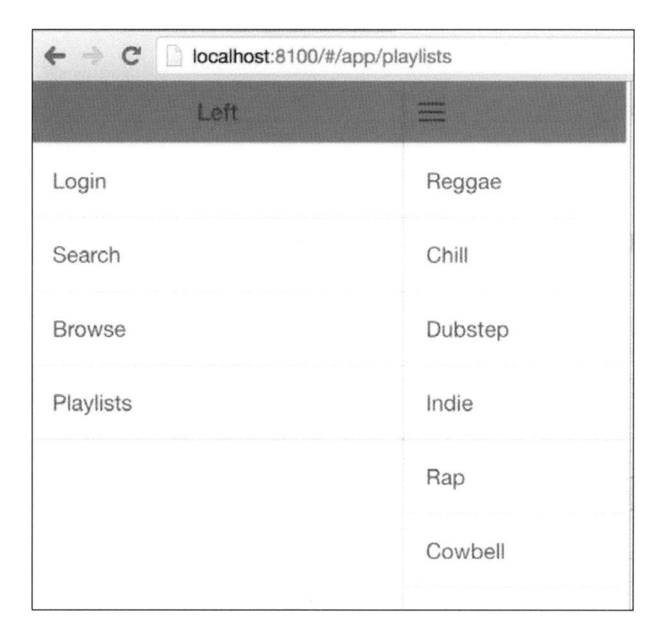

The heading text is black. We would like it to be close to white. If you open `_bar.scss`, you will find a section like this:

```
.title {
      color: #fff;
    }
```

Looking at this, we know that this not a variable. So, in this case, we will override the class itself. In our `ionic.app.scss`, after we include the Ionic CSS framework, we will add this:

```
.bar.bar-stable .title{
       color:#eee;
}
```

Once you save the file, you can see the title text color change. But, if you notice, the hamburger menu remains black. We want to change that as well. If you open the browser's development tools and inspect the hamburger menu, you will find a button like this:

```
<button class="button button-icon button-clear ion-navicon" menu-
toggle="left"></button>
```

In the styles section of this element in the development tools, you will find a class `bar-stable button button-clear`, which is setting the color to `#444`. Now, we have to track down this variable and reset it.

Since the first part of the class is `.bar-stable`, we know that the definition may be from `_bar.scss`. Inside `_bar.scss`, you will find a section like this:

```
.bar-stable {
  .button {
    @include button-style($bar-stable-bg, $bar-stable-border,
$bar-stable-active-bg, $bar-stable-active-border, $bar-stable-
text);
    @include button-clear($bar-stable-text, $bar-title-font-size);
  }
}
```

Do notice the mixin `button-clear`. We will open `_mixins.scss` and search for this mixin. The mixin looks something like:

```
@mixin button-clear($color, $font-size:"") {
  &.button-clear {
    border-color: transparent;
```

```
    background: none;
    box-shadow: none;
    color: $color;

    @if $font-size != "" {
      font-size: $font-size;
    }
  }
  &.button-icon {
    border-color: transparent;
    background: none;
  }
}
```

And, as you can see from here, the first argument to the mixin is set as `$color`. So, we know which variable to override.

Back in the `ionic.app.scss` file, we will override `$bar-stable-text` variable:

```
$bar-stable-text: #eee;
```

Before including the Ionic framework SCSS. Save the file and you will see the following screenshot:

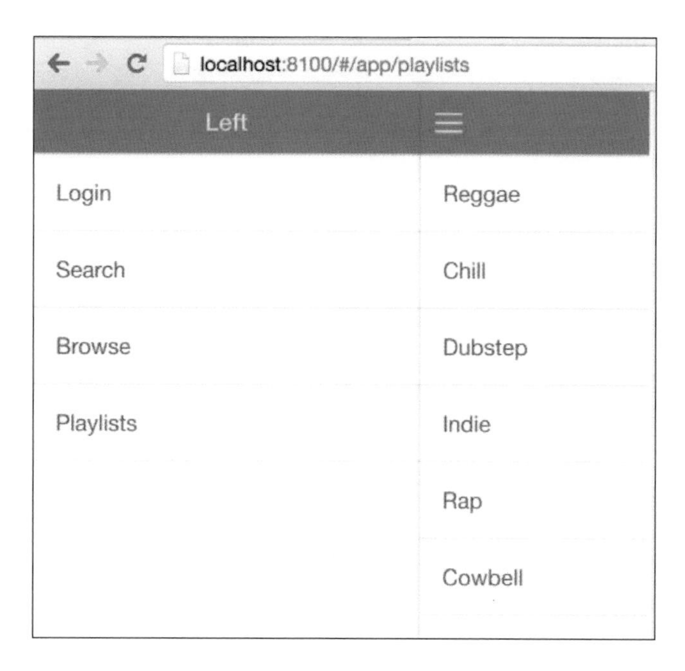

Next, we will change the base color of the font to a shade of teal. For this, we will override the variable `$base-color`. Now we will add some more padding to the list items. Again, you can head to `_items.scss`, and you will find this:

```
padding: $item-padding;
```

You can override the `$item-padding` to 30px.

Next, I want each of the items to have a light green background color. Since this property does not have a variable, we will override the class itself:

```
.item-complex .item-content{
        background:#E0F2F1;
        color:#00695C;
}
```

If you save the file and head to the browser, you will see the following screenshot:

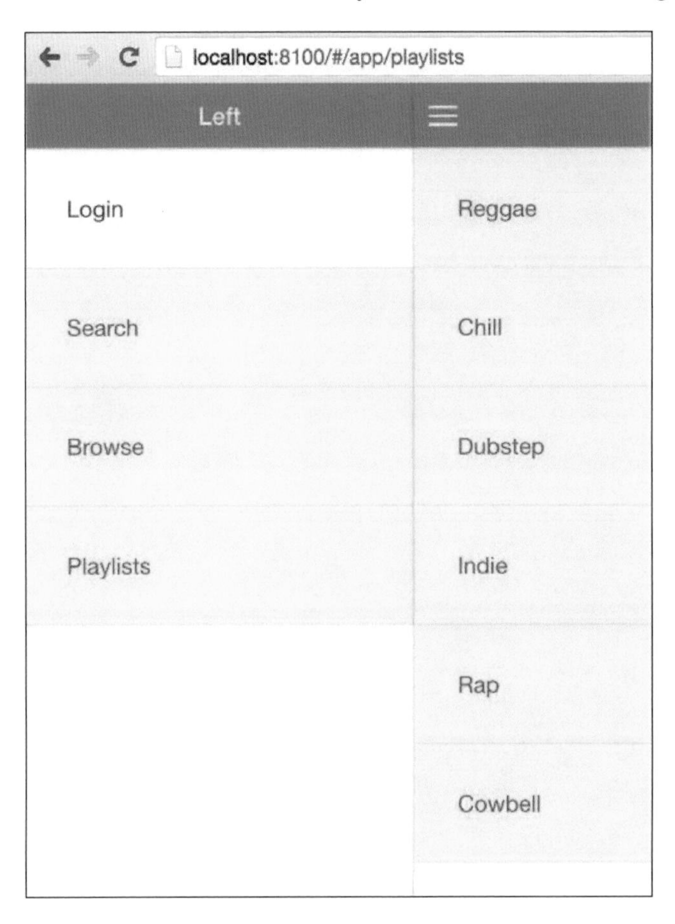

If you click on the login link, a modal popup will appear. In the popup, you will notice that the **Login** button uses the positive class for styling. Let's override that too using the following values:

```
$button-positive-bg: #00BFA5;
$button-positive-border: #00BFA5;
$button-positive-active-bg: #80CBC4;
$button-positive-active-border: #80CBC4;
$button-positive-text: #eee;
```

You can get the list of variables from the `button-style` mixin used for the `button-positive` class. Here we are taking care of both states of the `button` class.

The **Login** modal will look like this:

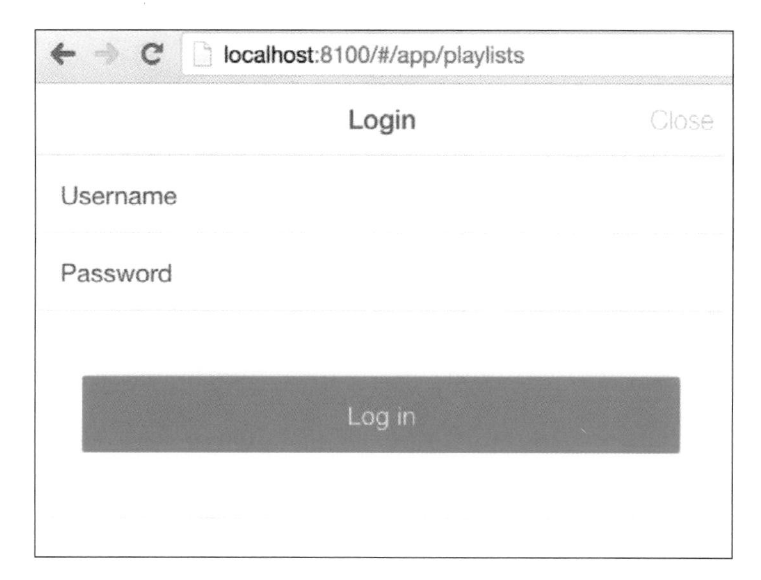

Everything looks good now, except for the border color of list items and the active background color when a list item is selected. Let's fix that too. If you open `_items.scss`, you should be able to see the `item-style` mixin, which takes the `$item-default-border` as the second argument. This value is applied as the border color. We will override this:

```
$item-default-border: #009688;
```

And finally the active background color. Under the link and button active states section, you will notice a mixin item-active-style. The first argument is `$item-default-active-bg`, which is the active background color. We will override this in our `ionic.app.scss`:

```
$item-default-active-bg: #B2DFDB;
```

The completed `ionic.app.scss` file looks like this:

```
// override all $stable themed components
$stable: #009688;


// override the burger menu color
$bar-stable-text: #eee;


// override app base color
$base-color: #00695C;


// increase the item padding
$item-padding : 30px;


// override buttons
$button-positive-bg: #00BFA5;
$button-positive-border: #00BFA5;
$button-positive-active-bg: #80CBC4;
$button-positive-active-border: #80CBC4;
$button-positive-text: #eee;


// border & active bg color
$item-default-border: #009688;
$item-default-active-bg: #B2DFDB;



// The path for our ionicons font files, relative to the built CSS in
www/css
$ionicons-font-path: "../lib/ionic/fonts" !default;


// Include all of Ionic
```

```
@import "www/lib/ionic/scss/ionic";

// Override title color
.bar.bar-stable .title{
        color:#eee;
}

// Override the item background and color
.item-complex .item-content{
       background:#E0F2F1;
       color:#00695C;
}
```

Our final app should look like this:

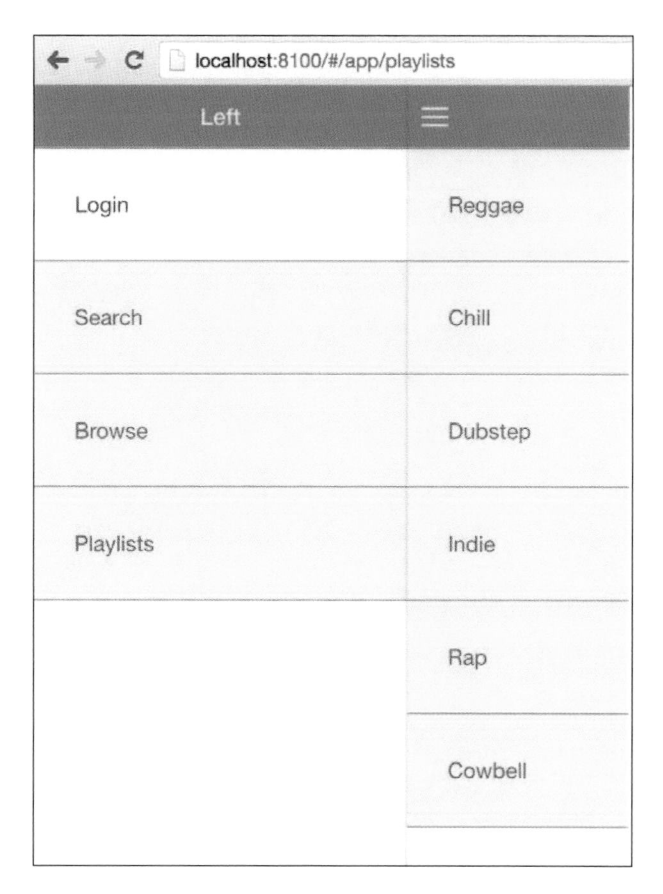

This was a quick and basic example of how you theme an Ionic app using SCSS. You can add a few more components to the app, and try theming them for practice.

I have shown a practical approach to how you can find variables and mixins in the Ionic SCSS setup. This knowledge can be used in any Ionic SCSS project to implement theming by overriding variables and reusing mixins.

Summary

In this chapter, we took a look at theming Ionic apps. We started off by setting up SCSS and then went through the Ionic SCSS file structure. Then, we overrode variables to change the theme of the application. Finally, we took a sample app and modified its look.

In the next chapter, we are going to look at various Ionic directives and services, which will help us in building Hybrid apps with ease.

5

Ionic Directives and Services

Reiterating our journey so far, we have started off by understanding the importance of AngularJS as a client-side MVW framework. We have gone through Apache Cordova, where and how it fits in to the entire hybrid application development stack. Then we introduced Ionic, explaining what it is and how it enables us to build hybrid applications with ease. In *Chapter 3, Ionic CSS Components and Navigation*, we saw how Ionic could be used as a CSS-only framework for your mobile web development, and in *Chapter 4, Ionic and SCSS*, we saw how we could theme those components using the power of SCSS.

In this chapter, we are going to take a look at Ionic directives and services, which provides reusable components and functionality that help us in developing applications even faster.

By the end of this chapter, you will be able to:

- Understand Ionic directives
- Understand Ionic services

Ionic directives and services

Ionic has components that are purely CSS-driven and it has components that need the magic of JavaScript to make them complete. Since Ionic uses AngularJS as its JavaScript framework, all reusable user interface components will be written in the form of directives and all reusable pieces of JavaScript functionality will be written in the form of services.

A few examples of Ionic directives are as follows:

- Navigation (`ion-nav-view`)
- Content (`ion-content`, `ion-pane` and `ion-refresher`)
- Headers and Footers (`ion-header-bar` and `ion-footer-bar`)
- Lists (`ion-list` and `ion-item`)
- Tabs (`ion-tabs` and `ion-tab`)
- Side menu (`ion-side-menus` and `ion-side-menu`)

A few examples of Ionic services are as follows:

- Platform (`$ionicPlatform`)
- Scroll (`$ionicScrollDelegate`)
- Modals (`$ionicModal`)
- Navbar (`$ionicNavBarDelegate`)
- History (`$ionicHistory`)
- Popup (`$ionicPopup`)

In the next section of the chapter, we will be going through some of the Ionic directives and services and understanding how to work with them. We will be working with Ionic core directives and services interchangeably, depending on the feature.

For this chapter, you can also access the code, raise issues, and chat with the author at GitHub (`https://github.com/learning-ionic/Chapter-5`).

The Ionic Platform service

The first service we are going to deal with is the Ionic Platform service (`$ionicPlatform`). This service provides device-level hooks that you can tap into to better control your application's behavior.

We will start off with the very basic `ready` method. This method is fired once the device is ready or immediately, if the device is already ready.

To try out Ionic Platform services, we will be scaffolding a blank app and then working with the services. Before we scaffold the blank app, we will create a folder named `chapter5`. Inside that folder, we will run the following command:

```
ionic start -a "Example 16" -i app.example.sixteen example16 blank
```

Once the app is scaffolded, if you open `www/js/app.js`, you should find a section such as:

```
.run(function($ionicPlatform) {
  $ionicPlatform.ready(function() {
    // Hide the accessory bar by default (remove this to show the
accessory bar above the keyboard
    // for form inputs)
    if(window.cordova && window.cordova.plugins.Keyboard) {
      cordova.plugins.Keyboard.hideKeyboardAccessoryBar(true);
    }
    if(window.StatusBar) {
      StatusBar.styleDefault();
    }
  });
})
```

All the Cordova-related code needs to be written inside the `$ionicPlatform.ready` method, as this is the point in the app life cycle where all the plugins are initialized and ready to be used.

You can see that the `$ionicPlatform` service is injected as a dependency to the `run` method. It is highly recommended to use `$ionicPlatform.ready` method inside other AngularJS components such as controllers and directives, where you are planning to interact with Cordova plugins.

In the preceding `run` method, note that we are hiding the keyboard accessory bar by setting:

```
cordova.plugins.Keyboard.hideKeyboardAccessoryBar(true);
```

You can override this by setting the value to `false`. Also, do notice the `if` condition before the statement. It is always better to check for variables related to Cordova before using them.

The `$ionicPlatform` service comes with a handy method to detect the hardware back button event. A few (Android) devices have a hardware back button and, if you want to listen to the back button pressed event, you will need to hook into the `onHardwareBackButton` method on the `$ionicPlatform` service:

```
var hardwareBackButtonHandler = function() {
  console.log('Hardware back button pressed');
  // do more interesting things here
}
        $ionicPlatform.onHardwareBackButton(hardwareBackButtonHandl
er);
```

This event needs to be registered inside the `$ionicPlatform.ready` method, preferably inside AngularJS's `run` method. The `hardwareBackButtonHandler` callback will be called whenever the user presses the device's back button.

A simple functionally that you can do with this handler is to ask the user if they want to really quit your app, making sure that they have not accidently hit the back button.

Sometimes this may be annoying. Thus, you can provide a setting in your app whereby the user selects if he/she wants to be alerted when they try to quit. Based on this, you can either defer registering the event or you can unsubscribe to it.

The code for the preceding logic will look something like this:

```
.run(function($ionicPlatform) {
    $ionicPlatform.ready(function() {
        var alertOnBackPress =
localStorage.getItem('alertOnBackPress');

        var hardwareBackButtonHandler = function() {
            console.log('Hardware back button pressed');
            // do more interesting things here
        }

        function manageBackPressEvent(alertOnBackPress) {
            if (alertOnBackPress) {
                $ionicPlatform.onHardwareBackButton(hardwareBackButto
nHandler);
            } else {
                $ionicPlatform.offHardwareBackButton(hardwareBackButt
onHandler);
            }
        }

        // when the app boots up
```

```
        manageBackPressEvent(alertOnBackPress);

        // later in the code/controller when you let
        // the user update the setting
        function updateSettings(alertOnBackPressModified) {
            localStorage.setItem('alertOnBackPress',
alertOnBackPressModified);
            manageBackPressEvent(alertOnBackPressModified)
        }

    });
})
```

In the preceding code snippet, we are looking in `localStorage` for the value of `alertOnBackPress`. Next, we create a handler named `hardwareBackButtonHandler`, which will be triggered when the back button is pressed. Finally, a utility method named `manageBackPressEvent()` takes in a Boolean value that decides whether to register or de-register the callback for `HardwareBackButton`.

With this set up, when the app starts we call the `manageBackPressEvent` method with the value from `localStorage`. If the value is present and is equal to `true`, we register the event; otherwise, we do not. Later on, we can have a settings controller that lets users change this setting. When the user changes the state of `alertOnBackPress`, we call the `updateSettings` method passing in if the user wants to be alerted or not. The `updateSettings` method updates `localStorage` with this setting and calls the `manageBackPressEvent` method, which takes care of registering or de-registering the callback for the hardware back pressed event.

This is one powerful example that showcases the power of AngularJS when combined with Cordova to provide APIs to manage your application easily.

This example may seem a bit complex at first, but most of the services that you are going to consume will be quite similar. There will be events that you need to register and de-register conditionally, based on preferences. So, I thought this would be a good place to share an example such as this, assuming that this concept will grow on you by the time you finish the chapter.

registerBackButtonAction

The `$ionicPlatform` also provides a method named `registerBackButtonAction`. This is another API that lets you control the way your application behaves when the back button is pressed.

By default, pressing the back button executes one task. For example, if you have a multi-page application and you are navigating from page one to page two and then you press the back button, you will be taken back to page one. In another scenario, when a user navigates from page one to page two and page two displays a pop-up dialog when it loads, pressing the back button here will only hide the pop-up dialog but will not navigate to page one.

The `registerBackButtonAction` method provides a hook to override this behavior. The `registerBackButtonAction` method takes the following three arguments:

- `callback`: This is the method to be called when the event is fired
- `priority`: This is the number that indicates the priority of the listener
- `actionId` (optional): This is the ID assigned to the action

By default the priority is as follows:

- Previous view = `100`
- Close side menu = `150`
- Dismiss modal = `200`
- Close action sheet = `300`
- Dismiss popup = `400`
- Dismiss loading overlay = `500`

So, if you want a certain functionality/custom code to override the default behavior of the back button, you will be writing something like this:

```
var cancelRegisterBackButtonAction =
$ionicPlatform.registerBackButtonAction(backButtonCustomHandler,
201);
```

This listener will override (take precedence over) all the default listeners below the priority value of `201`—that is dismiss modal, close side menu, and previous view but not above the priority value.

When the `$ionicPlatform.registerBackButtonAction` method executes, it returns a function. We have assigned that function to the `cancelRegisterBackButtonAction` variable. Executing `cancelRegisterBackButtonAction` de-registers the `registerBackButtonAction` listener.

The on method

Apart from the preceding handy methods, `$ionicPlatform` has a generic `on` method that can be used to listen to all of Cordova's events (`https://cordova.apache.org/docs/en/edge/cordova_events_events.md.html`).

You can set up hooks for application `pause`, `application resume`, `volumedownbutton`, `volumeupbutton`, and so on, and execute a custom functionality accordingly.

You can set up these listeners inside the `$ionicPlatform.ready` method as follows:

```
var cancelPause = $ionicPlatform.on('pause', function() {
            console.log('App is sent to background');
            // do stuff to save power
        });

var cancelResume = $ionicPlatform.on('resume', function() {
            console.log('App is retrieved from background');
            // re-init the app
        });

        // Supported only in BlackBerry 10 & Android
var cancelVolumeUpButton = $ionicPlatform.on('volumeupbutton',
function() {
            console.log('Volume up button pressed');
            // moving a slider up
        });

var cancelVolumeDownButton = $ionicPlatform.on('volumedownbutton',
function() {
            console.log('Volume down button pressed');
            // moving a slider down
        });
```

The `on` method returns a function that, when executed, de-registers the event.

Now you know how to control your app better when dealing with mobile OS events and hardware keys.

Headers and footers

Using the `ion-header-bar` and `ion-footer-bar` directives, you can add a fixed header and a fixed footer to your app.

A sample structure would look like this:

```
<ion-header-bar align-title="center" class="bar-assertive">
        <div class="buttons">
            <button class="button button-royal" ng-
click="doSomething()">Left Button</button>
        </div>
        <h1 class="title">Fixed Header</h1>
        <div class="buttons">
            <button class="button button-royal">Right
Button</button>
        </div>
    </ion-header-bar>
    <ion-content>
        <div class="padding">
            <h3>Content</h3>
            <p>Lorem ipsum dolor sit amet, consectetur adipisicing
elit, sed do eiusmod
            tempor incididunt ut labore et dolore magna aliqua. Ut
enim ad minim veniam,
            quis nostrud exercitation ullamco laboris nisi ut
aliquip ex ea commodo
            consequat. Duis aute irure dolor in reprehenderit in
voluptate velit esse
            cillum dolore eu fugiat nulla pariatur. Excepteur sint
occaecat cupidatat non
            proident, sunt in culpa qui officia deserunt mollit
anim id est laborum. </p>
        </div>
    </ion-content>
    <ion-footer-bar align-title="left" class="bar-energized">
        <div class="buttons">
            <button class="button button-dark">Left Button</button>
        </div>
        <h1 class="title">Fixed Footer</h1>
        <div class="buttons" ng-click="doSomething()">
            <button class="button button-dark">Right
Button</button>
        </div>
</ion-footer-bar>
```

This result will look like this:

Content

Next, we will take a look at content-related directives. The first is the `ion-content` directive.

ion-content

The `ion-content` directive is used as a content area. This directive has a bunch of options that let you control the content area better. You can use the `ion-content` with Ionic's custom scroll view or with the browser's default overflow scrolling.

At the time of writing, a full-blown `ion-content` directive consisted of the following attributes:

```
<ion-content
  delegate-handle=""
  direction=""
  locking=""
  padding=""
  scroll=""
  overflow-scroll=""
  scrollbar-x=""
  scrollbar-y=""
```

```
    start-x=""
    start-y=""
    on-scroll=""
    on-scroll-complete=""
    has-bouncing=""
    scroll-event-interval="">
    <h1>Heading!</h1>
  </ion-content>
```

The explanation of the key attributes of the `ion-content` is as follows:

- `scroll`: This decides whether to allow scrolling (default: `true`)
- `overflow-scroll`: This is to use browser's overflow scrolling
- `on-scroll`: This is the function/expression to be executed when the content is scrolled
- `on-scroll-complete`: This is the function/expression to be executed when the content scrolling is completed
- `scroll-event-interval`: This is the interval before calling on-scroll (default: `10` milliseconds)
- `scrollbar-x`: This shows a horizontal scrollbar (default: `true`)
- `scrollbar-y`: This shows a vertical scrollbar (default: `true`)
- `locking`: This is lock scrolling (default: `true`)
- `direction`: This indicates which way to scroll (`x`, `y` (default), `xy`)
- `has-bouncing`: This allows you to scroll past the edge of the content (iOS: `true`, Android: `false`)

ion-scroll

You can also control the scrolling of content using the `ion-scroll` directive. This directive is used in place of the `ion-content` directive.

The usage is quite simple:

```
<ion-view ng-controller="MyAppCtrl" cache-view="false">
    <ion-scroll zooming="true" direction="xy" style="width: 300px;
height: 300px">
        <div style="width: 1000px; height: 1000px; background-
color:teal"></div>
    </ion-scroll>
</ion-view>
```

It is important to set the height of the scroll box as well as the height of the inner content to enable scrolling.

If you want a center scrolling area, use `ion-content`.

We will talk about `ion-view` in the next section.

ion-refresher

Another handy directive for managing content is `ion-refresher`. This is a simple pull-to-refresh directive that is added to a scroll view (`ion-content` or `ion-scroll`).

To test this example, we will scaffold a new blank project:

```
ionic start -a "Example 17" -i app.example.seventeen example17
blank
```

Using the cd command, go to the `example17` folder and run this:

```
ionic serve
```

This will launch the blank template.

In this example, we will be implementing a pull-to-refresh. We will create a factory that will spoof a HTTP call and return an array of objects. The object is a dummy hash that has two properties for display purposes.

This factory would be invoked from `AppCtrl`, which is the default controller for our view. This controller will also implement the `doRefresh` method, which will be called when the user pulls to refresh. This method will talk to the factory and get random data and the response data will be appended to the existing list.

We will define the following data factory in `www/js/app.js` after the `config` method:

```
.factory('DataFactory', function($timeout, $q) {

    var API = {
        getData: function(count) {
            // Spoof a network call using promises
            var deferred = $q.defer();

            var data = [],
                _o = {};
            count = count || 3;

            for (var i = 0; i < count; i++) {
```

```
                    _o = {
                        // http://stackoverflow.com/a/8084248/1015046
                        random: (Math.random() +
1).toString(36).substring(7),
                        time: (new Date()).toString().substring(15,
24)
                    };

                    data.push(_o);
                };

                $timeout(function() {
                    // success response!
                    deferred.resolve(data);
                }, 1000);

                return deferred.promise;
            }
        };

        return API;
})
```

The preceding example can be implemented with a simple set timeout, rather than promises. But since AngularJS is heavily driven by promises, we are implementing the factory with promises and, personally, I think this is the way to go.

In the preceding factory, we have used AngularJS's `$q` service, which helps us return results in an asynchronous fashion, similar to an HTTP request. We are creating an object with a random alphanumeric string as one property and a substring of the date that returns time as the second property. This data is used for display purposes only and does not have any meaning.

Our app controller will be defined as follows in `www/js/app.js`:

```
.controller('AppCtrl', function($scope, DataFactory) {
    $scope.items = [];

    $scope.doRefresh = function() {
        DataFactory.getData(3)
            .then(function(data) {
                // extend the $scope.items array with the response
                // array from getData();
```

```
                // http://stackoverflow.com/a/1374131/1015046
                Array.prototype.push.apply($scope.items, data);
            }).finally(function() {
                // Stop the ion-refresher from spinning
                $scope.$broadcast('scroll.refreshComplete');
            });
    }

    // load data on page load
    DataFactory.getData(3).then(function(data) {
        $scope.items = data;
    });
})
```

In the preceding controller, we are injecting `DataFactory` as a dependency to the controller. We call the `getData` method when the controller gets initialized. The `getData` method will return three records that we will assign to the list.

Next, we define the `doRefresh` method that gets invoked when the user pulls to refresh. This method also calls the `getData` method of `DataFactory` and returns the data. We then append the response array from the `getData` method to our scope variable.

Do notice that we are appending the data to the existing array. In the case of a pull-to-refresh, you would prepend the data, as the user would like to see the updated data on top. Finally, we broadcast the `scroll.refreshComplete` event, which hides the refreshing icon/spinner.

Now, we will update our `www/index.html` body section as follows:

```
<body ng-app="starter" ng-controller="AppCtrl">
    <ion-header-bar class="bar-stable">
        <h1 class="title">Pull To Refresh</h1>
    </ion-header-bar>
    <ion-content>
        <ion-refresher pulling-text="Pull to refresh..." on-
refresh="doRefresh()">
        </ion-refresher>
        <ion-list>
            <ion-item collection-repeat="item in items">
                <h2>Random Key : {{item.random}}</h2>
                <p>Time : {{item.time}}</p>
            </ion-item>
        </ion-list>
    </ion-content>
</body>
```

Notice that we have added `ion-refresher` as the direct child of `ion-content`. We have used `collection-repeat` instead of `ng-repeat`.

> The `collection-repeat` allows an app to show huge lists of items of high performance than `ng-repeat`. You can read more about `collection-repeat` at `http://ionicframework.com/docs/api/directive/collectionRepeat/`.

Save all the files, head to the browser, and you should see the following screenshot:

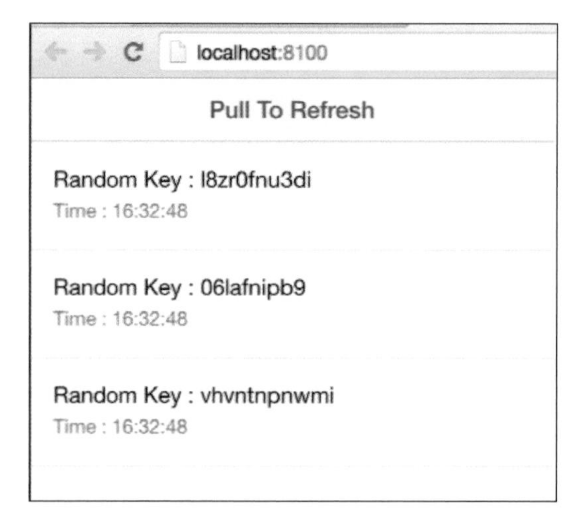

Now, using your mouse, you can pull down the page and you should see this:

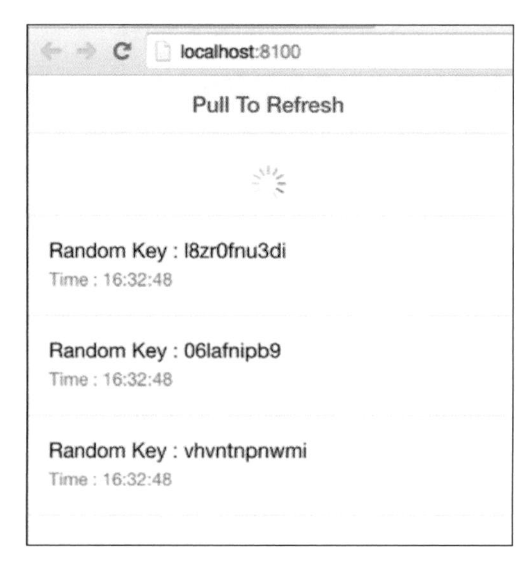

Once the promise is resolved, the data will be sent back to the controller and that data is appended to the item's arrays. Once that is done, `scroll.refreshComplete` is fired and the loading icon/spinner is hidden. The updated page looks like this:

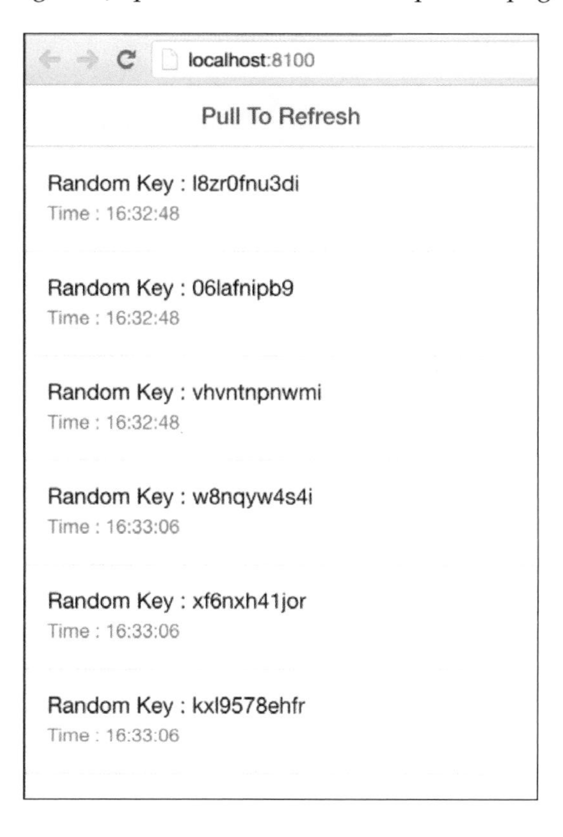

You can set pull-to-refresh text, the pull-down icon, as well as the spinner using the pulling-text, pulling-icon and spinner attributes on the `ion-refresher` directive. You can take a look at other possible options at `http://ionicframework.com/docs/api/directive/ionRefresher/`.

ion-infinite-scroll

Similar to the `ion-refresher`, Ionic provides another handy directive named `ion-infinite-scroll`. When the user reaches the end of a list, this directive invokes a method similar to `doRefresh` in the preceding example and updates the list.

The difference between `ion-refresher` and `ion-infinite-scroll` is that `ion-refresher` is used when a user explicitly wants to load a list, whereas `ion-infinite-scroll` is used when the list auto-updates as the user scrolls.

To add `ion-infinite-scroll` to our preceding example, we will update the body section as follows:

```
<body ng-app="starter" ng-controller="AppCtrl">
    <ion-header-bar class="bar-stable">
        <h1 class="title">Pull To Refresh</h1>
    </ion-header-bar>
    <ion-content>
        <ion-refresher pulling-text="Pull to refresh..." on-
refresh="doRefresh()">
        </ion-refresher>

        <ion-list>
            <ion-item collection-repeat="item in items">
                <h2>Random Key : {{item.random}}</h2>
                <p>Time : {{item.time}}</p>
            </ion-item>
        </ion-list>

        <ion-infinite-scroll on-infinite="loadMore()"
distance="1%">
        </ion-infinite-scroll>
    </ion-content>
</body>
```

Notice that `ion-infinite-scroll` is added after the list and it has an attribute named `on-infinite`. The value of this attribute will be evaluated when the distance is 1 percent. I have also left `ion-refresher` from the preceding example as it is. Since this is an example, I wanted to show how you could use both `ion-refresher` and `ion-infinite-scroll` in one example.

In a real-time news feed app, you would want to do something like the following. When the user pulls down, you would want to show the latest news and, when the user scrolls down, you would want to show the old news.

The updated version of `AppCtrl` with the `loadMore` method will be:

```
.controller('AppCtrl', function($scope, DataFactory) {
    $scope.items = [];

    $scope.doRefresh = function() {
        DataFactory.getData(3)
            .then(function(data) {
                // extend the $scope.items array with the response
                // array from getData();
                // http://stackoverflow.com/a/1374131/1015046
                Array.prototype.push.apply($scope.items, data);
            }).finally(function() {
                // Stop the ion-refresher from spinning
                $scope.$broadcast('scroll.refreshComplete');
            });
    }

    $scope.loadMore = function() {
        DataFactory.getData(3)
            .then(function(data) {
                // extend the $scope.items array with the response
                // array from getData();
                // http://stackoverflow.com/a/1374131/1015046
                Array.prototype.push.apply($scope.items, data);
            }).finally(function() {
                // Stop the ion-refresher from spinning
                $scope.$broadcast('scroll.infiniteScrollComplete');
            });
    }

    // load data on page load
    DataFactory.getData(3).then(function(data) {
        $scope.items = data;
    });
})
```

We have added the `loadMore` method to the scope. It has almost the same definition as `doRefresh`, except we are broadcasting `scroll.infiniteScrollComplete` here to notify that refresh is completed.

If you save all the files and head back to the browser you should see that `ion-infinite-scroll` starts making calls till the visible portion of the screen is filled with data.

When you pull down to refresh, the list will again be updated. But remember that we are not pre-pending to the list, so the data will be added at the end.

$ionicScrollDelegate

Ionic also provides a service to control scrolling views. It is named `$ionicScrollDelegate`. The `$ionicScrollDelegate` service provides API methods to scroll, zoom, and get the position of the scroll and so on.

In the earlier example, we can add a button to the header named `Scroll to Top`. When the user clicks on it, we will use `$ionicScrollDelegate` to scroll to the top, if the user is somewhere down the list.

The updated `ion-header-bar` looks like this:

```
<ion-header-bar class="bar-stable">
        <h1 class="title">Pull To Refresh</h1>
        <button class="button" ng-click="scrollToTop()">Scroll to
Top</button>
</ion-header-bar>
```

Then, we will add the `scrollToTop` definition in our app controller after injecting `$ionicScrollDelegate` as a dependency:

```
$scope.scrollToTop = function() {
        $ionicScrollDelegate.scrollTop();
    }
```

Now, however far the user goes down the list, he/she can press the scroll to the top button in the header to come right back up to the top of the list, as shown here:

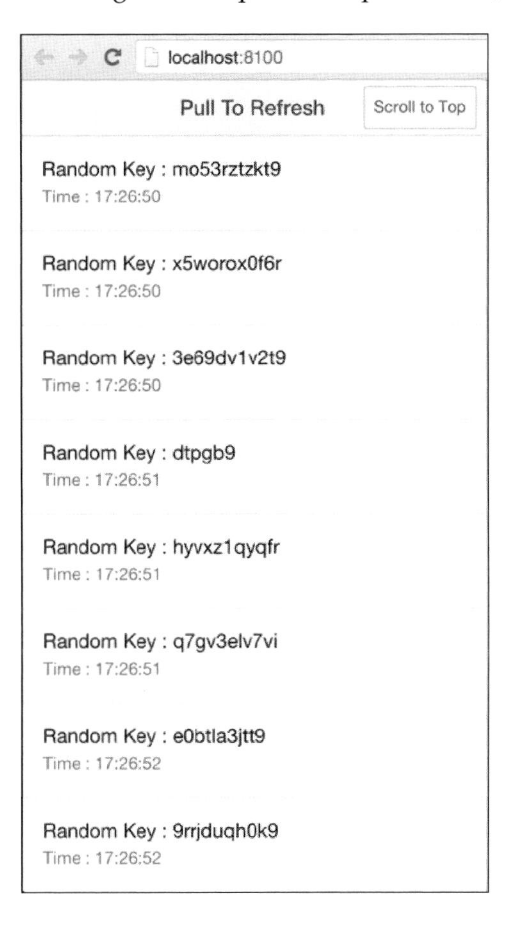

You can read more about `$ionicScrollDelegate` at `http://ionicframework.com/docs/api/service/$ionicScrollDelegate/`.

Navigation

The next component we are going to take a look at is the navigation component. The navigation component has a bunch of directives as well as a couple of services.

The first directive we are going to take a look at is `ion-nav-view`.

In *Chapter 3, Ionic CSS Components and Navigation*, we have already seen the Ionic state router and we have understood how it works. We have also seen that `ui-view` in the AngularUI Router is analogous to `ion-nav-view` in Ionic.

When the app boots up, `$stateProvider` will look for the default state and then will try to load the corresponding template inside the `ion-nav-view`.

ion-view

The next directive we are going to take a look at is the `ion-view` directive. The `ion-view` directive is the child of `ion-nav-view`. This directive is used as a container to display content and header bar information. When the application state changes, the corresponding view enters and exists the parent, `ion-nav-view`.

Views in Ionic are cached to improve performance. When a view leaves the `ion-nav-view`, its elements are left in the DOM and its scope is disconnected from the `$watch` cycle. When any previously cached view enters `ion-nav-view`, its scope is reconnected and the existing element is reactivated.

To try out an example, we will scaffold a new blank app:

```
ionic start -a "Example 18" -i app.example.eighteen example18
blank
```

Using the `cd` command, go to the `example18` folder and run this:

```
ionic serve
```

This will launch the blank app.

Next, we will add a router to this app, which has two states. Open `www/js/app.js` and add the following `config` section after the `run` method:

```
.config(function($stateProvider, $urlRouterProvider) {
    $stateProvider
        .state('page1', {
            url: '/page1',
            templateUrl: 'page1.html'
        })
        .state('page2', {
```

```
            url: '/page2',
            templateUrl: 'page2.html'
        });

    $urlRouterProvider.otherwise('/page1');
})
```

We have created two states, one for `page1` and another for `page2`. Next, we will update our `www/index.html` body section:

```
<body ng-app="starter">
    <ion-nav-bar></ion-nav-bar>
    <ion-nav-view></ion-nav-view>

    <!-- Templates -->
    <script type="text/ng-template" id="page1.html">
        <ion-view view-title="Title">
            <ion-content>
                <h3>Page 1</h3>
                <button class="button button-dark" ui-
sref="page2">
                    Navigate to Page 2
                </button>
            </ion-content>
        </ion-view>
    </script>
    <script type="text/ng-template" id="page2.html">
        <ion-view view-title="Title">
            <ion-content>
                <h3>Page 2</h3>
                <button class="button button-dark" ui-
sref="page1">
                    Navigate to Page 1
                </button>
            </ion-content>
        </ion-view>
    </script>
</body>
```

We have an `ion-nav-view` directive, where the `ion-view` content gets injected. We are creating our views using the `script` tag syntax. This approach of loading templates is efficient, as AngularJS does not need to make an AJAX call to fetch the template. But this approach is not developer/maintenance-friendly.

The `ion-view` directive has a child directive named `ion-content`. Every time a new template enters into the view, it is cached. You can set attributes on the `ion-view` directive to control the look and feel related to that view's state, as well as the cache behavior.

For instance, in the preceding snippet, we have added an attribute named `view-title` to the `ion-view` tag. This value is set as the page title, as well as the title for the navigation bar, if the `ion-nav-bar` tag is present.

To disable the caching of templates, you can set `cache-view` as `false` on the `ion-view` directive. We can also control whether the `nav-bar` should be visible or not by setting `hide-nav-bar` to `true` or `false`.

The `ion-view` directive with the preceding attributes would look like this:

```
<ion-view view-title="Title" cache-view="false" hide-nav-
bar="false" hide-back-button="true" can-swipe-back="false">
```

We can also control whether the back button should be shown in case there is a back button inside the navigation bar. We will look into this when we work with the `ion-nav-bar` directive.

To test `example18` so far, you can run this:

```
ionic server
```

Ionic view events

Ionic view has a bunch of life cycle methods that you can hook on to perform custom actions. We will add a new `run` method, as shown in the following section, to `example18`. Inside this `run` method, we have added listeners to the `$ionicview` events. Open `www/js/app.js` and add the following `run` method:

```
.run(function($ionicPlatform, $rootScope) {
    // View Life Cycle
    $rootScope.$on('$ionicView.loaded', function(event, view) {
        console.log('Loaded..', view.stateName);
    });

    $rootScope.$on('$ionicView.beforeEnter', function(event, view)
{
        console.log('Before Enter..', view.stateName);
    });

    $rootScope.$on('$ionicView.afterEnter', function(event, view)
{
```

```
        console.log('After Enter..', view.stateName);
    });

    $rootScope.$on('$ionicView.enter', function(event, view) {
        console.log('Entered..', view.stateName);
    });

    $rootScope.$on('$ionicView.leave', function(event, view) {
        console.log('Left..', view.stateName);
    });


    $rootScope.$on('$ionicView.beforeLeave', function(event, view)
{
        console.log('Before Leave..', view.stateName);
    });


    $rootScope.$on('$ionicView.afterLeave', function(event, view)
{
        console.log('After Leave..', view.stateName);
    });

    $rootScope.$on('$ionicView.unloaded', function(event, view) {
        console.log('View unloaded..', view.stateName);
    });

})
```

You can register multiple `run` methods in a single module.

And when we navigate from page 1 to page 2, you will see the following screenshot:

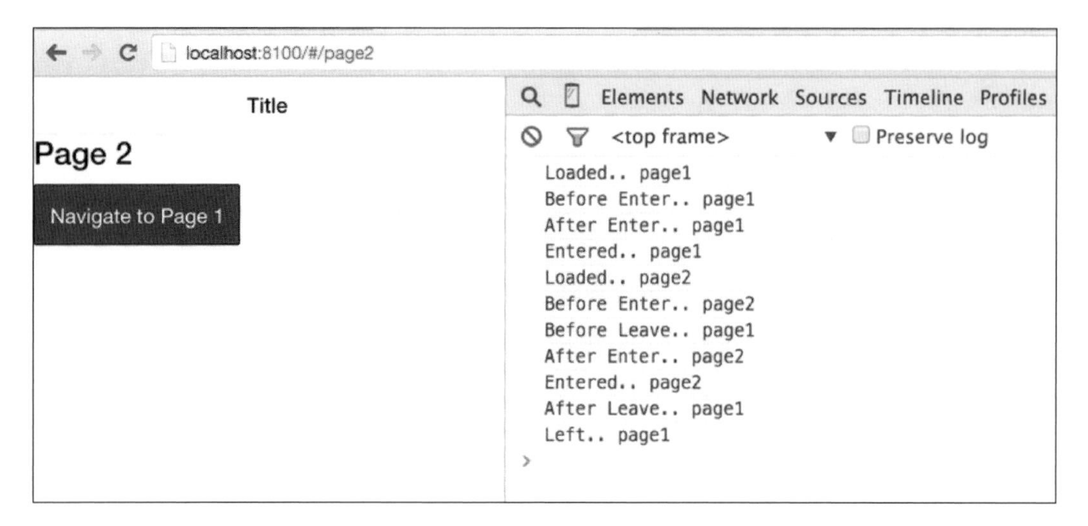

You can trace the order in which the events are fired and hook on to them, depending on your requirements.

`$ionicView.loaded` and `$ionicView.unloaded` will only work on `$rootScope` and not on `$scope` of the controller. You can hook on to the remaining events with the controller scope as well.

ion-nav-bar

When working with a multi-page app, the `ion-nav-bar` directive is your good friend. This directive takes care of changing the page's title bar as the application's state changes. In the `example18` app we have added a simplified version of `ion-nav-bar`.

Now, we will take a look at a slightly more complicated version. Replace the existing `ion-nav-bar` directive in `www/index.html` with the following code:

```
<ion-nav-bar class="bar-assertive">
        <ion-nav-buttons side="left">
            <button class="button button-energized" ng-
click="leftyClick()">
                Left Button
            </button>
        </ion-nav-buttons>
```

```
        <ion-nav-back-button class="button-clear">
            <i class="ion-arrow-left-c"></i> Back
        </ion-nav-back-button>
        <ion-nav-buttons side="right">
            <button class="button button-energized" ng-
click="rightyClick()">
                Right Button
            </button>
        </ion-nav-buttons>
</ion-nav-bar>
```

As you can see from the preceding code snippet, `ion-nav-bar` can have `ion-nav-buttons` as a child directive, as well as `ion-nav-back-button`.

The `ion-nav-buttons` is used to place buttons in the header navigation bar. The updated page should look like this:

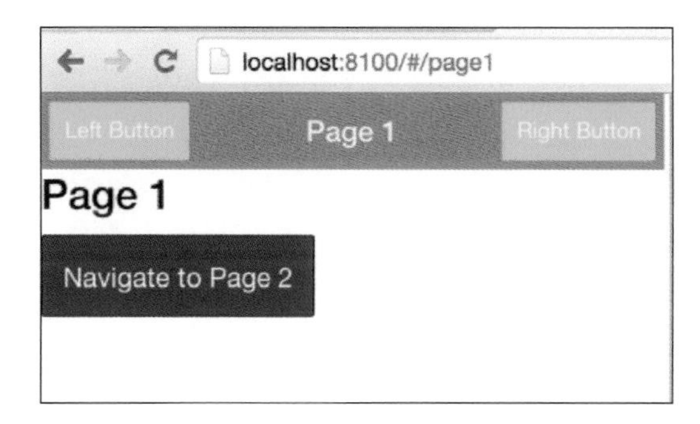

You can define `leftyClick()` and `rightyClick()` functionally and they will be fired when the buttons are clicked. You can either add a Header Controller and define these methods and add the Header Controller to the `ion-nav-bar` or you can define the `leftyClick()` and `rightyClick()` methods on root scope as well, which is not ideal. In a real-time scenario, typically in the top right-hand corner, you would have a **Logout** button, an **Options** button, or an **Add** button, depending on the nature of the app.

The `ion-nav-bar` directive also hosts the `ion-nav-back-button` directive. This directive takes care of adding the back button automatically when the user navigates from one page to another. If we navigate from page 1 to page 2, you will see the following view:

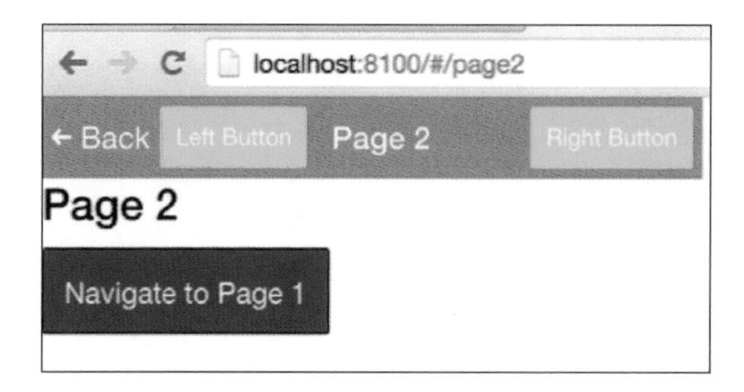

As you can see, the back button automatically appears in the left-top corner of the page, pushing the left button away from its position.

> The `ion-nav-bar` directive will work correctly only if the content of the template is wrapped in an `ion-view` tag.

This takes us back to the attributes on the `ion-view` tag. You can set the `hide-nav-bar` attribute to `false` on `ion-view`; this will show the navigation bar for the current page or you can set `back-button` to `false` to disable showing the back button for that page.

Modify page 2's `ion-view` as follows:

```
<ion-view view-title="Page 2" hide-nav-bar="false" hide-back-
button="true">
```

Then, navigate to page 2 from page 1, you will see that the back button does not appear:

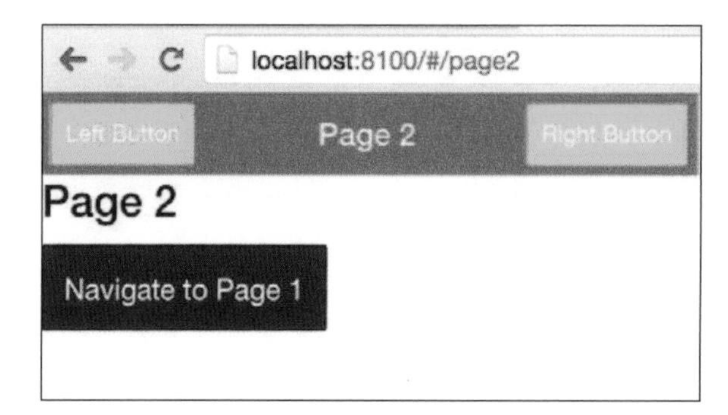

ion-nav-buttons

Ionic also provides you with fine-grained control over the buttons that appear in the header bar. If you declare `ion-nav-buttons` inside `ion-view`, in the template, these will override the ones from the `ion-nav-bar` directive.

We will update the `page2` template as follows:

```
<script type="text/ng-template" id="page2.html">
        <ion-view view-title="Page 2" hide-nav-bar="false" hide-
back-button="true">
            <ion-nav-buttons side="left">
                <button class="button button-calm" ng-
click="settingsClick()">
                    Settings
                </button>
            </ion-nav-buttons>
            <ion-nav-buttons side="right">
                <button class="button button-calm" ng-
click="optionsClick()">
                    Options
                </button>
            </ion-nav-buttons>
            <ion-content>
                <h3>Page 2</h3>
                <button class="button button-dark" ui-
sref="page1">
                    Navigate to Page 1
                </button>
            </ion-content>
        </ion-view>
    </script>
```

Do remember that we are not modifying the `ion-nav-buttons` directive in the `ion-nav-bar` directive:

```
<ion-nav-bar class="bar-assertive">
        <ion-nav-buttons side="left">
            <button class="button button-energized" ng-
click="leftyClick()">
                Left Button
            </button>
        </ion-nav-buttons>
        <ion-nav-back-button class="button-clear">
            <i class="ion-arrow-left-c"></i> Back
        </ion-nav-back-button>
```

```
        <ion-nav-buttons side="right">
            <button class="button button-energized" ng-
click="rightyClick()">
                Right Button
            </button>
        </ion-nav-buttons>
    </ion-nav-bar>
```

If you save the file and head back to the browser, page 1 will look as before:

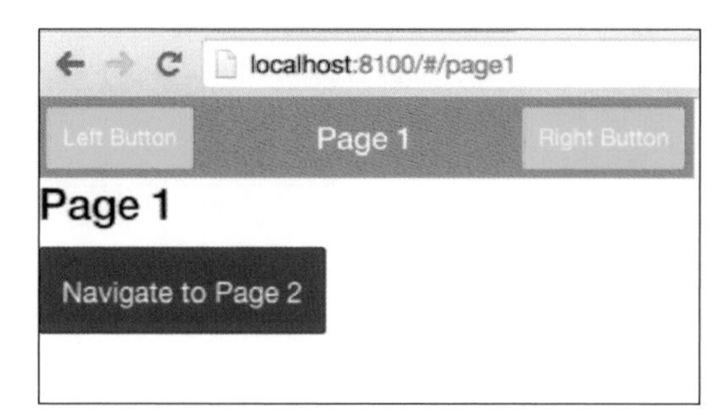

However, page 2 will now show the `ion-nav-button` directive from within the template:

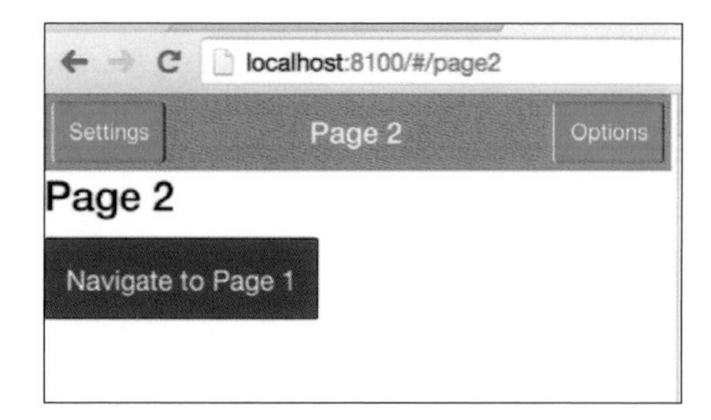

$ionicNavBarDelegate

The `ion-nav-bar` can be controlled from within the controller as well using the `$ionicNavBarDelegate` service.

To understand this better, we will update our templates by adding two controllers: `PageOneCtrl` for `page1.html` and `PageTwoCtrl` for `page2.html`.

The updated templates would look like this:

```
<script type="text/ng-template" id="page1.html">
        <ion-view ng-controller="PageOneCtrl">
            <ion-content>
                <h3>Page 1</h3>
                <button class="button button-dark" ui-
sref="page2">
                    Navigate to Page 2
                </button>
            </ion-content>
        </ion-view>
</script>
<script type="text/ng-template" id="page2.html">
        <ion-view ng-controller="PageTwoCtrl">
            <ion-content>
                <h3>Page 2</h3>
                <button class="button button-dark" ui-
sref="page1">
                    Navigate to Page 1
                </button>
            </ion-content>
        </ion-view>
</script>
```

Do notice that we have removed all the attributes/directives on `ion-view` and then added `ng-controller`.

We will update our `www/js/app.js` and add the two controllers we have declared:

```
.controller('PageOneCtrl', function($scope, $ionicNavBarDelegate)
{
    $ionicNavBarDelegate.title('Page 1');
})

.controller('PageTwoCtrl', function($scope, $ionicNavBarDelegate)
{
    $ionicNavBarDelegate.title('Page 2');
    $ionicNavBarDelegate.showBackButton(false);
})
```

We are setting the page title for `page1` and `page2` and we are setting `showBackButton` as `false` for `page2`. When you save all the files and go back to the browser, you should see the expected output.

Other properties that you can control using `$ionicNavBarDelegate` are as follows:

- `align`: This is used to align the title and buttons in the directions: left, right, and center (default)
- `showBar`: This is use to set or get if the `ion-nav-bar` is shown

$ionicHistory

Another very valuable navigation service is `$ionicHistory`. The `$ionicHistory` keeps track of all the views and captures how a user navigates between them.

The beauty of the `$ionicHistory` service is that it supports parallel history, unlike browsers, where only the pages visited in a given order are stored. Storing parallel history is very helpful when you have an interface such as tabs and each tab has its own set of pages.

The `$ionicHistory` is capable of capturing tab-level history; that is, when a user selects tab 2, navigates a few pages deep inside tab 2, selects tab 1 and hits the back button; the application will not take the user to the last page in tab 2 but rather the parent of the tabs page or will exit the app if the tabs view is the first page.

Back to the example at hand, we will update `PageTwoCtrl` as follows:

```
.controller('PageTwoCtrl', function($scope, $ionicNavBarDelegate,
$ionicHistory) {
    $ionicNavBarDelegate.title('Page 2');
    $ionicNavBarDelegate.showBackButton(false);
    console.log($ionicHistory.viewHistory())
})
```

We are injecting `$ionicHistory` as a dependency to `PageTwoCtrl` and we are console-logging the view history.

If we save the file and head back to the browser, navigating from page 1 to page 2, we should see this:

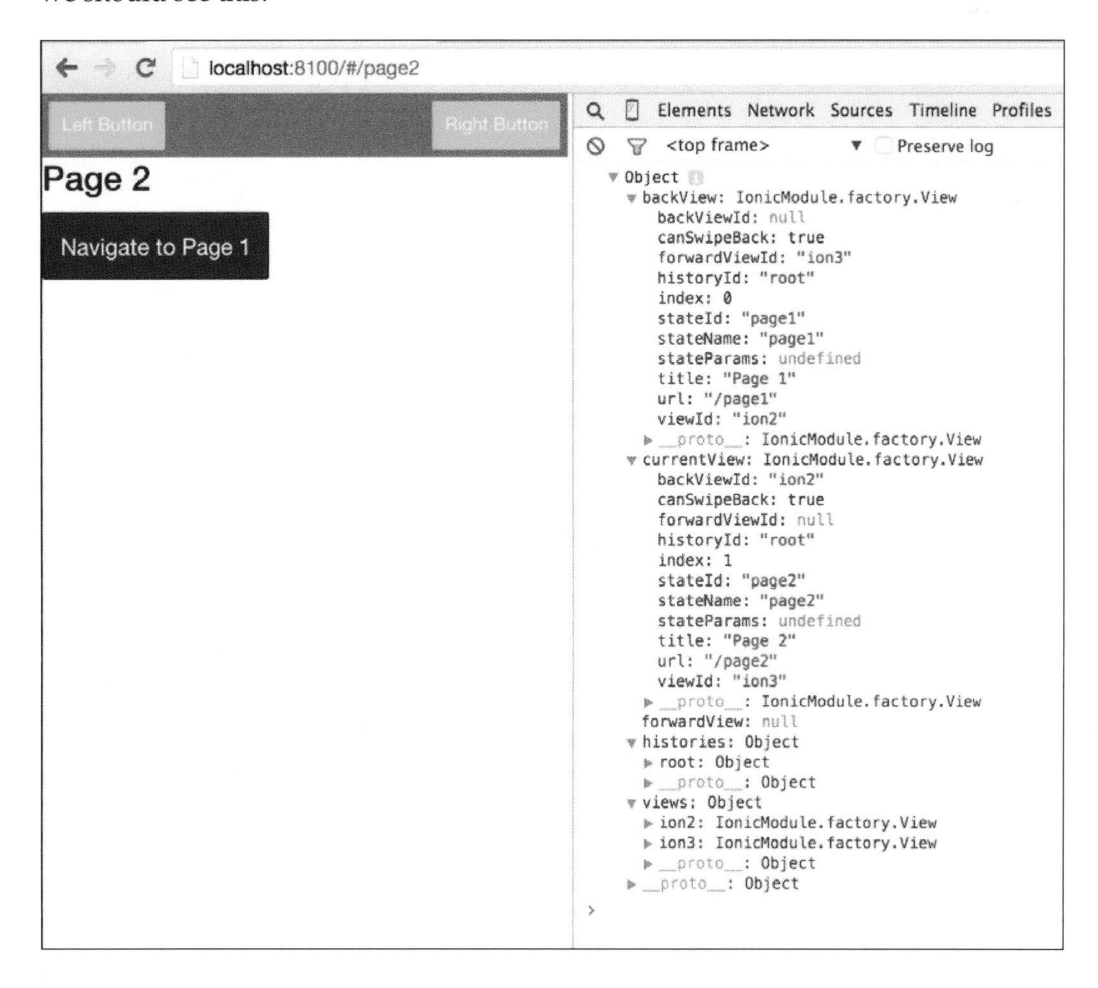

The `viewhistory` method returns an object that has details of `backView` (previous view), `currentView`, `Histories`, and all the views in the application.

You can access this object when you want to know how the user has navigated to the current page; the view history method is very helpful in such scenarios.

You can also use the `$ionicHistory` service to access individual properties of the view history method such as:

- `currentView`: This returns the app's current view.
- `currentHistoryId`: This returns the ID of the parent container of the current view.

- `currentTitle`: This gets or sets the current view's title.
- `backView`: This returns the view before the current view in the history stack.
- `backTitle`: This gets the previous view's title.
- `forwardView`: This returns the forward view in the history stack. Forward view is valid if a user navigated from page 1 to page 2 and then back to page 1. Here page 2 is the `forwardView`.
- `currentStateName`: This returns the current state name.

To quickly test the preceding properties, we will update our `PageOneCtrl` and `PageTwoCtrl` as shown here:

```
.controller('PageOneCtrl', function($scope, $ionicNavBarDelegate,
$ionicHistory) {

    $ionicNavBarDelegate.title('Page 1');

    console.log('currentView', $ionicHistory.currentView());
    console.log('currentHistoryId', $ionicHistory.currentHistoryId());
    console.log('currentTitle', $ionicHistory.currentTitle());
    console.log('backView', $ionicHistory.backView());
    console.log('backTitle', $ionicHistory.backTitle());
    console.log('forwardView', $ionicHistory.forwardView());
    console.log('currentStateName', $ionicHistory.currentStateName());

})

.controller('PageTwoCtrl', function($scope, $ionicNavBarDelegate,
$ionicHistory) {

    $ionicNavBarDelegate.title('Page 2');
    $ionicNavBarDelegate.showBackButton(false);

    console.log('viewHistory', $ionicHistory.viewHistory());
})
```

Now, when we navigate to page 1, we should see the properties logged:

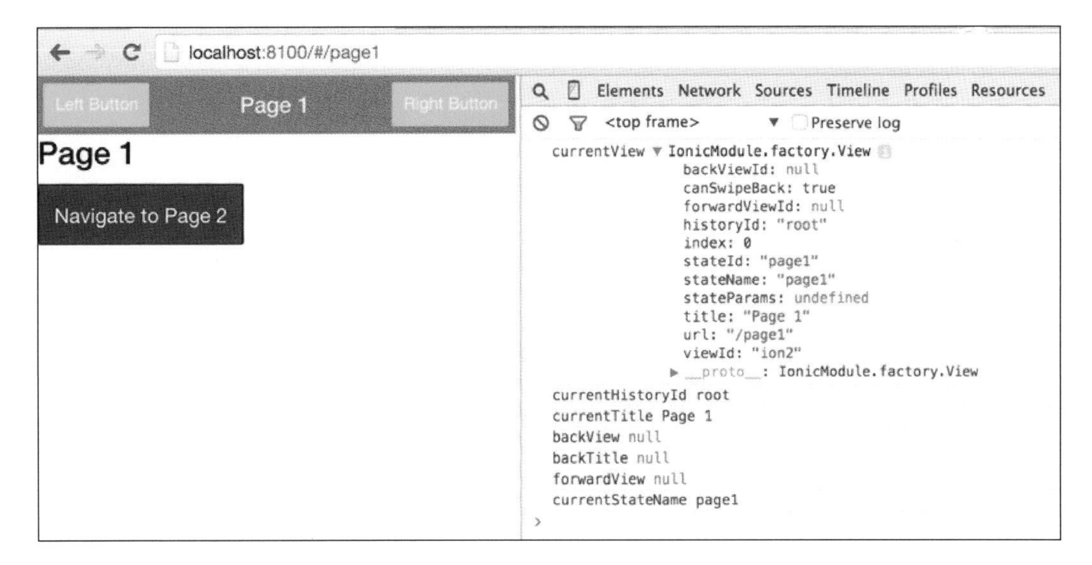

Then, when you navigate to **Page 2**, we will see the same values as we have seen earlier:

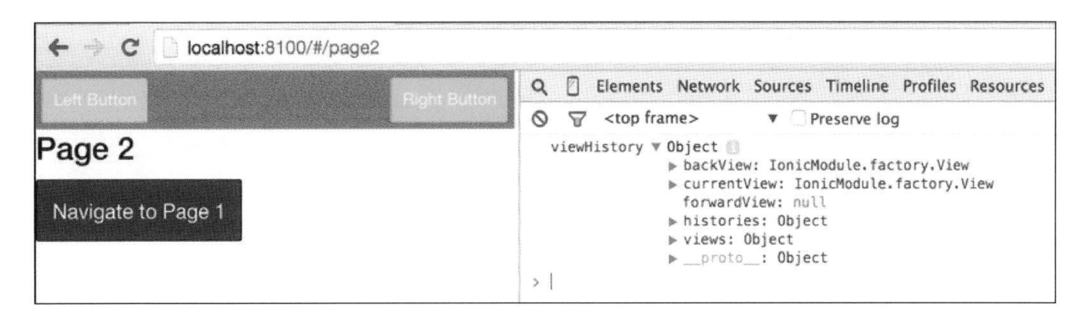

Finally, when you navigate back to **Page 1**, you will see the `forwardView` value populated:

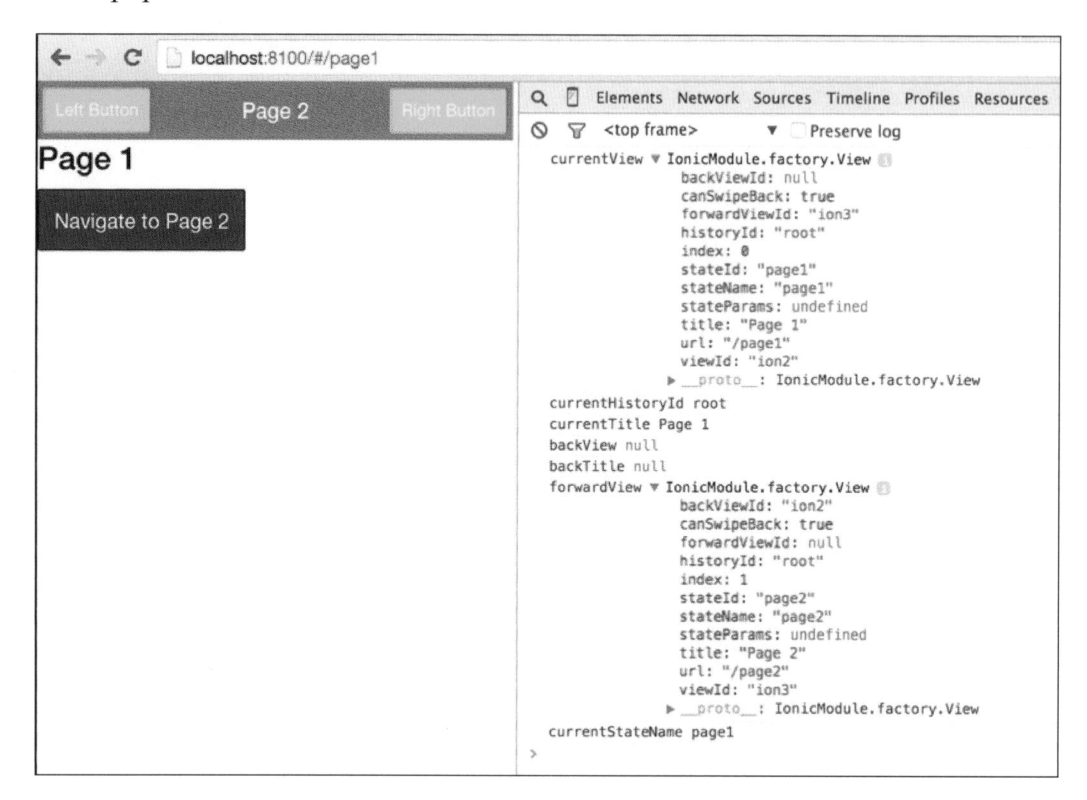

I have set `cache-view="false"` on the `ion-view` directives for both page 1 and page 2; hence `backView` is `null` in the preceding screenshot.

The `$ionicHistory` has three more methods on it:

- `goBack`: By default, the state route goes one view back. But you can specify how many views you would like to go back by passing in a negative integer to the `goBack` method. The default value is `-1`, hence it navigates back one view. If you execute `goBack(-2)`, the view that is 2 pages back will be shown. `goBack` does not cross history stacks and, if a value greater (for example, `-100`) than the available history stack is passed, the view navigates to the first page.
- `clearHistory`: This clears the history stack except for the current view.
- `clearCache`: This removes all cached views.

Using `$ionicHistory`, you can also control how the next view will behave using the `nextViewOptions` method.

You can control the following options:

- `disableAnimate`: This disables the animation on the next view
- `disableBack`: This sets the `backView` to `null` for the next view
- `historyRoot`: The next view will be the root of the history stack

If we add the preceding properties to our existing `PageOneCtrl`:

```
.controller('PageOneCtrl', function($scope, $ionicNavBarDelegate,
$ionicHistory) {

    $ionicNavBarDelegate.title('Page 1');

    console.log('currentView', $ionicHistory.currentView());
    console.log('currentHistoryId', $ionicHistory.currentHistoryId());
    console.log('currentTitle', $ionicHistory.currentTitle());
    console.log('backView', $ionicHistory.backView());
    console.log('backTitle', $ionicHistory.backTitle());
    console.log('forwardView', $ionicHistory.forwardView());
    console.log('currentStateName', $ionicHistory.currentStateName());

    $ionicHistory.nextViewOptions({
        disableAnimate: true,
        disableBack: true,
        historyRoot: true
    });
})
```

If we navigate to page 2, the output in the console will be as follows:

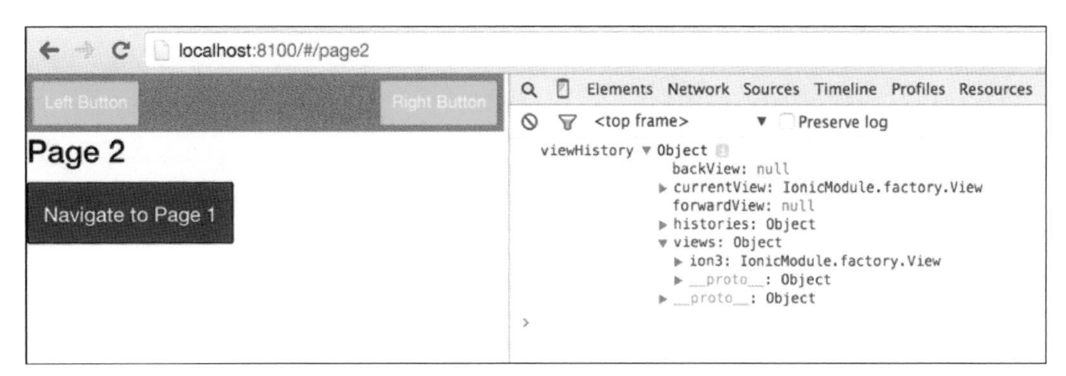

You will also notice that, when you click on **Navigate to Page 2**, the animation/transition is disabled, the `backView` here is set to `null`, and finally the `views` property has only one view: `page2`.

You can use these options to control the behavior of your app history state.

Tabs and side menu

To understand navigation a bit better, we will explore the `tabs` directive and the `side menu` directive.

We will scaffold the `tabs` template and go through the directives related to tabs; run this:

```
ionic start -a "Example 19" -i app.example.nineteen example19 tabs
```

Using the `cd` command, go to the `example19` folder and run this:

```
ionic serve
```

This will launch the tabs app.

If you open `www/index.html` file, you will notice that this template uses `ion-nav-bar` to manage the header with `ion-nav-back-button` inside it.

Next open `www/js/app.js` and you will find the application states configured:

```
.state('tab.dash', {
    url: '/dash',
    views: {
      'tab-dash': {
        templateUrl: 'templates/tab-dash.html',
        controller: 'DashCtrl'
      }
    }
  })
```

Do notice that the `views` object has a named object: `tab-dash`. This will be used when we work with the `tabs` directive. This name will be used to load a given view when a tab is selected into the `ion-nav-view` directive with the name `tab-dash`.

If you open `www/templates/tabs.html`, you will find a markup for the tabs component:

```
<ion-tabs class="tabs-icon-top tabs-color-active-positive">

  <!-- Dashboard Tab -->
```

```
    <ion-tab title="Status" icon-off="ion-ios-pulse" icon-on="ion-ios-pulse-strong" href="#/tab/dash">
      <ion-nav-view name="tab-dash"></ion-nav-view>
    </ion-tab>

    <!-- Chats Tab -->
    <ion-tab title="Chats" icon-off="ion-ios-chatboxes-outline" icon-on="ion-ios-chatboxes" href="#/tab/chats">
      <ion-nav-view name="tab-chats"></ion-nav-view>
    </ion-tab>

    <!-- Account Tab -->
    <ion-tab title="Account" icon-off="ion-ios-gear-outline" icon-on="ion-ios-gear" href="#/tab/account">
      <ion-nav-view name="tab-account"></ion-nav-view>
    </ion-tab>

  </ion-tabs>
```

The `tabs.html` will be loaded before any of the child tabs load, since tab state is defined as an abstract route.

The `ion-tab` directive is nested inside `ion-tabs` and every `ion-tab` directive has an `ion-nav-view` directive nested inside it. When a tab is selected, the route with the same name as the `name` attribute on the `ion-nav-view` will be loaded inside the corresponding tab.

Very neatly structured!

> You can read more about `tabs` directive and its services at `http://ionicframework.com/docs/nightly/api/directive/ionTabs/`.

Next, we are going to scaffold an app using the side menu template and go through the navigation inside it; run this:

```
ionic start -a "Example 20" -i app.example.twenty example20 sidemenu
```

Using the `cd` command, go to the `example20` folder and run this:

```
ionic serve
```

This will launch the side menu app.

We start off exploring with `www/index.html`. This file has only the `ion-nav-view` directive inside the body. Next, we open `www/js/app/js`. Here, the routes are defined as expected. But one thing to notice is the name of the views for search, browse, and playlists. It is the same—`menuContent`—for all:

```
.state('app.search', {
    url: "/search",
    views: {
      'menuContent': {
        templateUrl: "templates/search.html"
      }
    }
})
```

If we open `www/templates/menu.html`, you will notice the `ion-side-menus` directive. It has two children, `ion-side-menu-content` and `ion-side-menu`. The `ion-side-menu-content` displays the content for each menu item inside the `ion-nav-view` named `menuContent`. This is why all the menu items in the state router have the same view name.

The `ion-side-menu` is displayed on the left-hand side of the page. You can set the location on the `ion-side-menu` to the right to show the side menu on the right or you can have two side menus.

Do notice the `menu-toggle` directive on the button inside `ion-nav-buttons`. This directive is used to toggle the side menu.

If you want to have the menu on both sides, your `menu.html` will look as follows:

```
<ion-side-menus enable-menu-with-back-views="false">
  <ion-side-menu-content>
    <ion-nav-bar class="bar-stable">
      <ion-nav-back-button>
      </ion-nav-back-button>

      <ion-nav-buttons side="left">
        <button class="button button-icon button-clear ion-
navicon" menu-toggle="left">
        </button>
      </ion-nav-buttons>
      <ion-nav-buttons side="right">
        <button class="button button-icon button-clear ion-
navicon" menu-toggle="right">
        </button>
      </ion-nav-buttons>
    </ion-nav-bar>
    <ion-nav-view name="menuContent"></ion-nav-view>
```

```
  </ion-side-menu-content>

  <ion-side-menu side="left">
    <ion-header-bar class="bar-stable">
      <h1 class="title">Left</h1>
    </ion-header-bar>
    <ion-content>
      <ion-list>
        <ion-item menu-close ng-click="login()">
          Login
        </ion-item>
        <ion-item menu-close href="#/app/search">
          Search
        </ion-item>
        <ion-item menu-close href="#/app/browse">
          Browse
        </ion-item>
        <ion-item menu-close href="#/app/playlists">
          Playlists
        </ion-item>
      </ion-list>
    </ion-content>
  </ion-side-menu>
  <ion-side-menu side="right">
    <ion-header-bar class="bar-stable">
      <h1 class="title">Right</h1>
    </ion-header-bar>
    <ion-content>
      <ion-list>
        <ion-item menu-close ng-click="login()">
          Login
        </ion-item>
        <ion-item menu-close href="#/app/search">
          Search
        </ion-item>
        <ion-item menu-close href="#/app/browse">
          Browse
        </ion-item>
        <ion-item menu-close href="#/app/playlists">
          Playlists
        </ion-item>
      </ion-list>
    </ion-content>
  </ion-side-menu>
</ion-side-menus>
```

You can read more about `side menu` directive and its services at `http://ionicframework.com/docs/nightly/api/directive/ionSideMenus/`.

This concludes our journey through the navigation directives and services. Next, we will move to Ionic loading.

Ionic loading

The first service we are going to take a look at is `$ionicLoading`. This service is highly useful when you want to block a user's interaction from the main page and indicate to the user that there is some activity going on in the background.

To test this, we will scaffold a new blank template and implement `$ionicLoading`; run this:

```
ionic start -a "Example 21" -i app.example.twentyone example21 blank
```

Using the `cd` command, go to the `example21` folder and run this:

```
ionic serve
```

This will launch the blank template in the browser.

We will create an app controller and define the show and hide methods inside it. Open `www/js/app.js` and add the following code:

```
.controller('AppCtrl', function($scope, $ionicLoading, $timeout) {

    $scope.showLoadingOverlay = function() {
        $ionicLoading.show({
            template: 'Loading...'
        });
    };
    $scope.hideLoadingOverlay = function() {
        $ionicLoading.hide();
    };

    $scope.toggleOverlay = function() {
        $scope.showLoadingOverlay();

        // wait for 3 seconds and hide the overlay
        $timeout(function() {
            $scope.hideLoadingOverlay();
        }, 3000);
```

```
        };

    })
```

We have a function named `showLoadingOverlay`, which will call `$ionicLoading.show()`, and a function named `hideLoadingOverlay()`, which will call `$ionicLoading.hide()`. We have also created a utility function named `toggleOverlay()`, which will call `showLoadingOverlay()` and after 3 seconds will call `hideLoadingOverlay()`.

We will update our `www/index.html` body section as follows:

```
<body ng-app="starter" ng-controller="AppCtrl">
    <ion-header-bar class="bar-stable">
        <h1 class="title">$ionicLoading service</h1>
    </ion-header-bar>
    <ion-content class="padding">
        <button class="button button-dark" ng-click="toggleOverlay()">
            Toggle Overlay
        </button>
    </ion-content>
</body>
```

We have a button that calls `toggleOverlay()`.

If you save all the files, head back to the browser, and click on the **Toggle Overlay** button, you will see the following screenshot:

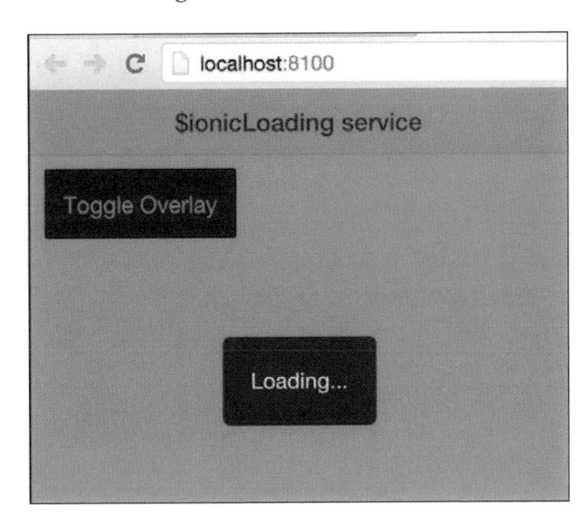

As you can see, the overlay is shown till the `hide` method is called on `$ionicLoading`.

You can also move the preceding logic inside a service and reuse it across the app. The service will look like this:

```
.service('Loading', function($ionicLoading, $timeout) {
    this.show = function() {
        $ionicLoading.show({
            template: 'Loading...'
        });
    };
    this.hide = function() {
        $ionicLoading.hide();
    };

    this.toggle= function() {
        var self  = this;
        self.show();

        // wait for 3 seconds and hide the overlay
        $timeout(function() {
            self.hide();
        }, 3000);
    };

})
```

Now, once you inject the `Loading` service into your controller or directive, you can use `Loading.show()`, `Loading.hide()`, or `Loading.toggle()`.

If you would like to show only a spinner icon instead of text, you can call the `$ionicLoading.show` method without any options:

```
$scope.showLoadingOverlay = function() {
        $ionicLoading.show();
    };
```

Then, you will see this:

You can configure the `show` method further. More information is available at `http://ionicframework.com/docs/nightly/api/service/$ionicLoading/`.

You can also use the `$ionicBackdrop` service to show just a backdrop. Read more about `$ionicBackdrop` at `http://ionicframework.com/docs/nightly/api/service/$ionicBackdrop/`.

You can also check out the `$ionicModal` service at `http://ionicframework.com/docs/api/service/$ionicModal/`; it is quite similar to the loading service.

The Action Sheet service

Action Sheet is a slide-up pane that shows a list of options. Generally, an action sheet is used to show contextual options when you have a list or grid of items. Typically, the action sheet service will be used when a user long-presses the list/grid item.

To test out the `$ionicActionSheet` service, we will scaffold a new blank app; run this:

```
ionic start -a "Example 22" -i app.example.twentytwo example22 blank
```

Using the `cd` command, go to the `example22` folder and run this:

```
ionic serve
```

This will launch the blank template in the browser.

Open `www/js/app.js` and we will add a new controller named `AppCtrl`:

```
.controller('AppCtrl', function($scope, $ionicActionSheet,
$timeout) {

    $scope.showOptions = function() {
        var hideSheet = $ionicActionSheet.show({
            buttons: [{
                text: 'Open'
            }, {
                text: 'Get Link'
            }],
            destructiveText: 'Delete',
            titleText: 'Options'

        });

        // hide the sheet after three seconds
        $timeout(function() {
            hideSheet();
        }, 3000);
    };

})
```

The `$ionicActionSheet.show` method returns a function that, when executed, closes the action sheet. The `show` method takes an object as an argument, which consists of the following properties:

- `buttons`: This shows a list of options/buttons
- `destructiveText`: This highlights a specific option as a dangerous operation
- `titleText`: This sets the title of the Action Sheet

Then, we will update the `body` section of our `www/index.html` as follows:

```
<body ng-app="starter" ng-controller="AppCtrl">
    <ion-pane>
      <ion-header-bar class="bar-stable">
        <h1 class="title">Action Sheet Example</h1>
      </ion-header-bar>
```

```
        <ion-content class="padding">
          <button class="button button-block button-dark" ng-
click="showOptions()">
            Show Options
          </button>
        </ion-content>
      </ion-pane>
    </body>
```

When you save all the files and head back to the browser, you will see the **Show Options** button. And when you click on it, you will see this:

The action sheet will hide after three seconds.

We will use this Action Sheet component in real time in *Chapter 8, Building a Message App*; there we will implement button handlers as well.

You can read more about Action Sheet at `http://ionicframework.com/docs/nightly/api/service/$ionicActionSheet/`.

Popover and Popup services

Popover is a contextual view that generally appears next to the selected item. This component is used to show contextual information or to show more information about a component.

To test this service, we will be scaffolding a new blank app:

```
ionic start -a "Example 23" -i app.example.twentythree example23
blank
```

Using the `cd` command, go to the `example23` folder and run this:

```
ionic serve
```

This will launch the blank template in the browser.

We will add a new controller to the blank project named `AppCtrl`. We will be adding our controller code in `www/js/app.js`:

```
.controller('AppCtrl', function($scope, $ionicPopover) {

    // init the popover
    $ionicPopover.fromTemplateUrl('button-options.html', {
        scope: $scope
    }).then(function(popover) {
        $scope.popover = popover;
    });

    $scope.openPopover = function($event, type) {
        $scope.type = type;
        $scope.popover.show($event);
    };

    $scope.closePopover = function() {
        $scope.popover.hide();
        // if you are navigating away from the page once
        // an option is selected, make sure to call
        // $scope.popover.remove();
    };

});
```

We are using the `$ionicPopover` service and setting up a popover from a template named `button-options.html`. We are assigning the current controller scope as the scope to the popover. We have two methods on the controller scope that will show and hide the popover. The `openPopover` method receives two options. One is the event and the second is the type of the button we are clicking (more on this in a moment).

Next, we update our `www/index.html` body section as follows:

```
<body ng-app="starter" ng-controller="AppCtrl">
    <ion-header-bar class="bar-positive">
        <h1 class="title">Popover Service</h1>
    </ion-header-bar>
    <ion-content class="padding">
        <button class="button button-block button-dark" ng-
click="openPopover($event, 'dark')">
            Dark Button
        </button>
        <button class="button button-block button-assertive" ng-
click="openPopover($event, 'assertive')">
            Assertive Button
        </button>
        <button class="button button-block button-calm" ng-
click="openPopover($event, 'calm')">
            Calm Button
        </button>
    </ion-content>
    <script id="button-options.html" type="text/ng-template">
        <ion-popover-view>
            <ion-header-bar>
                <h1 class="title">{{type}} options</h1>
            </ion-header-bar>
            <ion-content>
                <div class="list">
                    <a href="#" class="item item-icon-left">
                        <i class="icon ion-ionic"></i> Option One
                    </a>
                    <a href="#" class="item item-icon-left">
                        <i class="icon ion-help-buoy"></i> Option
Two
                    </a>
                    <a href="#" class="item item-icon-left">
                        <i class="icon ion-hammer"></i> Option
Three
                    </a>
```

```
                    <a href="#" class="item item-icon-left" ng-
click="closePopover()">
                        <i class="icon ion-close"></i> Close
                    </a>
                </div>
            </ion-content>
        </ion-popover-view>
    </script>
</body>
```

Inside `ion-content`, we have created three buttons, each themed with a different mood (dark, assertive, and calm). When a user clicks on the button, we show a popover that is specific to that button. For this example, all we are doing is passing in the name of the mood and showing the mood name as the heading in the popover. But you can definitely do more.

Do notice that we have wrapped our template's content inside `ion-popover-view`. This takes care of positioning the modal appropriately.

The template must be wrapped inside the `ion-popover-view` for the popover to work correctly.

When we save all the files and head back to the browser, we will see the three buttons. Depending on the button you click, the heading of the popover changes, but the options remain the same for all of them:

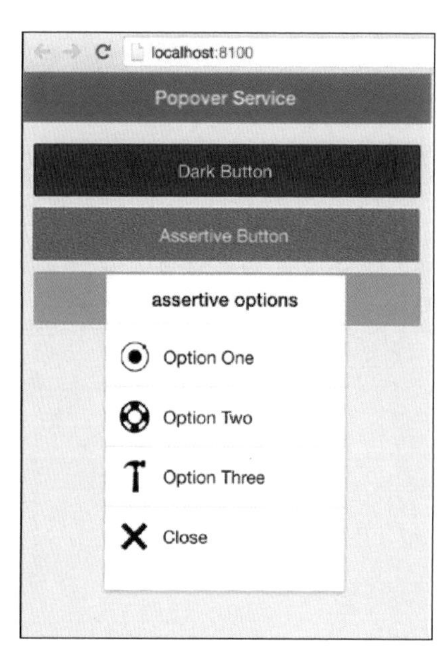

Then, when we click anywhere on the page or the close option, the popover closes.

If you are navigating away from the page when an option is selected, make sure to call:

```
$scope.popover.remove();
```

You can read more about Popover at `http://ionicframework.com/docs/api/controller/ionicPopover/`.

$ionicPopup

The next service we are going to take a look at is the `$ionicPopup` service. This service allows you to create popups that the user needs to respond in order to continue.

These popups are styled versions of JavaScript's native `alert`, `prompt`, and `confirm` methods.

To test this service, we will be scaffolding a new blank app; run this:

```
ionic start -a "Example 24" -i app.example.twentyfour example24 blank
```

Using the `cd` command, go to the `example24` folder and run this:

```
ionic serve
```

This will launch the blank template in the browser.

We will be implementing the show, confirm, and alert methods in an app style.

We will be using the `show` method to show a pin dialog, where the user needs to enter a pin. If the pin is valid, we show the user a secure area of our code. This secure area will have the buttons to show a confirm box and an alert box.

If the user cancels the pin dialog, we will take the user to an insecure area and ask the user to try again.

This example introduces a conditional content display approach using AngularJS and Ionic.

To get started, we will create a controller named `AppCtrl`. We will add the following `AppCtrl` code in our `www/js/app.js`:

```
.controller('AppCtrl', function($scope, $ionicPopup) {

    $scope.data = {};
    $scope.state = {};
```

```
    $scope.error = {};

    $scope.prompt = function() {
        // reset app states
        $scope.state.cancel = false;
        $scope.state.success = false;

        // reset error messages
        $scope.error.empty = false;
        $scope.error.invalid = false;

        var prompt = $ionicPopup.show({
            templateUrl: 'pin-template.html',
            title: 'Enter Pin to continue',
            scope: $scope,
            buttons: [{
                text: 'Cancel',
                onTap: function(e) {
                    $scope.state.cancel = true;
                }
            }, {
                text: '<b>Login</b>',
                type: 'button-assertive',
                onTap: function(e) {
                    $scope.error.empty = false;
                    $scope.error.invalid = false;
                    if (!$scope.data.pin) {
                        // disable close if the
                        // user does not enter
                        // a valid pin
                        $scope.error.empty = true;
                        e.preventDefault();
                    } else {
                        if ($scope.data.pin === '1234') {
                            $scope.state.success = true;
                            return $scope.data.pin;
                        } else {
                            $scope.error.invalid = true;
                            e.preventDefault();
                        }
                    }
                }
            }]
        });
```

```
    };

    $scope.confirm = function() {
        var confirm = $ionicPopup.confirm({
            title: 'Confirm Popup Heading',
            template: 'Are you sure you want to do that?'
        });
        confirm.then(function(res) {
            if (res) {
                console.log('Yes!');
            } else {
                console.log('Nooooo!!');
            }
        });
    };

    $scope.alert = function() {
        var alert = $ionicPopup.alert({
            title: 'You are secured!',
            template: 'You are inside a secure area!'
        });
        alert.then(function(res) {
            console.log('Yeah!! I know!!');
        });
    };

    // invoke the prompt on controller init.
    $scope.prompt();
})
```

Quite a lot of code! But it's quite simple.

We have created three objects on the scope named `data`, `state`, and `error`. These objects will be used to store data, application state, and errors for us.

We have added the prompt method. Here, we call the `$ionicPopup.show` method passing in the template and the definition for the tap method on the cancel button and the **Login** button. When the user clicks on the **Cancel** button of the prompt, we set the state object's `cancel` property to `true`. We will be using this property to toggle views.

When a user taps the **Login** button, we check if a valid pin is present. If not, we set the appropriate error message to `true`. If the user has entered a valid pin and if the value is equal to `1234`, we set the success property on the state object to `true`. This will toggle another view, which shows the **Confirm** and **Alert** buttons.

The `confirm` and `alert` methods are self-explanatory. They are set up using the `$ionicPopup.confirm`, and `$ionicPopup.alert` methods respectively. These methods return a promise, which is resolved when a button is clicked.

Finally, we invoke the `prompt` method to show the `Pin` dialog on controller load.

The updated body section of `www/index.html` will be as follows:

```
<body ng-app="starter" ng-controller="AppCtrl">
    <ion-pane ng-cloak>
        <ion-header-bar class="bar-positive">
            <h1 class="title">Super Secure App</h1>
        </ion-header-bar>
        <ion-content class="padding">
            <div class="card" ng-show="state.cancel">
                <div class="item item-divider">
                    Oops!! you cancelled!
                </div>
                <div class="item item-text-wrap">
                    To see the secure content enter pin
                    <button class="button button-assertive button-
block" ng-click="prompt()">
                        Try Again!
                    </button>
                </div>
            </div>
             <div class="card" ng-show="state.success">
                <div class="item item-divider">
                    You are viewing secure content!
                </div>
                <div class="item item-text-wrap">
                    <button class="button button-positive button-
block" ng-click="confirm()">
                        Show Confirm Dialog
                    </button>

                    <button class="button button-positive button-
block" ng-click="alert()">
                        Show Alert Dialog
                    </button>
                </div>
            </div>
        </ion-content>
    </ion-pane>
    <script type="text/ng-template" id="pin-template.html">
```

```
        <input type="password" ng-model="data.pin">
        <label ng-show="error.empty" class="assertive text-center
block padding">Please enter a valid Pin</label>
        <label ng-show="error.invalid" class="assertive text-
center block padding">Invalid Pin, Try Again!</label>
    </script>
</body>
```

We have added two card views; one shows when `state.cancel` is `true` and the other when `state.success` is `true`. Before the `end of body` tag, we have added our `pin-template.html` template.

Do notice that we have added the `ng-cloak` attribute to the `ion-pane` directive. This is to make sure that we do not show any content till the AngularJS processing is completed.

You can read more about `ng-cloak`, visit `https://docs.AngularJS.org/api/ng/directive/ngCloak`.

If you save all the files and head back to the browser, you will see this:

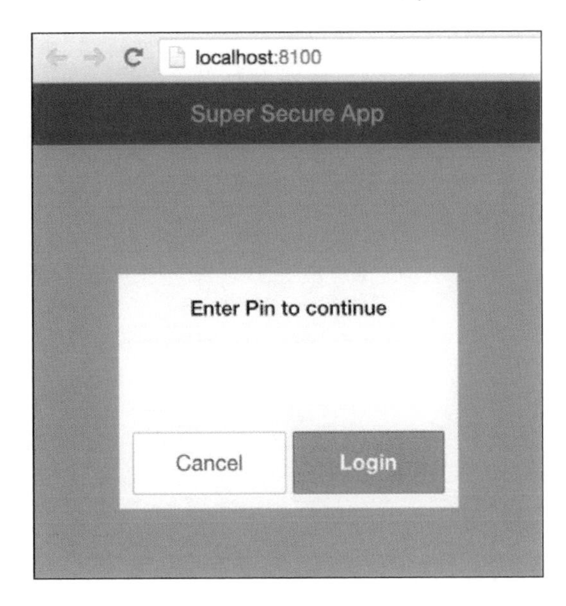

If you click on **Login** without entering valid data, you will see the following screenshot:

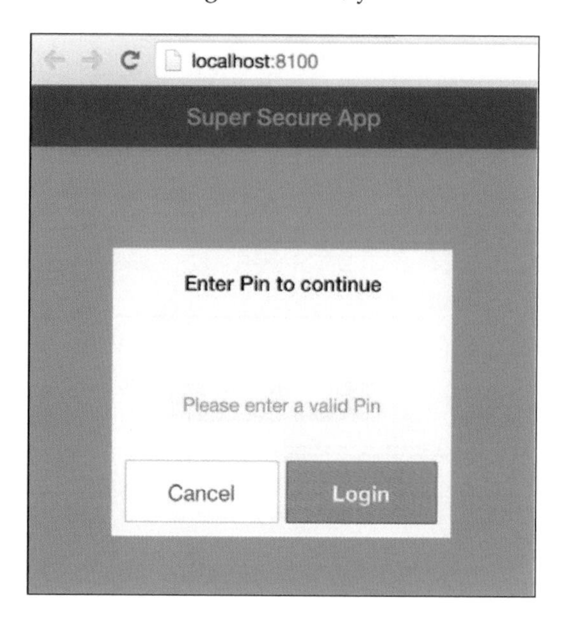

If you enter an invalid pin, you will see this:

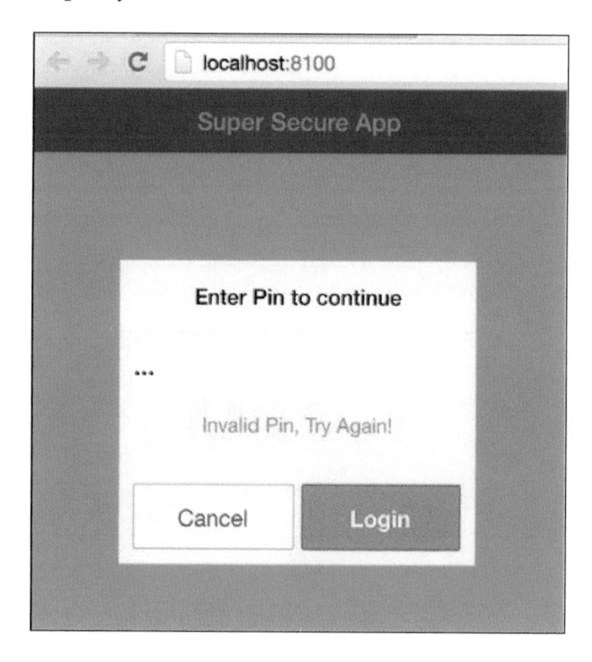

If you cancel the popup, you will be taken to an insecure area where you are given the option to try again:

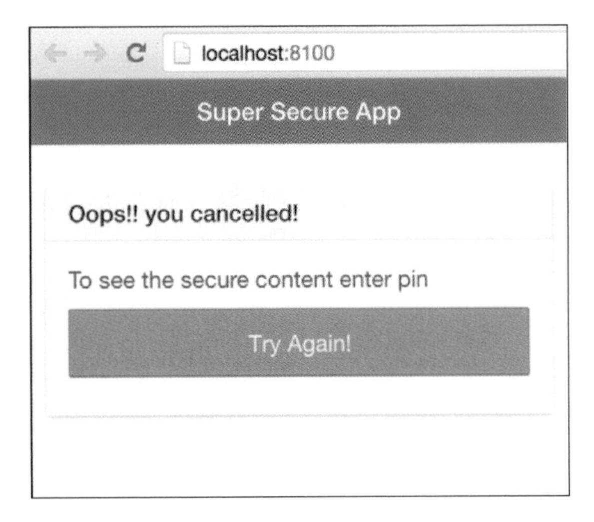

Finally, if you enter the correct pin, you will be taken to the secure area, where you should see the **Confirm** and **Alert** buttons. Clicking on them, you will see this:

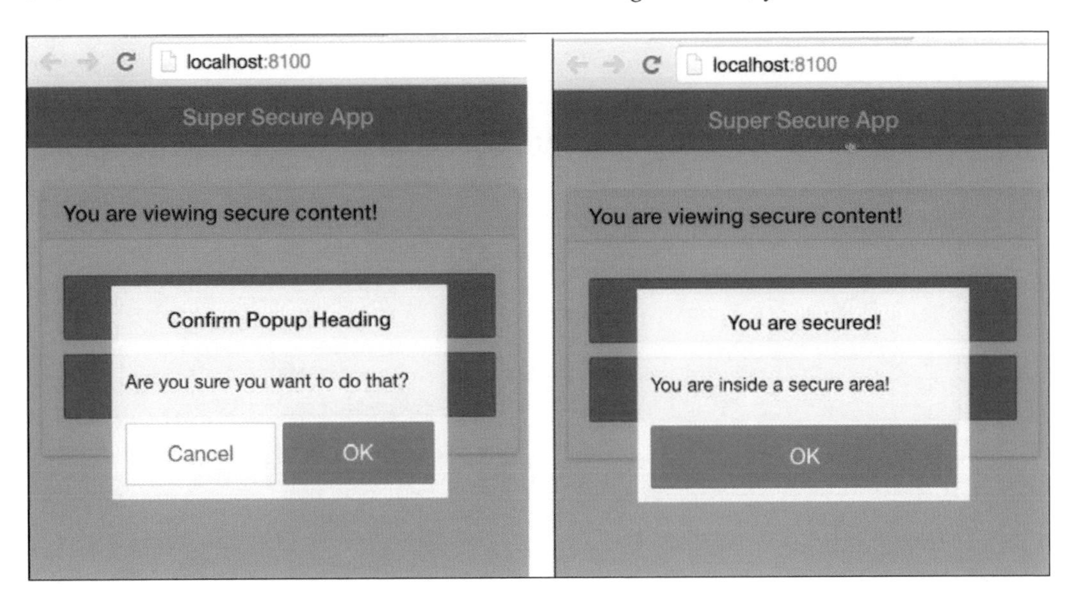

The preceding example not only discusses the `$ionicPopup` service, but also helps you understand how you can structure your application.

The preceding example is a single-page application. If you want, you can implement the same logic for a multiple application, where page 1 shows the popup, page 2 has insecure content, and page 3 has secure content. You can switch between pages depending on the user input.

The ion-list and ion-item directives

Since we are familiarizing ourselves with most of Ionic's directives and services, I thought it worth mentioning the `ion-list` and `ion-item` directives.

Lists are one of the most common display patterns when working with mobile apps. In Ionic, you can use the CSS version of the lists, as we have seen in *Chapter 3, Ionic CSS Components and Navigation*, or you can use the directive version of the lists.

The advantage of using the directive version of the list is that it provides additional attributes such as `ion-delete-button`, `ion-reorder-button`, and `ion-option-button`, which help us manage the lists better.

We will be testing these directives by scaffolding a new blank app; run this:

```
ionic start -a "Example 25" -i app.example.twentyfive example25 blank
```

Using the `cd` command, go to the `example25` folder and run this:

```
ionic serve
```

This will launch the blank template in the browser.

We will be implementing an example, provided in the Ionic docs, that covers all the aforementioned directives.

The following example is taken from `http://codepen.io/ionic/pen/JsHjf` and modified to add data via a factory.

First, we will create a factory that will dispatch random data for our lists. The factory is similar to the one we have used in `example17`, except the dataset returned is different:

```
.factory('DataFactory', function($timeout, $q) {

    var API = {
        getData: function(count) {
            // Spoof a network call using promises
```

```
            var deferred = $q.defer();

            var data = [],
                _o = {};
            count = count || 20;

            for (var i = 0; i < count; i++) {
                _o = {
                    // http://stackoverflow.com/a/8084248/1015046
                    id: i + 1,
                    title: (Math.random() +
1).toString(36).substring(7)
                };

                data.push(_o);
            };

            $timeout(function() {
                // success response!
                deferred.resolve(data);
            }, 1000);

            return deferred.promise;
        }
    };

    return API;
})
```

Here, we are returning an `id` and a `title` as properties of the object.

Next, we are going to create a controller named `AppCtrl` in `www/js/app.js`. This control will fetch data from the data factory and build the list. We will be also be providing definitions for the **Edit**, **Delete**, and **Option** buttons click inside it:

```
.controller('AppCtrl', function($scope, DataFactory) {

    $scope.items = [];

    $scope.data = {
        showDelete: false
    };

    $scope.edit = function(item) {
        alert('Edit Item: ' + item.id);
```

```
    };
    $scope.share = function(item) {
        alert('Share Item: ' + item.id);
    };

    $scope.moveItem = function(item, fromIndex, toIndex) {
        $scope.items.splice(fromIndex, 1);
        $scope.items.splice(toIndex, 0, item);
    };

    $scope.onItemDelete = function(item) {
        $scope.items.splice($scope.items.indexOf(item), 1);
    };

    // get data on page load
    DataFactory.getData().then(function(data) {
        $scope.items = data;
    });

})
```

Next, we update the `body` section of `www/index.html`:

```
<body ng-app="starter" ng-controller="AppCtrl">
    <!-- http://codepen.io/ionic/pen/JsHjf -->
    <ion-header-bar class="bar-positive">
        <div class="buttons">
            <button class="button button-icon icon ion-ios-minus-
outline" ng-click="data.showDelete = !data.showDelete;
data.showReorder = false"></button>
        </div>
        <h1 class="title">Ionic Lists</h1>
        <div class="buttons">
            <button class="button" ng-click="data.showDelete =
false; data.showReorder = !data.showReorder">
                Reorder
            </button>
        </div>
    </ion-header-bar>
    <ion-content>
        <ion-list show-delete="data.showDelete" show-
reorder="data.showReorder">
            <ion-item ng-repeat="item in items" item="item"
class="item-remove-animate">
                {{ item.id }}. {{ item.title }}
```

```
                <ion-delete-button class="ion-minus-circled" ng-
click="onItemDelete(item)">
                </ion-delete-button>
                <ion-option-button class="button-assertive" ng-
click="edit(item)">
                    Edit
                </ion-option-button>
                <ion-option-button class="button-calm" ng-
click="share(item)">
                    Share
                </ion-option-button>
                <ion-reorder-button class="ion-navicon" on-
reorder="moveItem(item, $fromIndex, $toIndex)"></ion-reorder-
button>
            </ion-item>
        </ion-list>
    </ion-content>
</body>
```

We have two buttons on the header bar that toggles the delete and reorder icons on the list. On the `ion-list` directive, we have used the `show-delete` and `show-reorder` attributes to show and hide the icons on the list item.

Inside each `ion-item` directive, we have added `ion-delete-button`, which calls the `onItemDelete` function; `ion-option-button`, which shows a **Share** or **Edit** button; and finally `ion-reorder-button`, which shows the re-order icon. When re-ordered, we call the `moveItem` method.

If you save all the files and head back to the browser, you will see this:

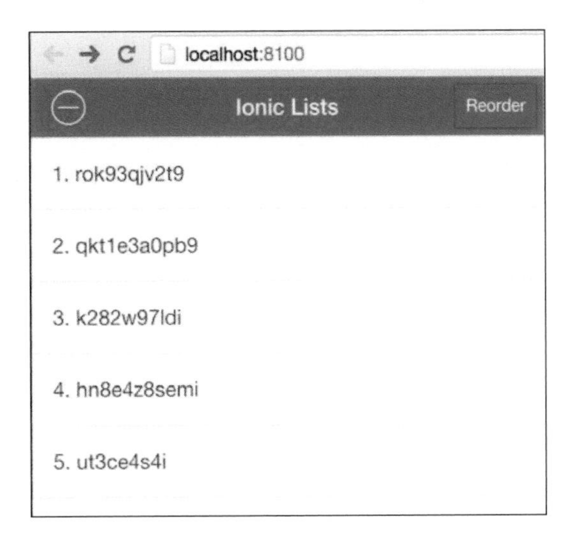

If you click on the delete icon in the header, you will see this:

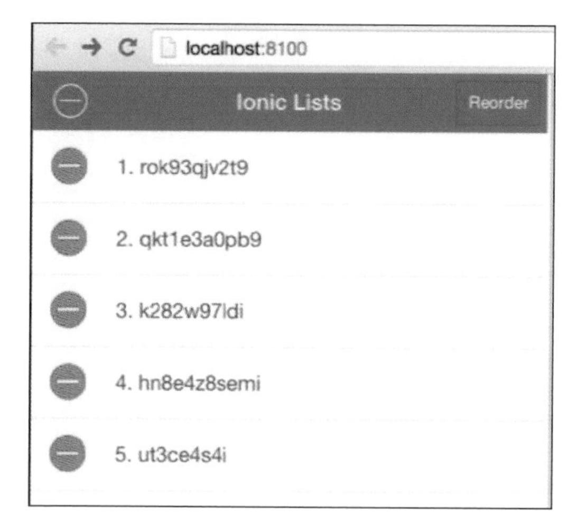

You can click on the delete icon that is to the left-hand side of the list item to delete it.

If you click on the reorder item in the header, you will see this:

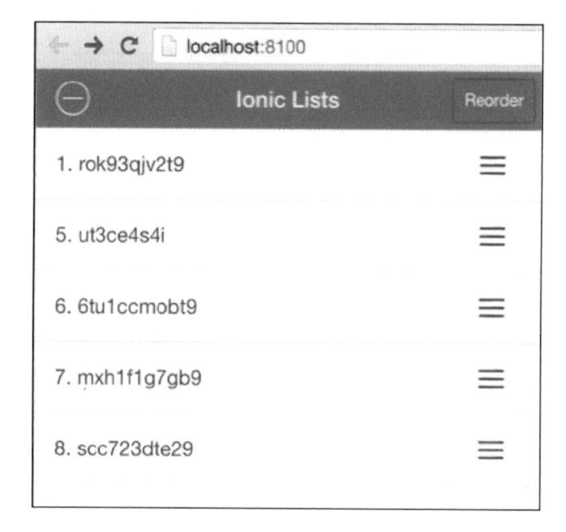

You can move the items around using the handle provided on each row. You can also close the reorder and swipe the items to the left-hand side to see the **Share** and **Edit** options:

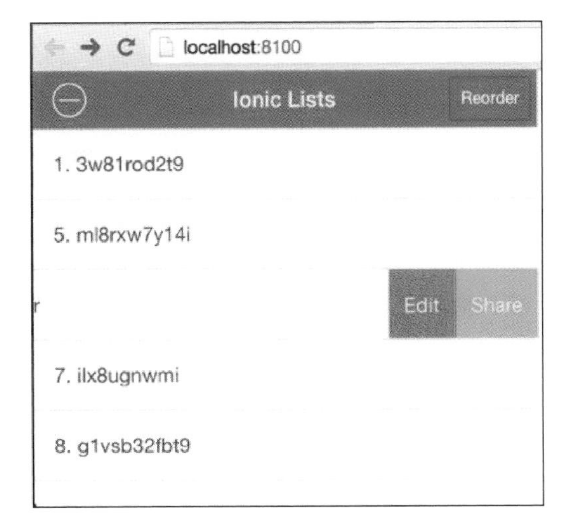

Re-order does not work well when you use `collection-repeat` instead of `ng-repeat`. You can read more at `https://github.com/driftyco/ionic/issues/1714`.

You can read more about lists at `http://ionicframework.com/docs/api/directive/ionList/`.

Gesture directives and services

The next set of directives and services are for gestures. If you did not already know, gestures are actions that a user performs on the screen when interacting with the application. An example of a gesture is pinching to zoom-out or pinching-in to zoom-in (just like on a smartphone).

Ionic supports these gestures and lets you handle them using the `$ionicGesture` service inside your controller or directive.

To make things more generic, I will explain one gesture directive and show how you can work with it. The same logic applies to all the other gestures.

We will be testing the `on-drag-up` directive by scaffolding a new blank app; run this:

```
ionic start -a "Example 26" -i app.example.twentysix example26 blank
```

Using the `cd` command, go to the `example26` folder and run this:

```
ionic serve
```

This will launch the blank template in the browser.

First, we will create a controller named `AppCtrl` in `www/js/app.js`.

```
.controller('AppCtrl', function($scope, $ionicGesture) {

    $scope.scopeGesture = 'None';
    $scope.delegateGesture = 'None';

    $scope.onDragUp = function() {
        $scope.scopeGesture = 'Drag up fired!'
    };

    // Event listener using event delegation
    // The logic below would be typically written in a directive
    // We have added this to the controller for illustration
purposes
    var $element =
angular.element(document.querySelector('#gestureContainer'));
    $ionicGesture.on('dragup', function() {
        $scope.delegateGesture = 'Drag up fired!';
    }, $element);
})
```

As mentioned earlier, we are implementing the `dragup` gesture. We have implemented the listener in two ways, one using the directive, which we will see in the HTML template, and the other using the `$ionicGesture.on` method.

Generally any DOM-related code would be written in a (custom) directive. Here, we have written this in a controller for illustration purposes. The event type is `dragup`. We are fetching the element from the DOM using the `document.querySelector` API and wrapping this HTML node in an AngularJS's element object. This is passed as the third argument to the `$ionicGesture.on` method.

Next, our `www/index.html` body section will be updated as follows:

```
<body ng-app="starter" ng-controller="AppCtrl">
    <ion-header-bar class="bar-dark">
        <h1 class="title">Gestures</h1>
    </ion-header-bar>
    <ion-content>
        <div class="card">
```

```
            <div id="gestureContainer" class="item text-center"
on-drag-up="onDragUp()">
                Drag me up!!
            </div>
        </div>
        <div class="card">
            <div class="item text-center">
                Scope Gesture : {{scopeGesture}}
                <br>
                Delegate Gesture : {{delegateGesture}}
            </div>
        </div>
    </ion-content>
</body>
```

We have created two card containers; the first one contains a `div` with the ID `gestureContainer` and the `on-drag-up` attribute will execute the `onDragUp` method when the event is fired.

The second card container consists of the `scopeGesture` value, which gets assigned when the `onDragUp` method is called. The `delegateGesture` will be set when the `dragup` event is fired from the `$ionicGesture.on` method.

If you save all the files and head back to the browser, you will see the two-card section. When you drag the content in the first card up, the second card content should be updated, as shown in the following screenshot:

Quite a simple way to manage gestures! The following table provides a list of gesture directives and their event type when used with the `$ionicGesture.on` method. You can use the preceding code example to implement any of the following gestures:

Gesture name	**Directive name**	**Event type (when using with `$ionicGesture.on()`)**
Drag up	`on-drag-up`	`dragup`
Drag down	`on-drag-down`	`dragdown`
Drag right	`on-drag-right`	`dragright`
Drag left	`on-drag-left`	`dragleft`
Drag	`on-drag`	`drag`
Swipe up	`on-swipe-up`	`swipeup`
Swipe down	`on-swipe-down`	`swipedown`
Swipe right	`on-swipe-right`	`swiperight`
Swipe left	`on-swipe-left`	`swipeleft`
Swipe	`on-swipe`	`Swipe`
Hold (touch > 500ms)	`on-hold`	`hold`
Tap (touch < 250ms)	`on-tap`	`tap`
Double tap	`on-double-tap`	`doubletap`
Touch	`on-touch`	`touch`
Release	`on-release`	`release`

You can also implement gesture handling using the `ionic.EventController` utility as well. You can read more at `http://ionicframework.com/docs/api/utility/ionic.EventController/#onGesture`.

By default, Ionic removes the 300ms tap delay that is added by the browser. The tap delay is added in the first place for the browser to differentiate between a tap and double-tap. If you want to enable the 300ms tap delay on any element, you can use the `data-tap-disabled` attribute. You can read more at `http://ionicframework.com/docs/api/page/tap/`.

Utilities

The final topic in this chapter explores a few utility services provided by Ionic. The first service we are going to take a look at is `$ionicConfigProvider`.

By default, Ionic plugs in the app configuration based on the environment it is running. And, depending on the environment, properties such as a transition will be applied. At the time of writing, Ionic officially supports Android and iOS only. However, Ionic can be used on other platforms as well.

All configurations are based on the environment the app is running in. If the environment is neither Android nor iOS, the configurations for iOS will be applied.

However, we can control these options using the `$ionicConfigProvider` service. You can override the default values as follows:

```
.config(function ($ionicConfigProvider) {

    $ionicConfigProvider.views.transition('none');
    $ionicConfigProvider.views.maxCache(10);

    $ionicConfigProvider.form.checkbox('circle'); //square or
circle

    $ionicConfigProvider.tabs.style('striped'); // striped or
standard

    $ionicConfigProvider.templates.maxPrefetch(10);

    $ionicConfigProvider.navBar.alignTitle('right');
})
```

You can also override values specific to a platform using the following approach:

```
.config(function($ionicConfigProvider) {

    // Checkbox style. Android defaults to square and iOS defaults
to circle.
    $ionicConfigProvider.platform.ios.form.checkbox('square');
    $ionicConfigProvider.platform.android.form.checkbox('circle');

})
```

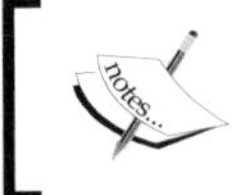

You can find the properties that you can override at `http://ionicframework.com/docs/api/provider/$ionicConfigProvider/`.

Ionic provides a set of utility methods on the `ionic.Platform` object. You can perform basic checks about the environment using the methods on this object:

```
.config(function() {
    console.log('ionic.Platform.isWebView()',
ionic.Platform.isWebView());
    console.log('ionic.Platform.isIPad()',
ionic.Platform.isIPad());
    console.log('ionic.Platform.isIOS()', ionic.Platform.isIOS());
    console.log('ionic.Platform.isAndroid()',
ionic.Platform.isAndroid());
    console.log('ionic.Platform.isWindowsPhone()',
ionic.Platform.isWindowsPhone());
})
```

You can read about other `ionic.Platform` methods at `http://ionicframework.com/docs/api/utility/ionic.Platform/`.

There is a set of utility methods that help you interact with the DOM as well. These are available inside the `ionic.DomUtil` object. A few methods on the `ionic.DomUtil` object are as follows:

```
.controller('AppCtrl', function($scope) {
    var $element = angular.element(document.
querySelector('#someElement'));
    console.log(ionic.DomUtil.getParentWithClass($element,
'.card'));
    console.log(ionic.DomUtil.getParentOrSelfWithClass($element,
'.card'));

    // requestAnimationFrame example
    function loop() {
        console.log('Animation Frame Requested');
        ionic.DomUtil.requestAnimationFrame(loop);
    }

    loop();
})
```

You can read about other `ionic.DomUtil` methods at `http://ionicframework.com/docs/api/utility/ionic.DomUtil/`.

Finally, we will take a look at the Event Controller object in Ionic. This consists of methods to hook and unhook events and gestures. You can also trigger events using the `ionic.EventController` trigger method.

The following section shows a quick example of how to use `ionic.EventController` for event/gesture binding, triggering, and unbinding.

Again you will be typically implementing the following logic in a directive and then applying the directive on the intended element:

```
.controller('AppCtrl', ['$scope', function($scope) {

    // Binding Events
    var $body = document.querySelector('body');

    var eventListener = function() {
        console.log('Body Tapped!');

        ionic.EventController.off('tap', eventListener, $body);
    };

    ionic.EventController.on('tap', eventListener, $body);

    ionic.EventController.trigger('tap', {
        target: $body
    });


    // Binding gestures
    var cancelSwipeUp;
    var gestureListener = function() {
        console.log('Body Swiped Up!');

        ionic.EventController.offGesture(cancelSwipeUp, 'swipeup',
gestureListener);
    }

    cancelSwipeUp = ionic.EventController.onGesture('swipeup',
gestureListener, $body);

    ionic.EventController.trigger('swipeup', {
        target: $body
    });


}])
```

Summary

In this chapter, we looked at various Ionic directives and services that help us develop applications easily. We started with the Ionic Platform service, then moved on to the Header and Footer directives. Next, we went through content-related directives and navigation-related directives and services. Next, we looked into overlays. Then, we quickly went through list directives, gestures, and utility services.

With this, we have finished going through Ionic itself. From the next chapter on, we will be utilizing these components to build simple and complex applications.

In the next chapter, we will be building a Book Store app, where a user can register and log in. The user can browse through a catalog of books and add them to the cart. The user can also check them out and view the shopping history in their profile. This application shows how to integrate Ionic with a secure RESTful backend service.

6
Building a Bookstore App

So far, we have looked at all the key elements of Ionic. In this chapter, we will build a Bookstore application using that knowledge. The main purpose of this chapter is to consolidate your understanding of Ionic and, at the same time, get a sense of integrating an Ionic app with an existing RESTful service.

[Do note that we will not be working with any server-side related code.]

The Bookstore app we are going to build is a simple multi-page Ionic client that lets a user browse through the books without any authentication. Only when the user wants to add a book to his cart or view his purchase history do we ask the user to login. This approach provides a better user experience by not forcing the user to login to see content, but rather allowing him to login only when needed.

Once the user is logged in, he/she can add books to the cart, view the cart, checkout the cart, and view purchases. A secure REST server will manage all the data for this application using JSON Web Tokens.

During the development process, we will work on the following topics:

- Understanding the end-to-end application architecture
- Setting up a server on a local machine or consume a hosted server
- Analyzing different views, controllers, and factories needed for the app and building these components
- Visually testing the application

[For this chapter, you can also access the code, raise issues, and chat with the author at GitHub (`https://github.com/learning-ionic/Chapter-6`).]

An introduction to the Bookstore application

In this chapter, we are going to build a Bookstore application. As explained earlier, a user can register and log in to the application. The user can browse through all the books in the store without any authentication. They can add books to cart, view their cart, and checkout the cart. Once the user makes a purchase, they can view it in their purchase history page.

The application features are quite simple but, to take the application to the next level, we will be integrating the application with a secure REST API server built, on Node.js, which uses JSON Web Tokens for authentication. Since we already have Node.js installed on the local machine, setting up a server should not be complicated. Or, in case you do not want to set up the server locally, you can find a link to the hosted version of the APIs in the next section.

Some end points such as Checkout and View Purchases are made secure with **JSON Web Tokens** (**JWT**). The server is set up in such a way that, if a REST client (such as the Ionic app) wants to fetch any application data; it needs to send a valid token with the request.

The flow of the application is as follows:

1. A user launches the app.
2. User can browse through the books without any authentication.
3. User wants to add an item to the cart or view purchases.
4. User attempts to register or login.
5. On successful register or login, the server along with the user data will send a token that is valid for 7 days.
6. If the client wants to perform any operations such as adding to the cart or viewing purchases, it needs to send a request to the appropriate REST end point with the token. If the token is valid and belongs to the user, we dispatch the data; otherwise, we forbid the user from accessing/updating the data.

We will understand the complete architecture of the application in the next section.

I have added a few technical features such as pagination and local storage to better manage the data. But I have not implemented it 100 percent. These pieces are to get you started on how to integrate these features with your ionic app.

A quick reminder: this is not a production-grade app, but will help you get started along those lines.

The Bookstore architecture

The following is a high-level view of all the components that are involved in building the bookstore application:

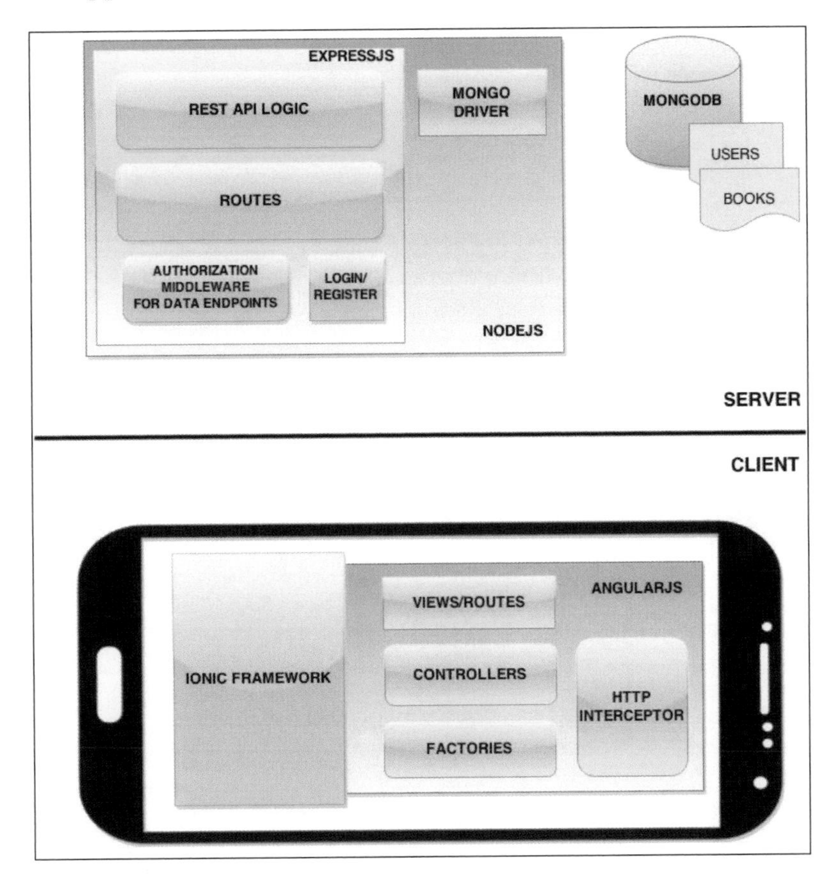

The server architecture

The secure REST server we are using for the application is built using Node.js/Express. MongoDB is used as the data persistence layer.

The data used in the application is generated via a Faker script (`https://www.npmjs.com/package/faker`). None of the data in the application is real and it is only used to prototype the app/fill the space. All the images and text are random.

Since the scope of this book is limited to Ionic, I will not be explaining how the server is built.

You can follow the following blog post to understand the server-side layer, how it is set up, and how JWTs work.

See Architecting a Secure RESTful Node.js app here: `http://thejackalofjavascript.com/architecting-a-restful-node-js-app/`.

You can find two implementations of a similar application, where I have built a Bucket list app using Node.js as the server-side and one more where I have built the same application using Firebase as the server-side. You can find more information in the following:

- Ionic Restify MongoDB: This an end-to-end Hybrid App:
  `http://thejackalofjavascript.com/an-end-to-end-hybrid-app/`
- Creating a Firebase Powered end-to-end Ionic application:
  `http://www.sitepoint.com/creating-firebase-powered-end-end-ionic-application/`

The server-side API documentation

I have provided documentation for the Bookstore REST API, where you can see all the endpoints, understand what input is expected for each route, and what the possible responses are, with expected exceptions.

You can find the documentation hosted here: `https://ionic-book-store.herokuapp.com/`.

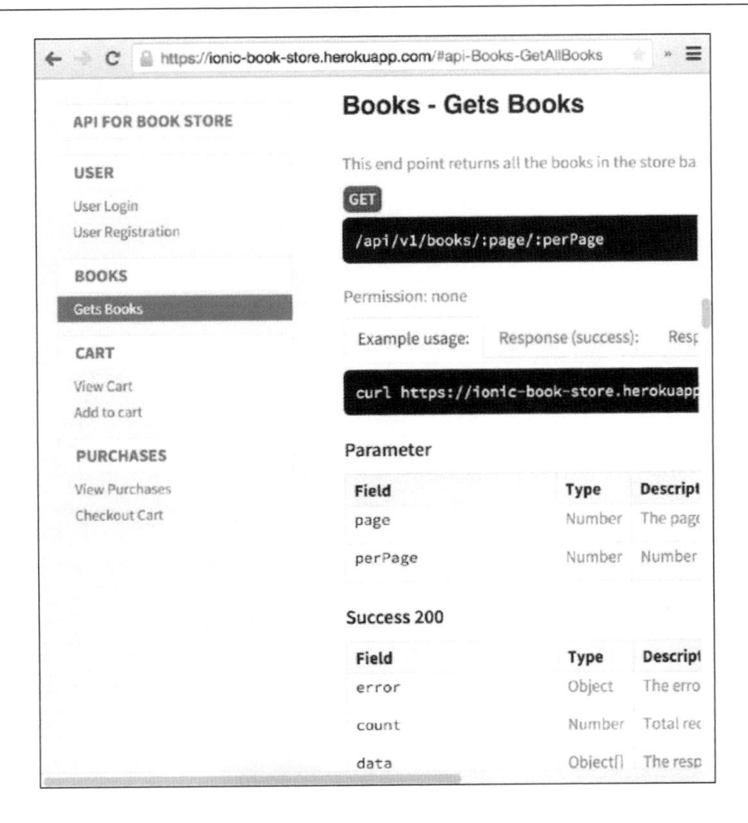

This documentation is not extensive but can be used quite easily with the details given in this chapter.

The client architecture

Coming to the client-side, we will have the following routes:

- Home (view all books)
- Login (tab component) / Register (tab component)
- View one book
- Add to cart
- View cart
- View purchases

We will have the following controllers:

- `AppCtrl`: This is an application-level controller (manage authentication)
- `BrowseCtrl`: This is used for viewing all books
- `BookCtrl`: This is used for viewing one book detail
- `CartCtrl`: This is used for viewing cart
- `PurchasesCtrl`: This is used for viewing purchases

We will have four sets of factories: one that manages Ionic loading, one that manages `localStorage`, one that manages authentication, and one that manages the data.

- `Loader`: This manages Ionic loading
- `LSFactory`: This manages local storage
- `AuthFactory`: This manages authentication
- `TokenInterceptor`: This manages tokens for every HTTP request
- `BooksFactory`: This is used to get all books
- `UserFactory`: This is the user login/register and cart, purchase API

We are going to use the HTML5 `localStorage` API to cache all the books locally to avoid fetching the books again and again. We will go through each of the factories as we start building the app.

Code on GitHub

I have hosted the client as well as the server code for this example on GitHub. I would recommend that you visit the repositories and check out the code. I will be adding updates or fixing any bugs reported by readers here.

I also encourage you to raise any issues you find and I will try my best to address them:

- Bookstore Ionic Client Repository
- Bookstore Node.js Server Repository

A Bookstore demo

The Bookstore app will be built using the side menu template. We will be using tabs, modals, loading, cards, lists and the grid system to build the application.

Before we proceed, you can take a quick peek at the application we are about to build at `https://ionic-book-store.herokuapp.com/app`.

The application will take some time to load, but once done, you will see something like this.

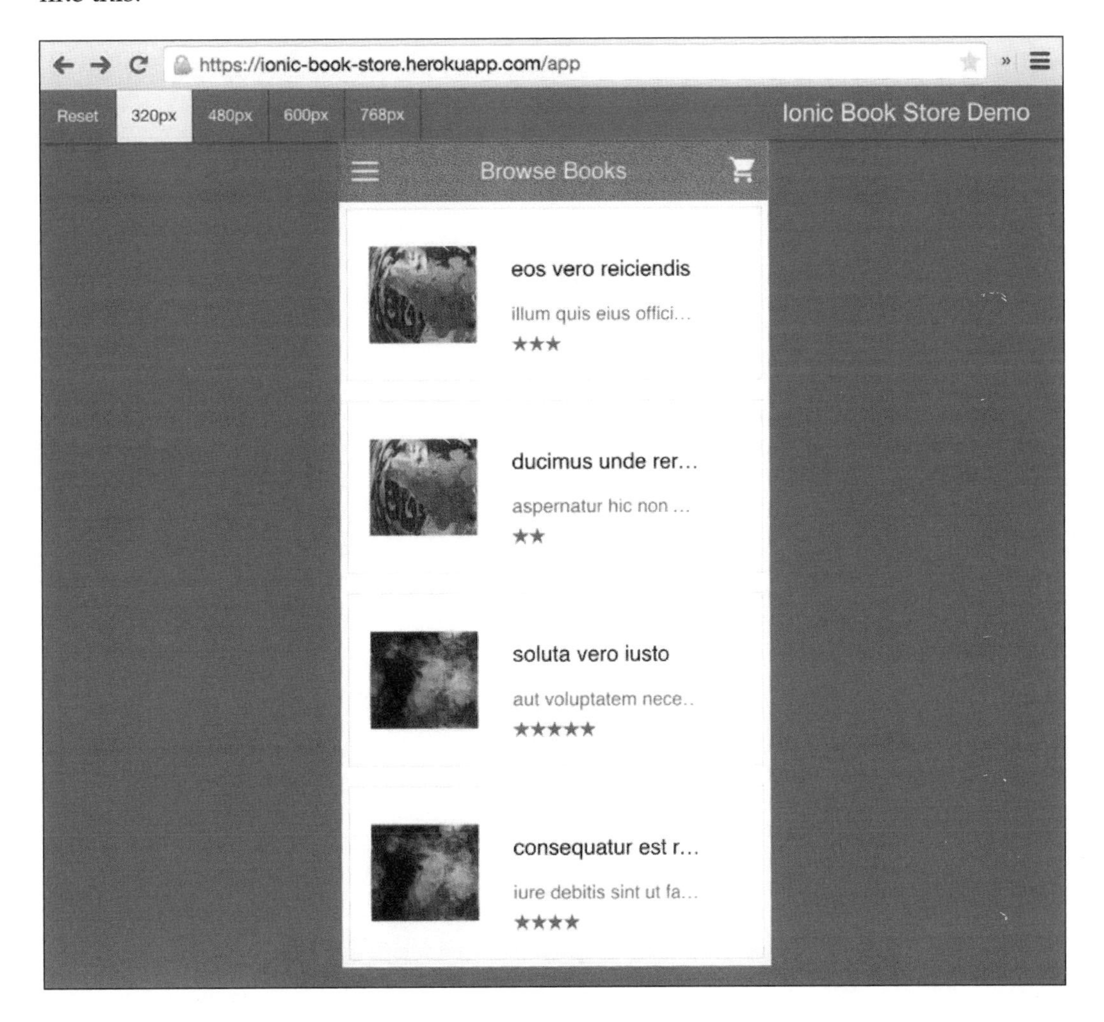

This is a live demo of the application we are going to build. You can click on the menu or the cart icon to view appropriate pages. You will be asked to login/register if you are trying to add to the cart or access the cart or purchases. You can create an account and test things out for yourself (it is free!).

Also, you can see a resolution bar on the top of the page to see how the app looks in different resolutions.

> Do note that all the data you see here is random faker data for prototyping purposes only.

The development flow

In this chapter, we are not going to develop the app feature-by-feature, view the output, and proceed to the next one. Rather, we will be developing the entire app at once and viewing the output at the end. If, at any point, you feel confused as to what the final result is, I highly encourage you check out the live version present at `https://ionic-book-store.herokuapp.com/app`.

Setting up the server

Since setting up the server is not a critical part of this book or this example app, you have two ways to do it:

1. Consume an existing REST API, which I have built.
2. Fork the server code, set up DB and run the server locally.

For option 1, you can check out the docs (`https://ionic-book-store.herokuapp.com/`) on readily available REST API end points and how to consume them.

For option 2, we will carry out the following operations:

Download and unzip the server code from: `https://github.com/arvindr21`.
If you are familiar with Node.js, this is a typical Express application that has JWT added to it.

For the database, you can either use your local instance of MongoDB or you can get a free MongoLab (`https://mongolab.com/`) account and use it. Or you can use my MongoLab URL for this. Do note that other people are also using this URL; so kindly be sensible about it.

Once you have decided on the connection, you need to open `server/db/connection.js` and update the connection string on line 2 as applicable; for example:

```
var db = mongojs('ionicbookstoreapp', ['users', 'books']);
```

Next, to generate some test data for the book API, open a terminal/prompt inside the `db` folder and run this:

```
node dbscript.js
```

This will generate 30 books for us to start working with the application.

> If you are using the MongoLab URL, you need not run the earlier step to add the books. They are already present.

Finally, to start the local server, use the `cd` command into the root of the `server` folder and run this:

```
node server.js
```

This will start the server on port `3000` and you can access the application on `http://localhost:3000`.

> Do not panic if you see an error when you navigate to `http://localhost:3000`. This is an API server; hence I have not added any UI to the home page.

You can open `http://localhost:3000/api/v1/books/1/10` and you should see the JSON data for about 10 books populate your browser. This means that you have successfully set up the server.

Again, if you are not comfortable with the **Do It Yourself** (**DIY**) approach, you can directly use the hosted REST endpoints. I will show you how easy it is to consume end points, irrespective of where your REST API is hosted.

Building the application

Now that we have our server set up and have an idea as to what we are going to build, let's start building it. We are going to perform the following steps, for us to easily build the app:

1. Scaffold the side menu template.
2. Refactor the template.

3. Build the authentication, local storage and REST API Factories.
4. Create controllers for each route and integrate them with the corresponding Factories.
5. Create templates and integrate with the Controller data.

Step 1 – Scaffolding the side menu template

The first thing we are going to do is scaffold a side menu template. Create a folder named `chapter6`. Open a terminal/prompt inside the `chapter6` folder and run this:

```
ionic start -a "Ionic Book Store" -i app.bookstore.ionic book-store
sidemenu
```

This will scaffold the side menu application. We will not be using theming in our Bookstore app, so there will be no SCSS setup.

Step 2 – Refactoring the template

In all the examples we have built so far, we have created components from scratch. But in this example, we are going to refactor the template.

Before we proceed, let's test whether everything is working fine. Using the `cd` command, go to the `book-store` folder and run this:

```
ionic serve
```

This will serve the scaffolded app. As mentioned in *Chapter 2, Welcome to Ionic*, open your development tool and set it up at the right hand section of the page. The app with development tools open will look like this:

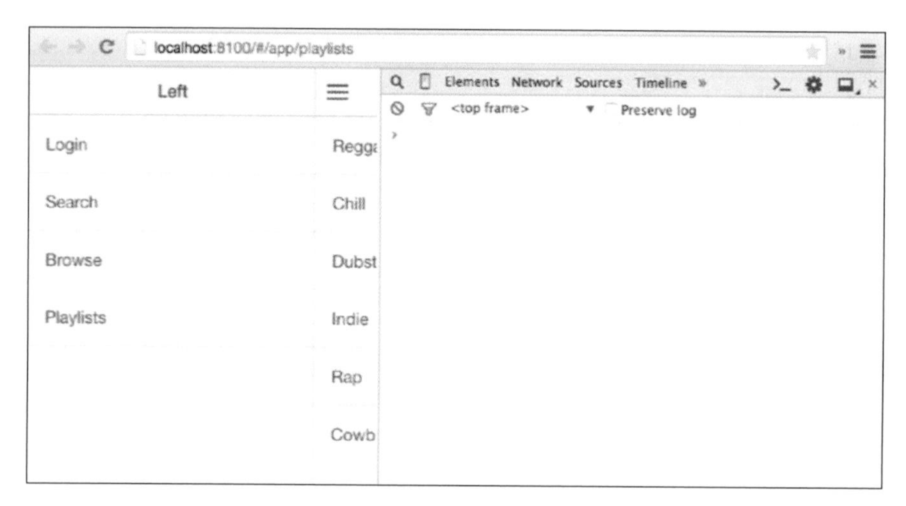

Refactoring the menu

The first thing we are going to refactor is the menu. We will replace the existing menu items with the ones we are going to use.

Open `www/templates/menu.html` and update the left-hand side `ion-side-menu` section as follows:

```
<ion-side-menu side="left">
        <ion-header-bar class="bar-assertive">
            <h1 class="title">Menu</h1>
        </ion-header-bar>
        <ion-content>
            <ion-list>
                <ion-item menu-close href="#/app/browse">
                    Browse Books
                </ion-item>
                <ion-item menu-close href="#/app/cart">
                    My Cart
                </ion-item>
                <ion-item menu-close href="#/app/purchases">
                    My Purchases
                </ion-item>
                <ion-item menu-close ng-show="isAuthenticated" ng-
click="logout()">
                    Logout
                </ion-item>
                <ion-item menu-close ng-hide="isAuthenticated" ng-
click="loginFromMenu()">
                    Login
                </ion-item>
            </ion-list>
        </ion-content>
</ion-side-menu>
```

We have added four menu items:

- **Browse books**: To view all the books
- **My cart**: To view the cart
- **My purchases**: To view all purchases
- **Login/logout**: A conditional menu item that changes based on the user's authentication status

Next, we will be updating the header or the `ion-side-menu-content` section at the top of `menu.html`:

```
<ion-side-menu-content>
        <ion-nav-bar class="bar-assertive">
            <ion-nav-back-button>
            </ion-nav-back-button>
            <ion-nav-buttons side="left">
                <button class="button button-icon button-clear
ion-navicon" menu-toggle="left">
                </button>
            </ion-nav-buttons>
            <ion-nav-buttons side="right">
                <!-- <button ng-show="isAuthenticated"
class="button button-icon button-clear ion-unlocked" ng-
click="logout()">
                </button> -->
                <a class="button button-icon button-clear ion-
android-cart" href="#/app/cart">
                </a>
            </ion-nav-buttons>
        </ion-nav-bar>
        <ion-nav-view name="menuContent"></ion-nav-view>
 </ion-side-menu-content>
```

We have modified the theme of the header to reflect an assertive mood. We have also added two buttons to the right. One is the logout, which I have commented out, and the other is the cart. This code shows how you can add icons to the header of the application.

Also do note that the commented out logout icon is a conditional icon. Only if the user is authenticated does it show up (if uncommented from the earlier code). Since I did not want two icons to the right of my title bar, I commented the logout button.

Also, update the `enable-menu-with-back-views` attribute value on `ion-side-menus` to `true`. Without this, you would not see the side menu icon when you are inside a child view.

If you save this file and go back to the browser, you will see the updated header and the menu:

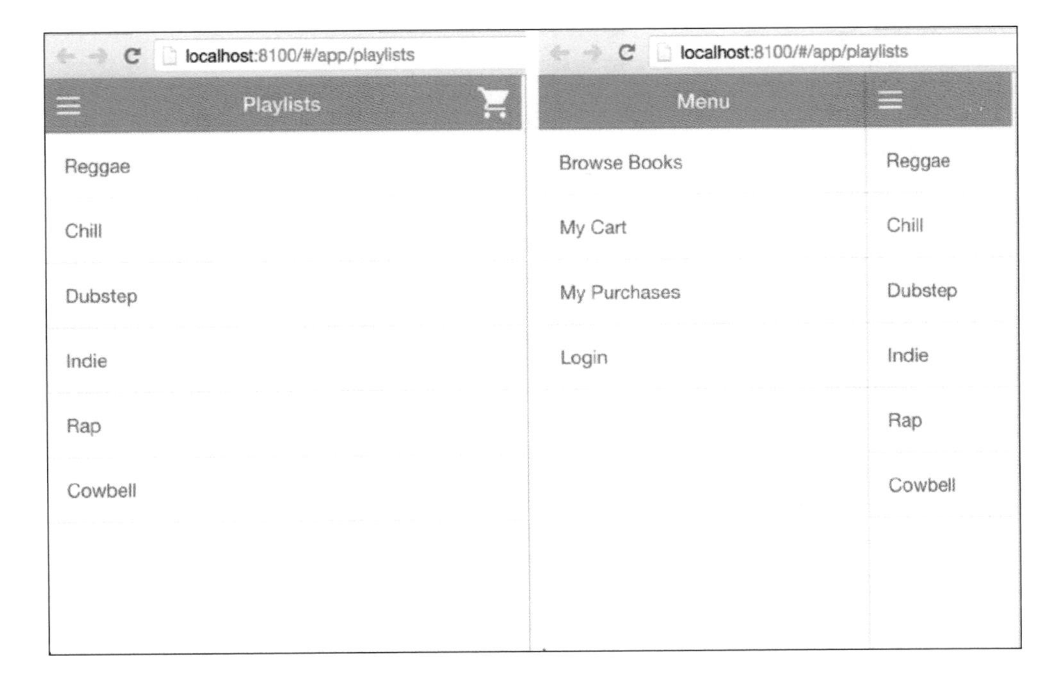

Refactoring the module name

Next, we are going to rename the module of the app. By default the module name set to the starter template is `starter`. We will rename it to `BookStoreApp`. The places to update are:

- Open `www/index.html` and rename `ng-app` directive value from starter to `BookStoreApp`.
- Open `www/js/app.js` and rename the angular module syntax as follows:

```
angular.module('BookStoreApp', ['ionic',
'BookStoreApp.controllers'])
```

- Open `www/js/controllers.js` and update `starter.controllers` to `BookStoreApp.controllers`.

This will take care of renaming the module in our app. From now on, we will be using `BookStoreApp` as the module namespace for the app.

Adding a run method and modifying routes

Now, we will configure the routes; open `www/js/app.js`. We will delete the existing `config` section here. Next, we will set up the `run` method to hold a few utility methods. Add the following `run` method to `www/js/app.js`:

```
.run(['$rootScope', 'AuthFactory',
    function($rootScope, , AuthFactory) {

        $rootScope.isAuthenticated = AuthFactory.isLoggedIn();

        // utility method to convert number to an array of
elements
        $rootScope.getNumber = function(num) {
            return new Array(num);
        }

    }
])
```

You attach multiple run methods to a module.

If you recall `menu.html`, we have added the capability to show and hide login/logout based on the value of `isAuthenticated`. This property is initialized here.

We also have a utility method named `getNumber`. We will get to it when we use it. All this method does is generate an array with the provided number as the length.

Next, we will add the routes. Below the `run` section, add the `config` section as follows:

```
.config(['$stateProvider', '$urlRouterProvider', '$httpProvider',
    function($stateProvider, $urlRouterProvider, $httpProvider) {

        // setup the token interceptor
        $httpProvider.interceptors.push('TokenInterceptor');

        $stateProvider

            .state('app', {
            url: "/app",
            abstract: true,
            templateUrl: "templates/menu.html",
```

```
        controller: 'AppCtrl'
    })

    .state('app.browse', {
        url: "/browse",
        views: {
            'menuContent': {
                templateUrl: "templates/browse.html",
                controller: 'BrowseCtrl'
            }
        }
    })

    .state('app.book', {
        url: "/book/:bookId",
        views: {
            'menuContent': {
                templateUrl: "templates/book.html",
                controller: 'BookCtrl'
            }
        }
    })

    .state('app.cart', {
        url: "/cart",
        views: {
            'menuContent': {
                templateUrl: "templates/cart.html",
                controller: 'CartCtrl'
            }
        }
    })


    .state('app.purchases', {
        url: "/purchases",
        views: {
            'menuContent': {
                templateUrl: "templates/purchases.html",
                controller: 'PurchasesCtrl'
            }
        }
    });
```

```
        // if none of the above states are matched, use this as
the fallback
        $urlRouterProvider.otherwise('/app/browse');
    }
])
```

Note that we could have edited the routes manually to produce what we need, but I thought this would be easier to illustrate.

Also note that, if you have kept the Ionic server running, you will see an error in the browser JavaScript console complaining about missing dependencies. The app will not function properly until we finish all the pieces of the code. You might as well kill the server till we are done.

The first thing we have added in the config is the `TokenInterceptor`. We will implement the `TokenInterceptor` when we are dealing with the authentication factory. I will refer back to here when we are working with `TokenInterceptor`.

The routes we have added are as follows:

- `/app`: This is an abstract route that manages the main view of the application
- `/browse`: This is the home page of the app, where we will list all the books
- `/book/:bookId`: This is used to view details about one book
- `/cart`: This is used to view the books in cart
- `/purchases`: This is used to view the list of purchases a user has made

The `login/register` tab interface will be a modal and not a route.

Refactoring templates

We can either go to one template at a time and refactor them as per our routes config or for the sake of simplicity we can (and will) delete all templates except `menu.html` from the `www/templates` folder and add empty HTML files for now.

After deleting all the templates except `menu.html`, we will create the following templates:

- `browse.html`
- `book.html`
- `cart.html`
- `purchases.html`
- `login.html`

You can leave all the templates blank for now. We will work with these templates at the end.

Step 3 – Building authentication, localStorage, and the REST API factory

Inside the `www/js` folder, create a file named `factory.js`. After that add a reference to this file in `www/index.html` after the reference to `controller.js` as follows:

```
<script src="js/factory.js"></script>
```

This file will hold all the factories. If you like, you can create one factory file for one feature. But for our example we will have all the factories in one file.

The first line we are going to add is the base URL for the REST API. You can either point the app to your local server or you can point it to the REST API hosted on Heroku.

Add the following to `www/js/factory.js`:

```
//var base = 'http://localhost:3000';
var base = 'https://ionic-book-store.herokuapp.com';
```

You can uncomment and use it as applicable.

Next, we will create a new module named `BookStoreApp.factory` that will hold all our factory definitions.

```
angular.module('BookStoreApp.factory', [])
```

Next, we will add the new module as a dependency to our main module `BookStoreApp`. Open `www/js/app.js` and update the `BookStoreApp` module definition as follows:

```
angular.module('BookStoreApp', ['ionic', 'BookStoreApp.controllers',
'BookStoreApp.factory'])
```

The Ionic loading factory

The first factory we are going to create is the Ionic loading factory. Below the AngularJS module definition, add this:

```
.factory('Loader', ['$ionicLoading', '$timeout',
function($ionicLoading, $timeout) {

    var LOADERAPI = {

        showLoading: function(text) {
            text = text || 'Loading...';
            $ionicLoading.show({
                template: text
            });
        },

        hideLoading: function() {
            $ionicLoading.hide();
        },

        toggleLoadingWithMessage: function(text, timeout) {
            $rootScope.showLoading(text);

            $timeout(function() {
                $rootScope.hideLoading();
            }, timeout || 3000);
        }

    };
    return LOADERAPI;
}])
```

We have the following three functions that help us in showing, hiding, and toggling Ionic loading:

- `showLoading`: This shows a blocking modal with the text provided or `Loading`.
- `hideLoading`: This hides the modal that was shown using `showLoading`.
- `toggleLoadingWithMessage`: This will show the modal with the provided message and hide it after the provided timeout or 3 seconds. This method will be used to show the blocked messages that get hidden automatically.

The localStorage factory

Next, we are going to add the `localStorage` factory. Below the Loader factory, add this:

```
.factory('LSFactory', [function() {

    var LSAPI = {

        clear: function() {
            return localStorage.clear();
        },

        get: function(key) {
            return JSON.parse(localStorage.getItem(key));
        },

        set: function(key, data) {
            return localStorage.setItem(key,
JSON.stringify(data));
        },

        delete: function(key) {
            return localStorage.removeItem(key);
        },

        getAll: function() {
            var books = [];
            var items = Object.keys(localStorage);

            for (var i = 0; i < items.length; i++) {
                if (items[i] !== 'user' || items[i] != 'token') {
                    books.push(JSON.parse(localStorage[items[i]]));
                }
            }

            return books;
        }

    };

    return LSAPI;

}])
```

This factory has an API that we can use to interact with the HTML5 `localStorage` API. We will be using local storage to save all the books. This way, we do not need to make calls to the server every time to fetch the books.

Since this is an example, we have not added a background process that checks for new books and updates the local storage. You can easily add one in your app.

The `clear`, `get`, `set`, and `delete` methods are wrappers for the `localStorage` API's `clear`, `getItem`, `setItem`, and `deleteItem` methods. Since we will be dealing with objects that need to be saved in local storage and local storage stores only strings, we have modified the `set` and `get` method such that we stringify the object before saving and parse the stringified text after fetching. This way, other methods can send objects to the `get` method and the data gets massaged here.

The `getAll` method will be used to fetch all the books we have saved in `localStorage`.

Do note that we have used the `Object.keys` method to convert the `localStorage` (array-like) object to an array.

You can read more about the `Object.keys` method at `https://developer.mozilla.org/en-US/docs/Web/JavaScript/Reference/Global_Objects/Object/keys`.

The Authentication factory

The next factory we are going to work with is the Authentication factory. Add the following code after the `LSFactory` definition:

```
.factory('AuthFactory', ['LSFactory', function(LSFactory) {

    var userKey = 'user';
    var tokenKey = 'token';

    var AuthAPI = {

        isLoggedIn: function() {
            return this.getUser() === null ? false : true;
        },

        getUser: function() {
            return LSFactory.get(userKey);
        },

        setUser: function(user) {
```

```
            return LSFactory.set(userKey, user);
        },

        getToken: function() {
            return LSFactory.get(tokenKey);
        },

        setToken: function(token) {
            return LSFactory.set(tokenKey, token);
        },

        deleteAuth: function() {
            LSFactory.delete(userKey);
            LSFactory.delete(tokenKey);
        }

    };

    return AuthAPI;

}])
```

This factory is dependent on `LSFactory` and manages the user authentication data. As mentioned earlier, when the user does a login or register, the server will send an access token along with a user object. These wrapper methods save the user data and token data in local storage using the `LSFactory` API.

Next, we will create the `TokenInterceptor` factory. If you remember, we have added a reference to the `TokenInterceptor` in our `www/js/app.js` file, the config section. We are telling AngularJS to call the `TokenInterceptor` every time it is making a HTTP request.

What are Interceptors?

When making AJAX calls using the `$http` service, there will be times (as with our app) where you would like to intercept the HTTP request and add some additional data before the request is fired. The piece of AngularJS code that lets you achieve this is an interceptor.

Interceptors are added to the `$httpProvider` interceptor using the following syntax:

```
$httpProvider.interceptors.push('MyInterceptor');
```

After setting up a factory/service named `MyInterceptor`, you can read more about Interceptors and how they work at `http://www.webdeveasy.com/interceptors-in-angularjs-and-useful-examples/`.

When this method is invoked, it will check if a token and a user object are present in the `localStorage`. If yes, it will attach them to the header of the request. If you recall, the add to cart, view cart, checkout, and view purchase routes need the user to be authenticated. This token is the only way the server knows if the user is authenticated and if the user is authorized to view the content.

Add the `TokenInterceptor` factory below the `AuthFactory` in `www/js/factory.js`:

```
.factory('TokenInterceptor', ['$q', 'AuthFactory', function($q,
AuthFactory) {

    return {
        request: function(config) {
            config.headers = config.headers || {};
            var token = AuthFactory.getToken();
            var user = AuthFactory.getUser();

            if (token && user) {
                config.headers['X-Access-Token'] = token.token;
                config.headers['X-Key'] = user.email;
                config.headers['Content-Type'] =
"application/json";
            }
            return config || $q.when(config);
        },

        response: function(response) {
            return response || $q.when(response);
        }
    };

}])
```

The REST API factory

Next, we will be creating two factories. One factory interacts with the REST API end points, which do not need authentication to get the data, and the other factory interacts with the REST API endpoints, which need authentication. This is just a logical separation. You can have both in one factory as well.

The first is `BooksFactory`. This factory has a `get` method that talks to the public `api/v1/books` endpoint:

```
.factory('BooksFactory', ['$http', function($http) {

    var perPage = 30;

    var API = {
        get: function(page) {
            return $http.get(base + '/api/v1/books/' + page + '/'
+ perPage);
        }
    };

    return API;
}])
```

The REST endpoint `/api/v1/books` has the ability to paginate data. You can send the `perPage` and `page` number; it will return the corresponding records. You can use this server side API to paginate the book data and load books on demand.

But, in this app, we are going to make only 1 call and fetch 30 records. You can implement an `ion-infinite-scroll` and load the books on demand as an exercise.

Next is the `UserFactory`. This factory consists of `login`, `register` REST endpoints, and four other methods to interact with the cart and purchase API.

Add the following `UserFactory` factory definition after the `BooksFactory`:

```
.factory('UserFactory', ['$http', 'AuthFactory',
    function($http, AuthFactory) {

        var UserAPI = {

            login: function(user) {
                return $http.post(base + '/login', user);
            },

            register: function(user) {
                return $http.post(base + '/register', user);
            },

            logout: function() {
                AuthFactory.deleteAuth();
```

```
            },

            getCartItems: function() {
                var userId = AuthFactory.getUser()._id;
                return $http.get(base + '/api/v1/users/' + userId
+ '/cart');
            },

            addToCart: function(book) {
                var userId = AuthFactory.getUser()._id;
                return $http.post(base + '/api/v1/users/' + userId
+ '/cart', book);
            },

            getPurchases: function() {
                var userId = AuthFactory.getUser()._id;
                return $http.get(base + '/api/v1/users/' + userId
+ '/purchases');
            },

            addPurchase: function(cart) {
                var userId = AuthFactory.getUser()._id;
                return $http.post(base + '/api/v1/users/' + userId
+ '/purchases', cart);
            }

        };

        return UserAPI;
    }
])
```

The `getCartItems`, `addToCart`, `getPurchases`, and `addPurchase` methods first get the user ID from the `localStorage` before making the REST call. This is how the REST endpoint needs the URL to be.

With this we have successfully added the required factory methods that manage the data, authentication, and REST interaction for us. We will talk about the response of each REST endpoint when we are dealing with appropriate controllers.

If your server is still running and you have done everything correctly, you should see an error about `BrowserCtrl`. That is okay; we will work on controllers next.

Step 4 – Creating controllers for each route and integrating with the factory

Now that we have our factories configured, we will be creating the required controllers. Again for simplicity sake, we will delete `AppCtrl`, `PlaylistsCtrl`, and `PlaylistCtrl` from the `www/js/controllers.js` file leaving only:

```
angular.module('BookStoreApp.controllers', [])
```

The application controller

The first controller we are going to add is the application controller or `AppCtrl`. This controller manages the login/register functionality. If any child controller such as the cart controller wants to force the user to login, before proceeding it will broadcast a `showLoginModal` on the scope and the `showLoginModal` listener will take care of managing the login/registration process. Once the user is successfully logged in, the cart controller will be notified to proceed.

We will be using the `$on` and `$broadcast` methods to trigger custom evens such as `showLoginModal`.

We will add the `AppCtrl` following the module definition in `www/js/controller.js`. We will be splitting the `AppCtrl` code into two pieces for a better explanation.

First, we will add the definition and all the needed dependencies:

```
.controller('AppCtrl', ['$rootScope', '$ionicModal',
'AuthFactory', '$location', 'UserFactory', '$scope', 'Loader',
    function($rootScope, $ionicModal, AuthFactory, $location,
UserFactory, $scope, Loader) {

}])
```

Next, we will register the `showLoginModal` event on the root scope. We will define the required methods here:

```
        $rootScope.$on('showLoginModal', function($event, scope,
cancelCallback, callback) {
            $scope.user = {
                email: '',
                password: ''
            };

            $scope = scope || $scope;

            $scope.viewLogin = true;

            $ionicModal.fromTemplateUrl('templates/login.html', {
```

```
                scope: $scope
            }).then(function(modal) {
                $scope.modal = modal;
                $scope.modal.show();

                $scope.switchTab = function(tab) {
                    if (tab === 'login') {
                        $scope.viewLogin = true;
                    } else {
                        $scope.viewLogin = false;
                    }
                }

                $scope.hide = function() {
                    $scope.modal.hide();
                    if (typeof cancelCallback === 'function') {
                        cancelCallback();
                    }
                }

                $scope.login = function() {
                    Loader.showLoading('Authenticating...');

UserFactory.login($scope.user).success(function(data) {

                        data = data.data;
                        AuthFactory.setUser(data.user);
                        AuthFactory.setToken({
                            token: data.token,
                            expires: data.expires
                        });

                        $rootScope.isAuthenticated = true;
                        $scope.modal.hide();
                        Loader.hideLoading();
                        if (typeof callback === 'function') {
                            callback();
                        }
                    }).error(function(err, statusCode) {
                        Loader.hideLoading();
                        Loader.toggleLoadingWithMessage(err.message);
                    });
```

```
                }

                $scope.register = function() {
                    Loader.showLoading('Registering...');

                    UserFactory.register($scope.user).
success(function(data) {

                        data = data.data;
                        AuthFactory.setUser(data.user);
                        AuthFactory.setToken({
                            token: data.token,
                            expires: data.expires
                        });

                        $rootScope.isAuthenticated = true;
                        Loader.hideLoading();
                        $scope.modal.hide();
                        if (typeof callback === 'function') {
                            callback();
                        }
                    }).error(function(err, statusCode) {
                        Loader.hideLoading();
                        Loader.toggleLoadingWithMessage(err.message);
                    });
                }
            });
        });
```

Next, we add two methods on the `$rootScope` property. These methods will be invoked from the `sidemenu`:

```
        $rootScope.loginFromMenu = function() {
            $rootScope.$broadcast('showLoginModal', $scope, null,
null);
        }

        $rootScope.logout = function() {
            UserFactory.logout();
            $rootScope.isAuthenticated = false;
            $location.path('/app/browse');
            Loader.toggleLoadingWithMessage('Successfully Logged
Out!', 2000);
        }
```

The `showLoginModal` event takes in three arguments:

- `scope`: The scope in which the modal needs to be created. If no scope is provided, the `AppCtrl` scope will be used.
- `cancelCallback`: The `callback` function to be executed when the user cancels the login/registration process.
- `callback`: The `callback` function that needs to be executed when the user is successfully registered/logged in.

Using the `$ionicModal` service, we create a modal from the `login.html` file. We will work with the templates in the next section.

The `login` and `register` methods take care of talking to the `UserFactory` login or `register` method respectively. Once the user is successfully logged in/registered, the response from the server looks like:


```
{
    "error": null,
    "data": {
        "token": "eyJ0eXAiOiJKV1QiLCJhbGciOiJIUzI1NiJ9.eyJleHAiOjE0
MzM1MjIwNzQ4MzYsInVzZXIiOnsiX2lkIjoiNTU2ODU5NjgyN2ZjY2JjMTZkNjA4MzBi
IiwiZW1haWwiOiJhQGEuY29tIiwibmFtZSI6ImEiLCJjYXJ0IjpbeyJpZCI6IjU1NjgzY
2Q4ZmJiMmUxOTI0ZjE4YTRlYSIsInF0eSI6MX1dLCJwdXJjaGFzZXMiOlt7IlB1cmNoYX
NlIG1hZGUgb24gMjktTWF5LTIwMTUgYXQgMTc6NTAiOlt7ImlkIjoiNTU2ODNjZDhmYmI
yZTE5MjRmMThhNGU4IiwicXR5IjoxfV19LHsiUHVyY2hhc2UgbWFkZSBvbiAyOS1NYXkt
MjAxNSBhdCAxNzo1OSI6W3siaWQiOiI1NTY4M2NkOGZiYjJlMTkyNGYxOGE0ZWIiLCJxd
HkiOjF9LHsiaWQiOiI1NTY4M2NkOGZiYjJlMTkyNGYxOGE0ZjYiLCJxdHkiOjF9LHsiaW
QiOiI1NTY4M2NkOGZiYjJlMTkyNGYxOGE0ZjgiLCJxdHkiOjF9XX0seyJQdXJjaGFzZSB
tYWRlIG9uIDI5LU1heS0yMDE1IGF0IDIwOjUxIjpbeyJpZCI6IjU1NjgzY2Q4ZmJiMmUx
OTI0ZjE4YTRlOCIsInF0eSI6MX0seyJpZCI6IjU1NjgzY2Q4ZmJiMmUxOTI0ZjE4YTRlY
SIsInF0eSI6MX0seyJpZCI6IjU1NjgzY2Q4ZmJiMmUxOTI0ZjE4YTRlZSIsInF0eSI6MX
1dfV19fQ.J0U0BZXhP6C1VWEHDT18BMOzkK_dvXP-xdGUiIr7-z8",
        "expires": 1433522074836,
        "user": {
            "_id": "5568596827fccbc16d60830b",
            "email": "a@a.com",
            "name": "a",
        }
    },
    "message": "Success"
}
```


We extract the `token` and `user` object from the response and set it to `localStorage` using the `AuthFactory setUser` and `setToken` methods. The `TokenInterceptor` while making REST calls will pick up this data and add it to the request.

The `loginFromMenu` and `logout` are called from the `Login/logout` menu item. All the `loginFromMenu` method does is broadcast a `showLoginModal` that will take care of user authentication.

The `logout` method calls the `UserFactory` logout method that takes care of clearing the user and token entries in the `localStorage`. It also resets the `isAuthenticated` property and redirects the user to the `/app/browse` page.

The browse controller

The next controller we are going to work with is the `BrowseCtrl`. This controller is responsible for showing all the books when the user launches the application. The first time the `BrowseCtrl` contacts the REST API endpoint to get the books (upon successful fetch) it saves them to `localStorage`. So, the next time (and henceforth) it will look in `localStorage` before making a call, saving battery, and data charges.

As an exercise, you can implement a background process to update the `localStorage` with the latest books from time to time.

```
.controller('BrowseCtrl', ['$scope', 'BooksFactory', 'LSFactory',
'Loader',
    function($scope, BooksFactory, LSFactory, Loader) {

        Loader.showLoading();

        // support for pagination
        var page = 1;
        $scope.books = [];
        var books = LSFactory.getAll();

        // if books exists in localStorage, use that instead of
making a call
        if (books.length > 0) {
            $scope.books = books;
            Loader.hideLoading();
        } else {
            BooksFactory.get(page).success(function(data) {

                // process books and store them
                // in localStorage so we can work with them later
on,
                // when the user is offline
```

```
                processBooks(data.data.books);

                $scope.books = data.data.books;
                $scope.$broadcast('scroll.infiniteScrollComplete');
                Loader.hideLoading();
            }).error(function(err, statusCode) {
                Loader.hideLoading();
                Loader.toggleLoadingWithMessage(err.message);
            });
        }

        function processBooks(books) {
            LSFactory.clear();
            // we want to save each book individually
            // this way we can access each book info. by it's _id
            for (var i = 0; i < books.length; i++) {
                LSFactory.set(books[i]._id, books[i]);
            };
        }

    }
])
```

Since our REST API supports pagination, we need to pass in the `page` number to get the data from and the `perPage`, which we have set in the `BooksFactory`. I have made the page number dynamic and set it up, so you can implement pagination and load books on demand.

But in this example we will be loading all 30 books at once.

The book controller

Once the user browses through all the books and wants to see details about a particular book, he/she will click on the book. At that point, we redirect the user to the `/book` page, which will trigger the `BookCtrl`. The `BookCtrl` will search for a book with the given id in `localStorage` and displays its details.

Add the `BookCtrl` after the `BrowseCtrl` in `www/js/controllers.js`:

```
.controller('BookCtrl', ['$scope', '$state', 'LSFactory',
'AuthFactory', '$rootScope', 'UserFactory', 'Loader',
```

```
    function($scope, $state, LSFactory, AuthFactory, $rootScope,
UserFactory, Loader) {

        var bookId = $state.params.bookId;

        $scope.book = LSFactory.get(bookId);

        $scope.$on('addToCart', function() {
            Loader.showLoading('Adding to Cart..');
            UserFactory.addToCart({
                id: bookId,
                qty: 1
            }).success(function(data) {
                Loader.hideLoading();
                Loader.toggleLoadingWithMessage('Successfully
added ' + $scope.book.title + ' to your cart', 2000);
            }).error(function(err, statusCode) {
                Loader.hideLoading();
                Loader.toggleLoadingWithMessage(err.message);
            });

        });

        $scope.addToCart = function() {
            if (!AuthFactory.isLoggedIn()) {
                $rootScope.$broadcast('showLoginModal', $scope,
null, function() {
                    // user is now logged in
                    $scope.$broadcast('addToCart');
                });
                return;
            }
            $scope.$broadcast('addToCart');
        }
    }
])
```

Using the `LSFactory.get(bookId)` we fetch the book from `localStorage`.

If you viewed the demo, you will have noticed that, on the book detail page, there is an **Add to Cart** button. The logic for add to cart is quite simple. If the user clicks on **Add to Cart**, we check if the user is logged in. If the user is not logged in, we broadcast a `showLoginModal` event and, once the user has successfully logged in, we broadcast the `addToCart`, which adds the present book to the cart.

If the user is already logged in, we broadcast `addToCart`.

The `addToCart` event builds an object taking in the current `bookid` and quantity (hardcoded to 1), and then calls the `UserFactory` `addToCart` method. This takes care of adding the book to the cart.

The cart controller

The next controller we are going to look at is the cart controller. This will be invoked when the user clicks on the cart icon present in the header or when the user clicks on the cart menu item from the side menu.

When the user clicks on the cart, we will check if the user is logged in. If the user is logged in, we fetch the user's cart items and show them. Otherwise, we broadcast `showLoginModal`, which will take care of the authentication. If the user cancels the login modal, we take the user back to `/app/browse`.

Once the user is successfully authenticated/logged in, we will broadcast the `getCart` event. The `getCart` calls the `UserFactory` `getCartItems` method and fetches all the cart items. Once the cart items are fetched, we assign them to the books property on `$scope`.

We will add the following `CartCtrl` after the `BookCtrl`:

```
.controller('CartCtrl', ['$scope', 'AuthFactory', '$rootScope',
'$location', '$timeout', 'UserFactory', 'Loader',
    function($scope, AuthFactory, $rootScope, $location, $timeout,
UserFactory, Loader) {

        $scope.$on('getCart', function() {
            Loader.showLoading('Fetching Your Cart..');
            UserFactory.getCartItems().success(function(data) {
                $scope.books = data.data;
                Loader.hideLoading();
            }).error(function(err, statusCode) {
                Loader.hideLoading();
                Loader.toggleLoadingWithMessage(err.message);
            });
```

```
        });

        if (!AuthFactory.isLoggedIn()) {
            $rootScope.$broadcast('showLoginModal', $scope, function()
{
                // cancel auth callback
                $timeout(function() {
                    $location.path('/app/browse');
                }, 200);
            }, function() {
                // user is now logged in
                $scope.$broadcast('getCart');
            });
            return;
        }

        $scope.$broadcast('getCart');

        $scope.checkout = function() {
           // we need to send only the id and qty
            var _cart = $scope.books;
            var cart = [];
            for (var i = 0; i < _cart.length; i++) {
                cart.push({
                    id: _cart[i]._id,
                    qty: 1 // hardcoded to 1
                });
            };

            Loader.showLoading('Checking out..');
            UserFactory.addPurchase(cart).success(function(data) {
                Loader.hideLoading();
                Loader.toggleLoadingWithMessage('Successfully checked
out', 2000);
                $scope.books = [];
            }).error(function(err, statusCode) {
                Loader.hideLoading();
                Loader.toggleLoadingWithMessage(err.message);
            });
        }
    }
])
```

We have added the `checkout` method on `$scope`. Once the user views his/her cart, they can check out the cart, and this method calls the `UserFactory` `addPurchase` method passing in the `cart` array. The `cart` array consists of objects that contain the book `id` and the `quantity` of the book (hardcoded to 1 unit) added to the cart.

The purchase controller

The final controller in our app is the purchase controller. This controller shows a list of purchases the current logged in user has made. As with the cart controller, we check if the user is logged to proceed. Once the user is logged in, we broadcast the `getPurchases` event. This will take care of contacting the purchases API via the `UserFactory` `getPurchases` method and gets the list of purchases:

```
.controller('PurchasesCtrl', ['$scope', '$rootScope',
'AuthFactory', 'UserFactory', '$timeout', 'Loader',
    function($scope, $rootScope, AuthFactory, UserFactory,
$timeout, Loader) {
        // http://forum.ionicframework.com/t/expandable-list-in-
ionic/3297/2
        $scope.groups = [];

        $scope.toggleGroup = function(group) {
            if ($scope.isGroupShown(group)) {
                $scope.shownGroup = null;
            } else {
                $scope.shownGroup = group;
            }
        };
        $scope.isGroupShown = function(group) {
            return $scope.shownGroup === group;
        };

        $scope.$on('getPurchases', function() {
            Loader.showLoading('Fetching Your Purchases');
            UserFactory.getPurchases().success(function(data) {
                var purchases = data.data;
                $scope.purchases = [];
                for (var i = 0; i < purchases.length; i++) {
                    var key = Object.keys(purchases[i]);
                    $scope.purchases.push(key[0]);
                    $scope.groups[i] = {
                        name: key[0],
                        items: purchases[i][key]
                    }
```

```
                    var sum = 0;
                    for (var j = 0; j < purchases[i][key].length;
j++) {
                        sum +=
parseInt(purchases[i][key][j].price);
                    };
                    $scope.groups[i].total = sum;
                };
                Loader.hideLoading();
            }).error(function(err, statusCode) {
                Loader.hideLoading();
                Loader.toggleLoadingWithMessage(err.message);
            });
        });

        if (!AuthFactory.isLoggedIn()) {
            $rootScope.$broadcast('showLoginModal', $scope,
function() {
                $timeout(function() {
                    $location.path('/app/browse');
                }, 200);
            }, function() {
                // user is now logged in
                $scope.$broadcast('getPurchases');
            });
            return;
        }

        $scope.$broadcast('getPurchases');
    }
])
```

We have added a couple of methods named `toggleGroup` and `isGroupShown`. These methods will be used when we are building the template. Once the response arrives, we format the data so that it can be organized as a nested list.

I recommend checking out the online version of this app for the view purchases feature before you proceed. That will give you a good understanding of what is going on in the code.

Step 5 – Creating templates and integrating with the controller data

Now that we have controllers ready with the data, we will build templates to present that data.

The Login template

The first template we are going to work with is `login.html`:

```
<ion-modal-view>
    <div class="tabs-striped tabs-background-assertive tabs-color-
light">
        <div class="tabs">
            <a class="tab-item" ng-class="{active : viewLogin}"
href="javascript:" ng-click="switchTab('login')">
                <i class="icon ion-locked"></i> Login
            </a>
            <a class="tab-item" ng-class="{active : !viewLogin}"
href="javascript:" ng-click="switchTab('register')">
                <i class="icon ion-person-add"></i> Register
            </a>
        </div>
    </div>
    <!-- login pane -->
    <ion-pane ng-show="viewLogin">
        <ion-header-bar>
            <h1 class="title">Login</h1>
            <div class="buttons">
                <button class="button button-assertive" ng-
click="hide()">Close</button>
            </div>
        </ion-header-bar>
        <ion-content>
            <form>
                <div class="list">
                    <label class="item item-input">
                        <span class="input-label">Email</span>
                        <input type="email" ng-model="user.email">
                    </label>
                    <label class="item item-input">
                        <span class="input-label">Password</span>
                        <input type="password" ng-
model="user.password">
                    </label>
```

```
                    <label class="item">
                        <button class="button button-block button-
assertive" ng-click="login()" ng-disabled="!user.email ||
!user.password" type="submit">Log in</button>
                    </label>
                </div>
            </form>
        </ion-content>
    </ion-pane>
    <!-- register pane -->
    <ion-pane ng-hide="viewLogin">
        <ion-header-bar>
            <h1 class="title">Register</h1>
            <div class="buttons">
                <button class="button button-assertive" ng-
click="hide()">Close</button>
            </div>
        </ion-header-bar>
        <ion-content>
            <form>
                <div class="list">
                    <label class="item item-input">
                        <span class="input-label">Name</span>
                        <input type="text" ng-model="user.name">
                    </label>
                    <label class="item item-input">
                        <span class="input-label">Email
Address</span>
                        <input type="text" ng-model="user.email">
                    </label>
                    <label class="item item-input">
                        <span class="input-label">Password</span>
                        <input type="password" ng-
model="user.password">
                    </label>
                    <label class="item">
                        <button class="button button-block button-
assertive" ng-click="register()" ng-disabled="!user.name || !user.
email || !user.password" type="submit" type="submit">Register</button>
                    </label>
                </div>
            </form>
        </ion-content>
    </ion-pane>
</ion-modal-view>
```

The `login` template has a tabs component that toggles between the **Login** and **Register** view. This tabs component is not an Ionic tab directive but rather the Tab CSS components made to look like tabs. On clicking on the tab icon, we will switch between the **Login** pane and **Register** pane by setting the `viewLogin` property to `true` or `false` using the `switchTab` method.

The completed login template looks as shown in the following. (You can click on the **Register** tab icon to see the register view as well:

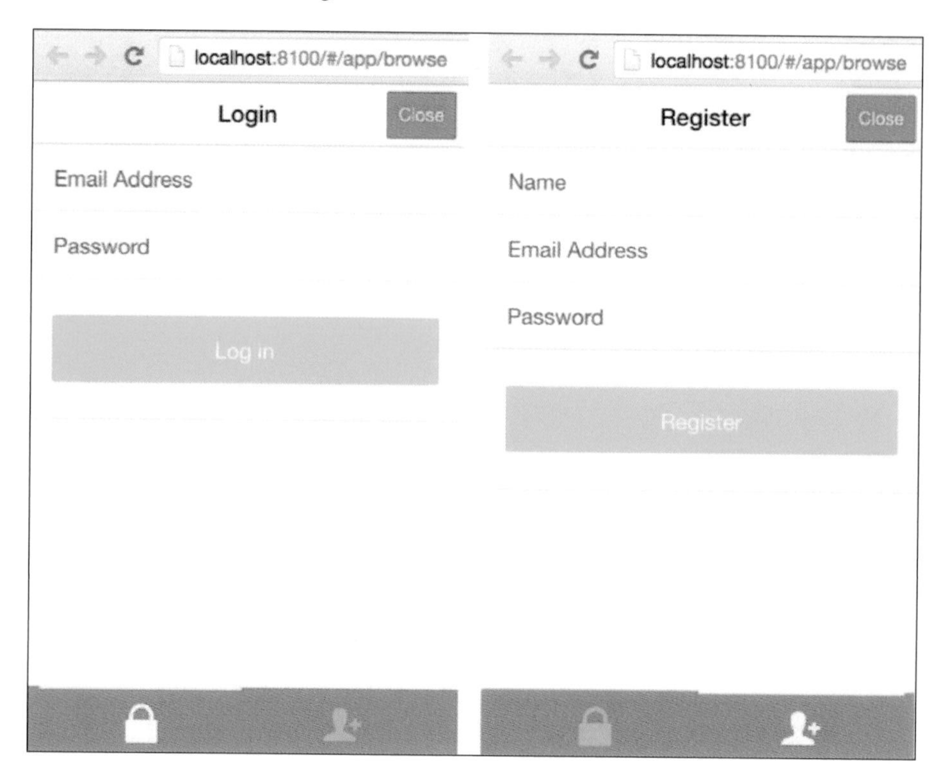

The Browse template

The next template we are going to build is the `Browse` template. This template will be used to show a list of books. Open `www/templates/browse.html` and update it as follows:

```
<ion-view view-title="Browse Books" hide-back-button="true">
    <ion-content>
        <ion-list>
            <div ng-repeat="book in books track by $index" class="row
responsive-sm" ng-if="$index % 2 == 0">
```

```
                    <ion-item class="col-50" ng-repeat="i in [$index, 
$index + 1]" ng-if="books[i] != null" ng-href="#/app/book/
{{::books[i]._id}}">
                        <div class="item-thumbnail-left">
                            <img ng-src="{{::book.image}}">
                            <h2>{{::books[i].title}}</h2>
                            <p>{{::books[i].short_description}}</p>
                            <p>
                                <i class="icon ion-star" ng-repeat="i 
in getNumber(books[i].rating) track by $index"></i>
                            </p>
                        </div>
                    </ion-item>
                </div>
            </ion-list>
        </ion-content>
</ion-view>
```

In the earlier template, I have used `{{::property}}` instead of `{{property}}`. The `{{::property}}` is how you implement one-way data binding in AngularJS. One-way data binding is ideal when the value of the property used in the template does not change after the initial bind.

Our app is a perfect example for that. Once the value is bound to the template, we are not updating it. This way, we can save AngularJS the pain of running digest loops on our variables.

You can get a better understanding of one-way data binding from `http://blog.thoughtram.io/angularjs/2014/10/14/exploring-angular-1.3-one-time-bindings.html`.

Here, we have used `ion-list` to display the books in a list. But to show how you can implement a grid using Ionic's grid system, I have written the template in the way described earlier.

In the earlier template, we show two columns of books unless the viewport is a mobile device. We have achieved the grid using two loops. The outer loop will have a class named `row` and the items in the inner loop have the class named `col-50`.

Also, we added the class `responsive-sm` to the outer loop telling Ionic's grid system so that, if the device is small, it should render the list in one column.

Quite interesting, right?

The rendered page for the mobile viewport looks like this:

The tablet version would look like this:

The Book template

When the user clicks on a book in the browse screen to view its details, we redirect the user to the `/book` page. Here we show the details of the book with the **Add to Cart** button. Add the following code to `www/templates/book.html`:

```
<ion-view view-title="{{::book.title}}" hide-back-button="true">
    <ion-content>
        <div class="list card">
            <div class="item item-avatar">
                <img ng-src="{{::book.author_image}}">
                <h2>{{::book.title}}</h2>
                <p>{{::book.release_date | date:'yyyy-MM-dd'}}</p>
                <p>{{::book.author}}</p>
            </div>
            <div class="item item-body">
                <img class="full-image" ng-src="{{::book.image}}">
                <p>
                    {{::book.long_description}}
                </p>
                <p class="row">
                    <label class="col">
                        Rating : <i class="icon ion-star" ng-
repeat="i in getNumber(book.rating) track by $index"></i>
                    </label>
                    <label class="col">
                        Price :
                        <label class="subdued">{{::book.price |
currency}} $</label>
                    </label>
                </p>
                <button class="button button-assertive button-
block" ng-click="addToCart()">
                    <i class="icon ion-checkmark"></i> Add to
Cart
                </button>
            </div>
        </div>
    </ion-content>
</ion-view>
```

The new thing to look out for in this template is the **Rating** section, where we have used an `ng-repeat` to print the stars dynamically, based on the rating value. We are using the `getNumber` method that we have defined in the `run` method.

The rendered book template looks like this:

The Cart template

The **Cart** template is quite the same as the **Browse** template, except that we have added a checkout button on top and a fall back message when there are no items in the cart. Update the `www/templates/cart.html` as follows:

```
<ion-view view-title="Your Cart" cache-view="false" hide-back-
button="true">
    <ion-content>
```

```
        <div class="padding">
            <button class="button button-block button-dark" ng-
show="books.length > 0" ng-click="checkout()">
                <i class="icon ion-checkmark"></i> Checkout Cart
            </button>
        </div>
        <ion-list>
            <div ng-repeat="book in books track by $index"
class="row responsive-sm" ng-if="$index % 2 == 0">
                <ion-item class="col-50" ng-repeat="i in [$index,
$index + 1]" ng-if="books[i] != null" ng-href="#/app/book/
{{::books[i]._id}}">
                    <div class="item-thumbnail-left">
                        <img ng-src="{{::book.image}}">
                        <h2>{{::books[i].title}}</h2>
                        <p>{{::books[i].short_description}}</p>
                        <p>{{::books[i].price}} $</p>
                        <p>
                            <i class="icon ion-star" ng-repeat="i
in getNumber(books[i].rating) track by $index"></i>
                        </p>
                    </div>
                </ion-item>
            </div>
        </ion-list>
        <div class="card" ng-show="books.length == 0">
            <div class="item item-text-wrap text-center">
                <h2>No Books in your cart!</h2>
                <br>
                <a href="#/app/browse">Add a few</a>
            </div>
        </div>
    </ion-content>
</ion-view>
```

The rendered view looks like this:

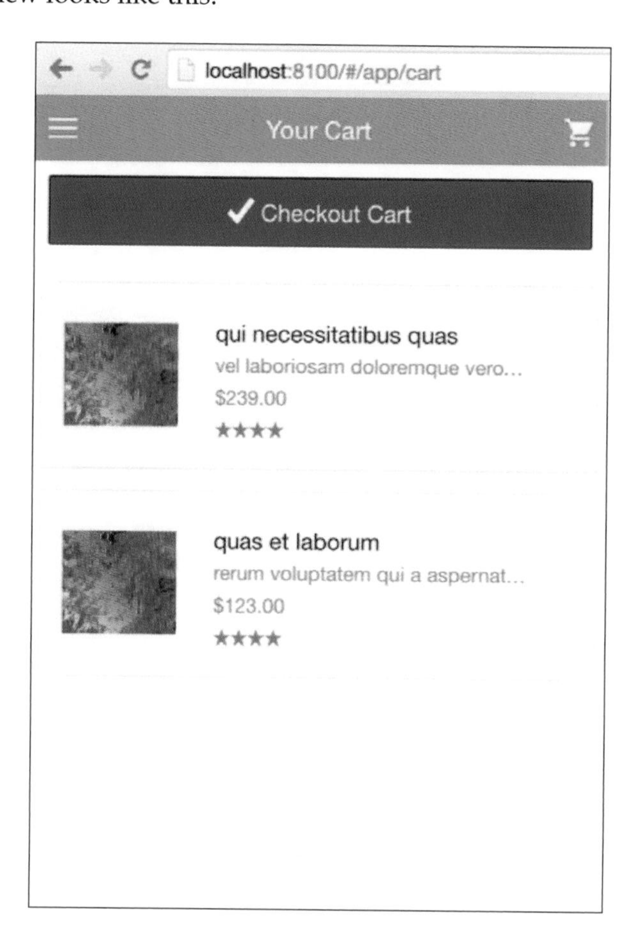

The Purchase template

And the final template is the purchase template. To add a variation to the way things are displayed, I have used a nested list to display a list of purchases instead of a master detail page. Master detail refers to listing all of the purchases on this purchases page; when a user clicks on it, we take the user to another page to show the details of the purchase (like the **Browse** and **Book** page).

So, all the purchases are grouped based on the time of purchase and are displayed as the first level list. When a user clicks on the group head, we show the list of books that were purchased under this group.

This is an accordion component. You can read more about the component `http://forum.ionicframework.com/t/expandable-list-in-ionic/3297/2`.

Open `www/templates/purchases.html` and update it as follows:

```
<ion-view view-title="Your Purchases" cache-view="false" hide-
back-button="true">
    <ion-content>
        <ion-list>
            <div ng-repeat="group in groups">
                <ion-item class="item-stable" ng-
click="toggleGroup(group)" ng-class="{active: isGroupShown(group)}">
                    <p><i class="icon" ng-
class="isGroupShown(group) ? 'ion-minus' : 'ion-plus'"></i>
 {{::group.name}}
                        <span class="badge badge-
positive">{{::group.items.length}}</span></p>
                    <p>You paid : {{::group.total | currency}}</p>
                </ion-item>
                <ion-item class="item-accordion" ng-repeat="item
in group.items" ng-show="isGroupShown(group)" ng-
href="#/app/book/{{::item._id}}">
                    <div class="item-thumbnail-left">
                        <img ng-src="{{::item.image}}">
                        <h2>{{::item.title}}</h2>
                        <p>{{::item.short_description}}</p>
                        <p>
                            <i class="icon ion-star" ng-repeat="i
in getNumber(item.rating) track by $index"></i>
                        </p>
                    </div>
                </ion-item>
            </div>
        </ion-list>
    </ion-content>
</ion-view>
```

If you save the file and head back to the browser, you should see:

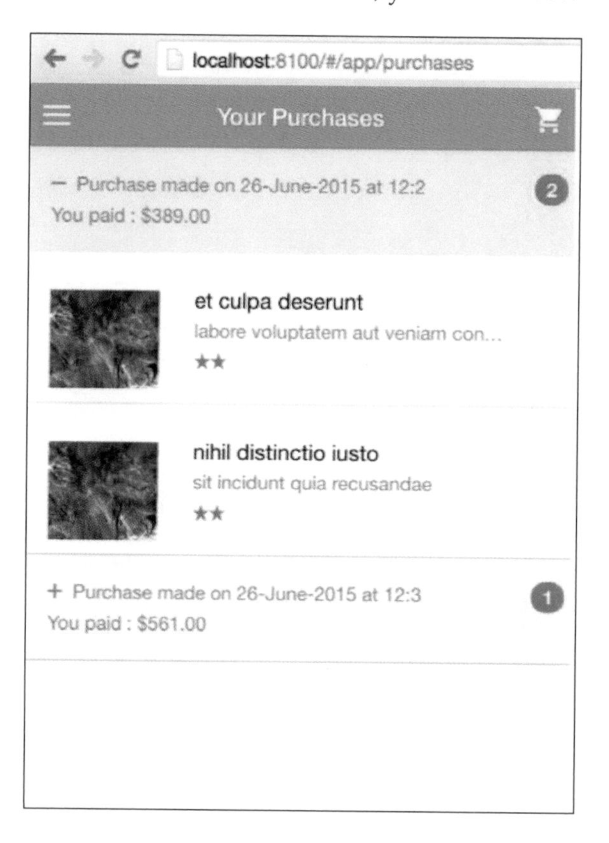

For the final finishing touches, we will add a couple of custom styles. Update `www/css/styles.css` as follows:

```
.item-thumbnail-left,
.item-thumbnail-left .item-content {
    min-height: 75px;
}

.ion-android-cart:before {
    font-size: 24px !important;
}

.item-thumbnail-left > img:first-child,
.item-thumbnail-left .item-image,
.item-thumbnail-left .item-content > img:first-child,
.item-thumbnail-left .item-content .item-image {
    top: 27px;
```

```
        left: 16px;
        padding-bottom: 10px;
    }

    .badge.badge-positive {
        position: absolute;
        right: 5px;
    }
```

Summary

In this chapter, we saw how to build an Ionic application consuming an existing REST API. We also saw how to consume a token-based server and handle routes that need authentication as opposed to those that don't. This hands-on example should consolidate a lot of the Ionic knowledge you have gained.

In the next chapter, we will look at Cordova plugins, as well as how to work with ngCordova.

7
Cordova and ngCordova

In this chapter, we are going to look at integrating device-specific features, such as network, battery status, cameras, and so on into any Ionic application. We will first look at Cordova plugins, and then work with ngCordova.

In this chapter, we will take a look at:

- Setting up a platform-specific SDK
- Working with the Cordova plugin API
- Working with ngCordova
- Testing a few ngCordova plugins

Setting up a platform-specific SDK

Before we start interacting with the device-specific features, we need to have the SDK for that device operating system set up on our local machine. Officially, Ionic supports only iOS, Android, and to a lesser extent Windows phone platforms. Nevertheless, Ionic can be used on any device.

The following are links on how to set up a mobile SDK on your machine.

Unfortunately, you cannot proceed further in this chapter (and book) without setting that up. Let's look at the following links:

- **Android**: http://cordova.apache.org/docs/en/5.0.0/guide_platforms_android_index.md.html#Android%20Platform%20Guide
- **iOS**: http://cordova.apache.org/docs/en/5.0.0/guide_platforms_ios_index.md.html#iOS%20Platform%20Guide
- **Windows Phone 8**: http://cordova.apache.org/docs/en/5.0.0/guide_platforms_wp8_index.md.html#Windows%20Phone%208%20Platform%20Guide

For other supported OS, you can check out http://cordova.apache.org/docs/en/5.0.0/guide_platforms_index.md.html#Platform%20Guides; I am referring to the documentation for Cordova 5.0.0.

In this book, we will work with Android and iOS only. You can follow a similar approach for other mobile platforms as well.

Before we proceed further, we will make sure the setup is completed, and is working as expected.

For this chapter, you can also access the code, raise issues, and chat with the author at GitHub (https://github.com/learning-ionic/Chapter-7).

The Android setup

Make sure you have the SDK installed and Android tools are in your path. Then, from anywhere on your machine in a terminal/prompt run:

```
android
```

This will launch the Android SDK manager. Make sure that you have the latest version of Android installed, or any specific version you are targeting.

Next, run the following command:

```
android avd
```

This will launch the Android Virtual Device manager. Make sure you have at least one AVD setup. If this isn't yet the case, you can easily do so by clicking on the **Create** button. You can fill the options as follows:

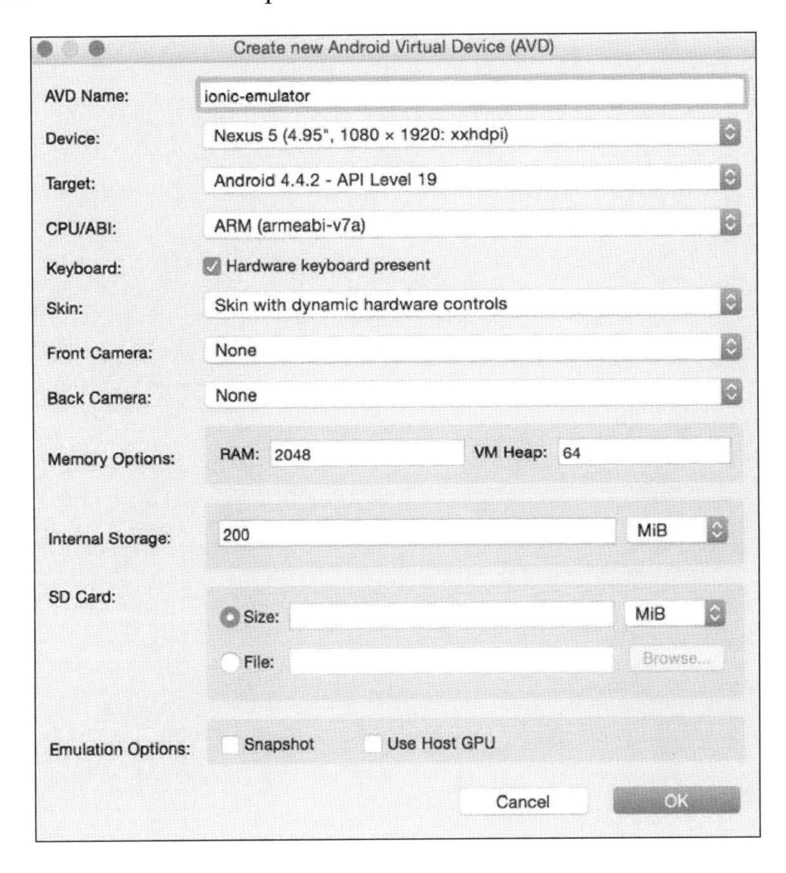

The iOS setup

Make sure you have Xcode and the required tools installed, and also have `ios-sim` and `ios-deploy` installed globally:

```
npm install -g ios-sim
npm install -g ios-deploy
```

iOS setup can be done only on an Apple machine. Windows developers cannot deploy iOS apps from Windows machines, as Xcode is required to do so.

Testing the setup

Let's take a look at how we can test the setup for Android and iOS.

Testing for Android

To test the setup, we will scaffold a new Ionic application, and emulate that using the Android and iOS emulators.

We will first scaffold a tabs application:

```
ionic start -a "Example 27" -i app.example.twentyseven example27 tabs
```

To test the tabs application, using the `cd` command go to the `example27` folder and run this:

```
ionic serve
```

This will launch the app in the browser and you should be able to see the tabs application.

To emulate the app on an Android emulator, first we need to add Android platform support for this project and then emulate it.

To add the Android platform, run this:

```
ionic platform add android
```

Once that is done, run the following command:

```
ionic emulate android
```

After some time, you will see the emulator launch, and the app will be deployed and executed inside the emulator:

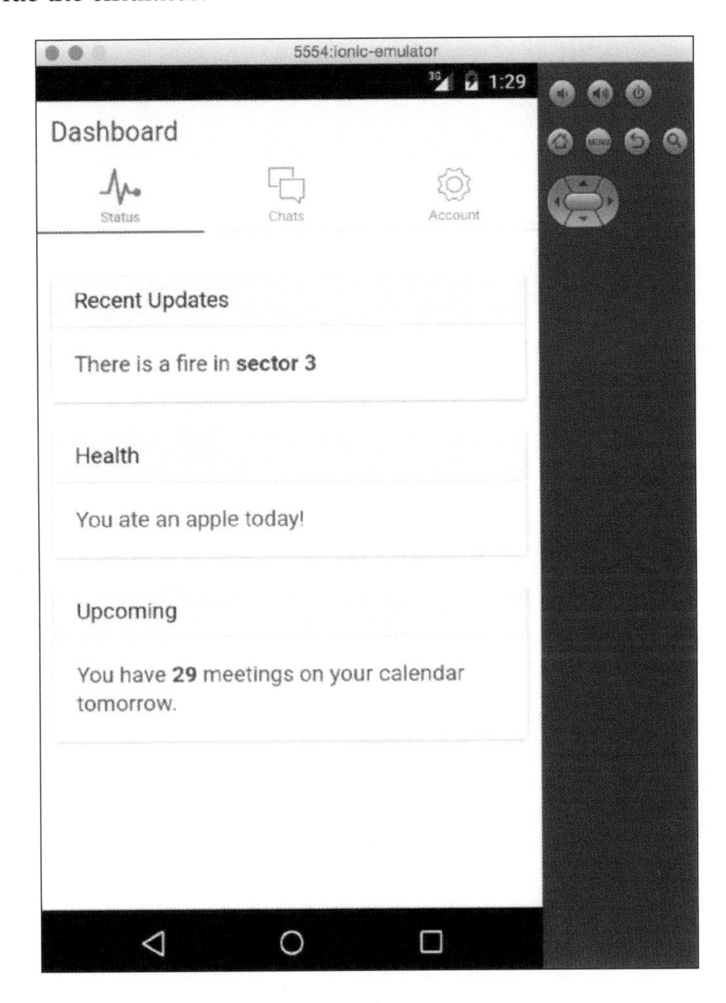

If you have already worked with native Android apps, you know how slow the Android emulator is. If you have not, it is quite slow.

An alternative to the Android emulator is Genymotion (`https://www.genymotion.com`). Ionic is nicely integrated with Genymotion as well.

Genymotion has two flavors, one free and the other for business. The free version has minimal features and is supposed to be for personal use only.

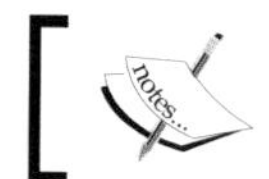

You can download a copy of Genymotion from https://www.genymotion.com/#!/store.

Once you have installed Genymotion, create a new virtual device with your preferred Android SDK. My config looks like this:

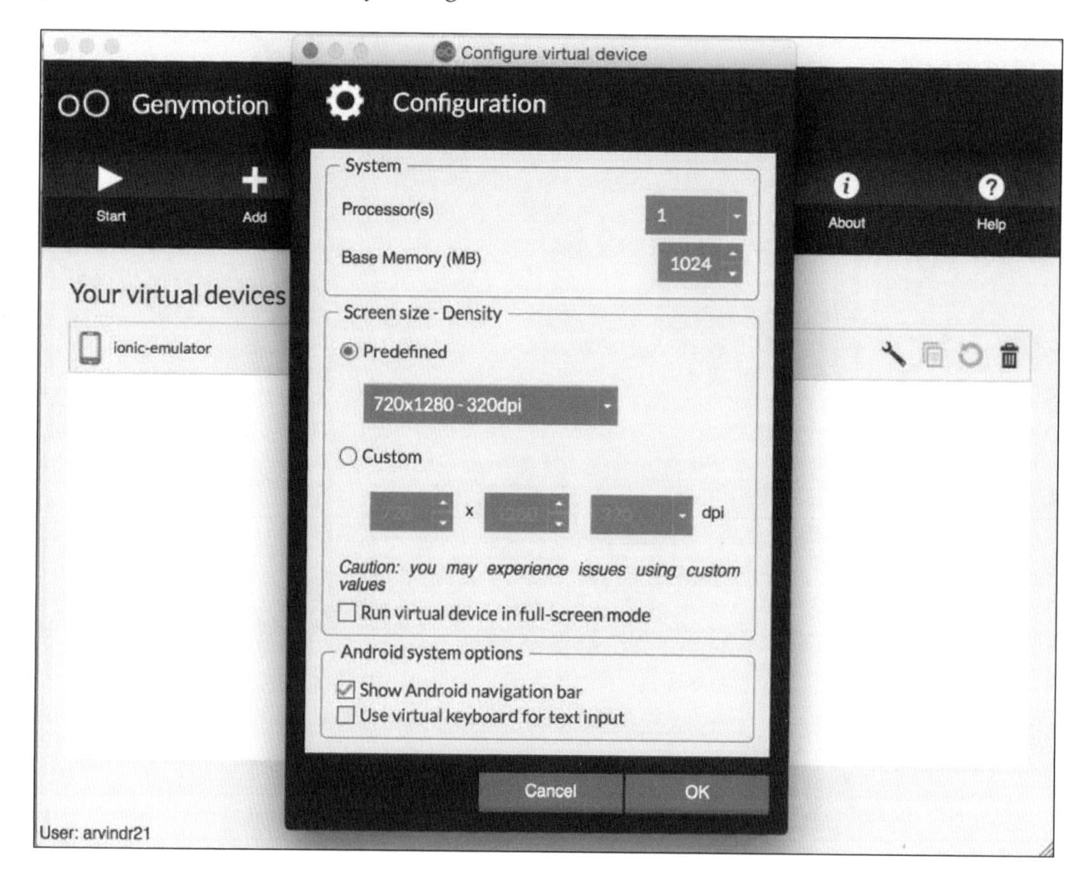

Next, we launch the emulator and let it run in the background.

Now that we have Genymotion running, we need to tell Ionic to emulate the app using Genymotion and not the Android emulator. For that we use:

```
ionic run android
```

Instead of this:

```
ionic emulate android
```

This will deploy the app to the Genymotion emulator and you can see the app immediately, unlike with the Android emulator.

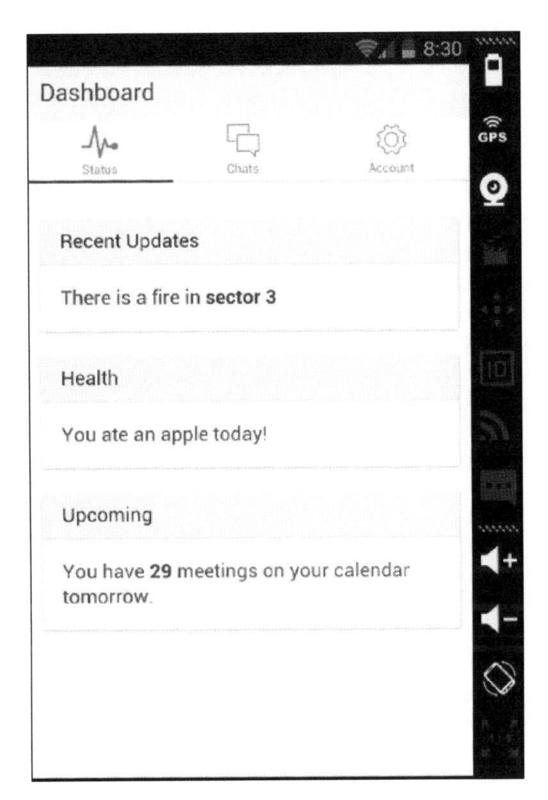

Make sure Genymotion is running in the background.

If Genymotion seems a bit large for your pocket, you can simply connect your Android mobile phone to your laptop and run this:

```
ionic run android
```

This will deploy the app to the actual device.

> To set up Android USB debugging, please refer to `http://developer.android.com/tools/device.html`.
>
> The earlier screenshots of Genymotion are taken from a personal edition, as I do not have a license for it. I generally use the iOS emulator in tandem with my Android mobile phone during the development phase. Once the entire development is completed, I purchase device time from online testing services, and test on the targeted devices.
>
> If you are facing an issue while connecting your Android mobile phone to your computer, please check if you are able to run `adb` device in the terminal/prompt and able to see your device listed here. You can find more information on **Android Debug Bridge** (**ADB**) at `http://developer.android.com/tools/help/adb.html`.

The earlier procedures are different ways to test the app for Android.

Testing for iOS

To test for iOS, we will first add iOS platform support as we did for Android, and then emulate it.

Run this:

```
ionic platform add ios
```

Then, run this:

```
ionic emulate ios
```

You should see the default emulator launch and, finally, the app will appear as follows:

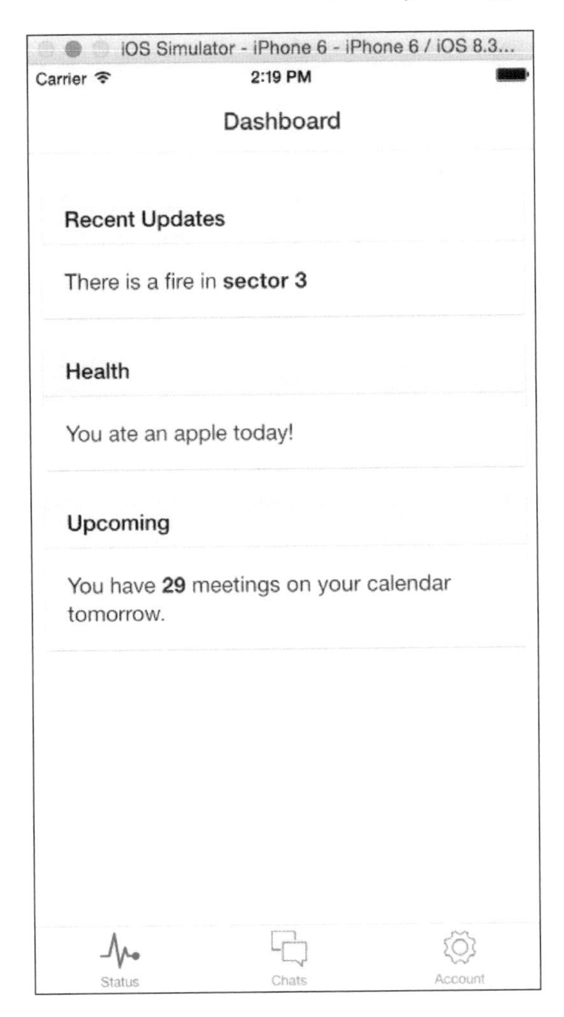

To deploy onto an Apple device, you can run this:

```
ionic run ios
```

Make sure you are able to emulate the app before moving further.

Getting started with Cordova plugins

According to the Cordova documentation:

> *"A plugin is a package of injected code that allows the Cordova web view within which the app renders to communicate with the native platform on which it runs. Plugins provide access to device and platform functionality that is ordinarily unavailable to web-based apps. All the main Cordova API features are implemented as plugins, and many others are available that enable features such as bar code scanners, NFC communication, or to tailor calendar interfaces."*

In other words, Cordova plugins are the window to your device-specific features. The Cordova/Phonegap team has already built the needed plugins to work with almost all device-specific features. There are community-contributed plugins as well that can provide customization wrappers around device-specific features.

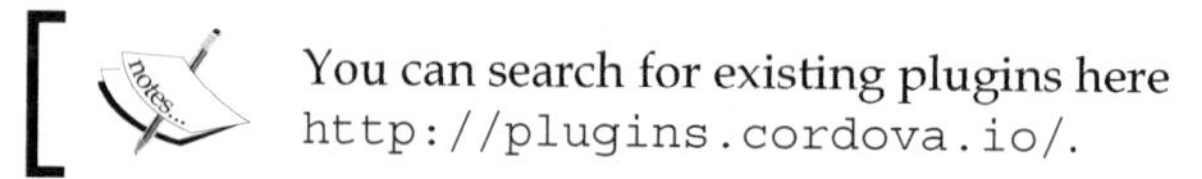

You can search for existing plugins here `http://plugins.cordova.io/`.

During the course of this chapter, we will be exploring a few plugins.

Do note that Cordova plugins are moving to NPM. By the time this book has been published; all the Cordova plugins will have completed the transition to NPM. For more information, visit `https://cordova.apache.org/announcements/2015/04/21/plugins-release-and-move-to-npm.html`.

To adjust to the earlier changes, as a developer you need not do anything from your side, except use Cordova CLI (a version greater than or equal to 5.0.0) to add plugins. This will take care of downloading the plugins from the appropriate registry.

The Ionic team has already merged a pull request to change dot notation to hyphenated notation. For more information, visit `https://github.com/driftyco/ionic-cli/pull/409`.

Since we are focusing on Ionic-specific development, we will add plugins using the Ionic CLI. Under the hood, Ionic CLI calls the Cordova CLI to do the necessary.

The Ionic plugin API

There are four main commands that you will be using while dealing with plugins.

Add a plugin

This CLI command is used to add a new plugin to the project, for example:

```
ionic plugin add org.apache.cordova.camera
```

Also, you can use this:

```
ionic plugin add cordova-plugin-camera
```

Remove a plugin

This CLI command is used to remove a plugin from the project, for example:

```
ionic plugin rm org.apache.cordova.camera
```

Also, you can use this:

```
ionic plugin rm cordova-plugin-camera
```

List added plugins

This CLI command is used to list all the plugins in the project, for example:

```
ionic plugin ls
```

Search plugins

This CLI command is used to search plugins from the command line, for example:

```
ionic plugin search scanner barcode
```

To test the earlier commands, we will scaffold a new project and execute them. Run the following command:

```
ionic start -a "Example 28" -i app.example.twentyeight example28
blank
```

When you download the blank project, the following plugins will be downloaded and setup:

`cordova-plugin-device`

`cordova-plugin-console`

`cordova-plugin-whitelist`

`cordova-plugin-splashscreen`

`com.ionic.keyboard`

To test the blank application, using the `cd` command go to the `example28` folder, and run this:

```
ionic serve
```

Let's search for the battery status plugin and add it to our project. Kill the server and run this:

```
ionic plugin search battery status
```

At the time of writing, one can see the following screenshot:

```
→  example28  ionic plugin search battery status
Updated the hooks directory to have execute permissions
running cordova plugin search battery status
npm http GET http://registry.cordova.io/-/all/since?stale=update_after&s
tartkey=1433066172224
npm http 200 http://registry.cordova.io/-/all/since?stale=update_after&s
tartkey=1433066172224
com.blueshift.cordova.battery - Battery
org.apache.cordova.battery-status - Cordova Battery Plugin
→  example28
```

When you run the command, you may see only the hyphenated versions, or both.

Depending on what plugin name you find, you can add that plugin to the project. So, in my case, to add the battery status plugin to the project, I would run this:

```
ionic plugin add org.apache.cordova.battery-status
```

This will add the battery status plugin (`https://github.com/apache/cordova-plugin-battery-status`) to our current project.

Also, do notice that, as soon as you run the preceding command, you will see the following screenshot:

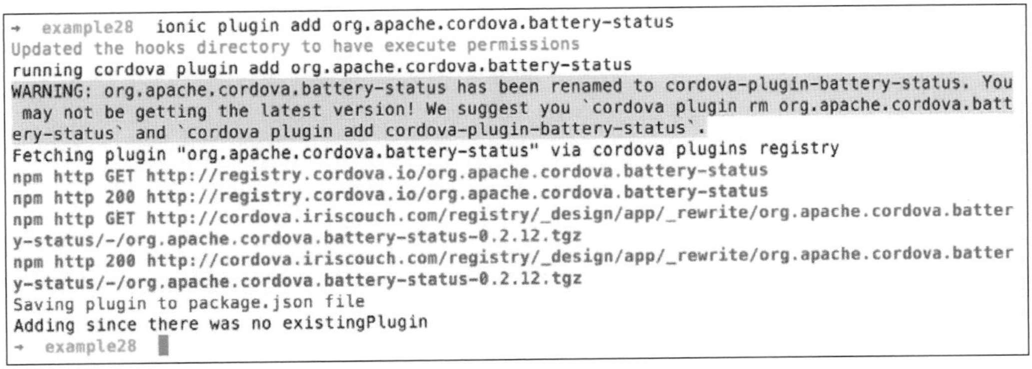

```
→ example28 ionic plugin add org.apache.cordova.battery-status
Updated the hooks directory to have execute permissions
running cordova plugin add org.apache.cordova.battery-status
WARNING: org.apache.cordova.battery-status has been renamed to cordova-plugin-battery-status. You
 may not be getting the latest version! We suggest you `cordova plugin rm org.apache.cordova.batt
ery-status` and `cordova plugin add cordova-plugin-battery-status`.
Fetching plugin "org.apache.cordova.battery-status" via cordova plugins registry
npm http GET http://registry.cordova.io/org.apache.cordova.battery-status
npm http 200 http://registry.cordova.io/org.apache.cordova.battery-status
npm http GET http://cordova.iriscouch.com/registry/_design/app/_rewrite/org.apache.cordova.batter
y-status/-/org.apache.cordova.battery-status-0.2.12.tgz
npm http 200 http://cordova.iriscouch.com/registry/_design/app/_rewrite/org.apache.cordova.batter
y-status/-/org.apache.cordova.battery-status-0.2.12.tgz
Saving plugin to package.json file
Adding since there was no existingPlugin
→ example28
```

The CLI prints out a warning that says that the plugin is renamed, and the downloaded plugin might not be the latest.

So, let's use the newer version. But, before we add the hyphenated version, we need to remove the already added plugin. Run this:

```
ionic plugin rm org.apache.cordova.battery-status
```

Add the plugin with the hyphenated name:

```
cordova plugin add cordova-plugin-battery-status
```

To view all the plugins that were installed, run this:

```
ionic plugin ls
```

Then, you should see the following screenshot:

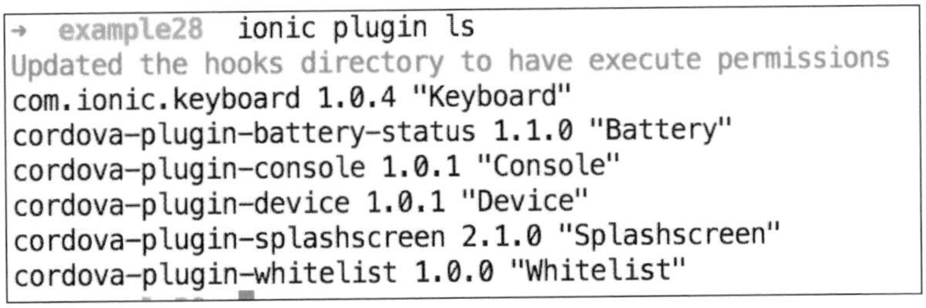

```
→ example28 ionic plugin ls
Updated the hooks directory to have execute permissions
com.ionic.keyboard 1.0.4 "Keyboard"
cordova-plugin-battery-status 1.1.0 "Battery"
cordova-plugin-console 1.0.1 "Console"
cordova-plugin-device 1.0.1 "Device"
cordova-plugin-splashscreen 2.1.0 "Splashscreen"
cordova-plugin-whitelist 1.0.0 "Whitelist"
```

As mentioned, `com.ionic.keyboard` is using hyphenated notation and the remaining are using the dot notation. You may see only hyphenated notation plugins when you run this command.

Before we go ahead and test the Battery status plugin, we need to use it in some way in our code. Open `www/js/app.js`. Inside the `run` method, towards the end of the `ionicPlatform.ready` callback, add the following code:

```
alert(device.model);

        window.addEventListener("batterystatus", onBatteryStatus,
false);

        function onBatteryStatus(info) {
            // Handle the online event
            alert("Level: " + info.level + " isPlugged: " +
info.isPlugged);
        }
```

We have added an alert to show the device model (the `cordova-plugin-device` plugin will be used) and then we have added an event listener to notify us when the battery status changes (the `cordova-plugin-battery-status` plugin will be used).

Now run this:

```
ionic serve
```

You should see no alert popup and, if you open the development tools, you will see an error that says: `device is not defined`.

This means that we cannot run the plugins directly in the browser; they need an environment to execute such as Android, iOS, or sometimes a browser itself.

Yes, a browser is another platform, like Android or iOS, where the `cordova.js` will work. The `cordova.js` is the library that bridges the gap between JavaScript API and the device-specific language. Depending on what type of plugin you are using, you can perform emulation from your browser as well.

Let's try this with the device and battery features. To add a browser platform, run this:

```
ionic platform add browser
```

Now, to run the app inside the browser environment, execute:

```
ionic run browser
```

This will launch a new instance of your default browser and run the app. Now you should see the alert for `device.model`. And, if you open the development tools, you should see this:

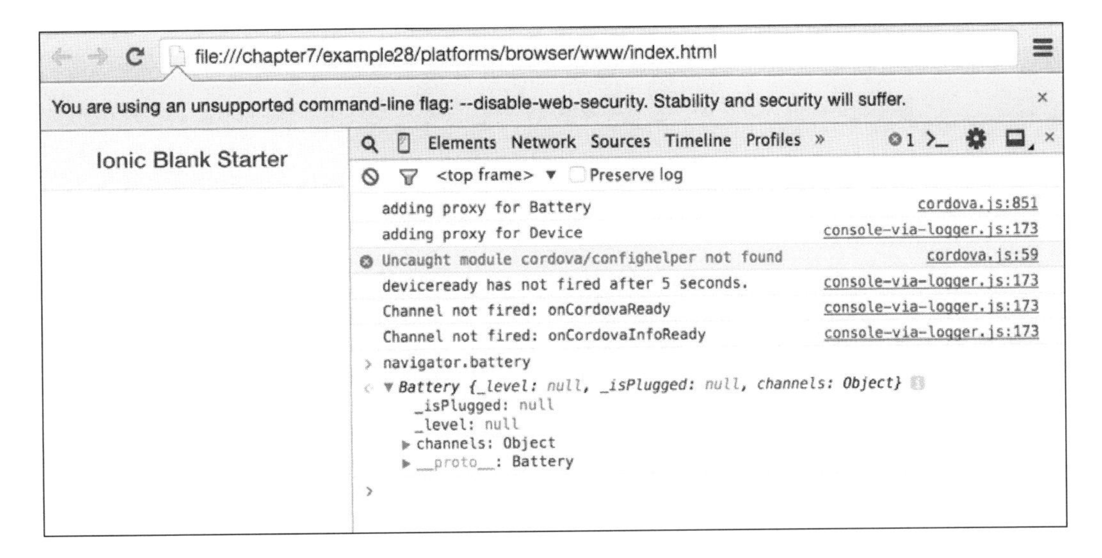

However, if you run `navigator.battery` in the console as shown earlier, you should see the `battery` object with `null` values in its properties.

To test the app (and plugin) properly, we need to add either an Android platform or an iOS platform:

```
ionic platform add android
```

You can also use this:

```
ionic platform add ios
```

Then execute any one of the following commands:

- `ionic emulate android`
- `ionic emulate ios`
- `ionic run android`
- `ionic run ios`

You should see the appropriate message:

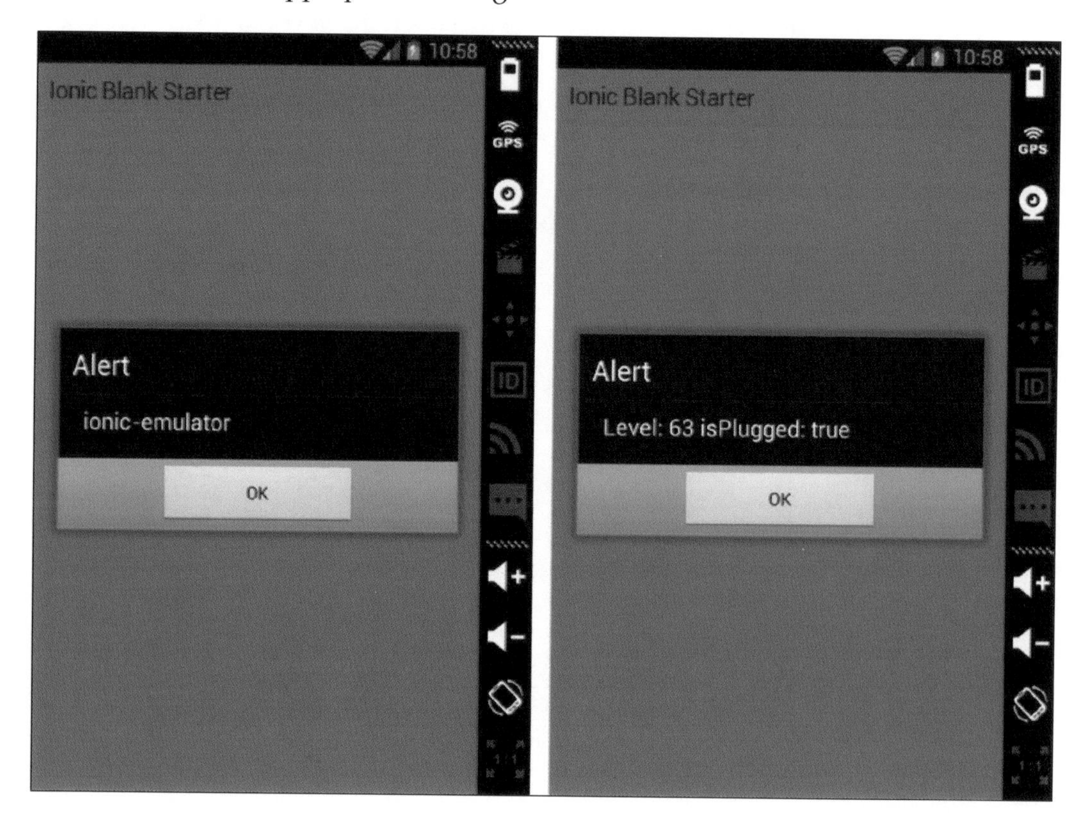

Now you know how to add Cordova plugins to your Ionic project and test them. In the next section, we will be working with ngCordova and a few more plugins.

The preceding screenshots from Genymotion are from my personal edition. These images are for illustration purposes only.

The Cordova whitelist plugin

Before we go ahead and start working with ngCordova, we are going to spend a moment on one of the key Cordova plugins - the whitelist plugin `https://github.com/apache/cordova-plugin-whitelist`.

From the Cordova documentation on the whitelist plugin:

> *"Domain whitelisting is a security model that controls access to external domains over which your application has no control. Cordova provides a configurable security policy to define which external sites may be accessed."*

So, if you want to have more control over how your app should behave when dealing with content from other sources, you should be working with the whitelist plugin. As you may have noticed, this plugin is already added to our Ionic project.

If this plugin is not added to the Ionic/Cordova project, you can do so easily by running:

```
ionic plugin add cordova-plugin-whitelist
```

Once the plugin is added, you can update the `config.xml` file with the navigation whitelist - the links that your app is allowed to open inside webview.

You will be adding:

```
<allow-navigation href="http://example.com/*" />
```

To allow links to `example.com` and if you want your webview to link to any website, you add this:

```
<allow-navigation href="http://*/*" />
<allow-navigation href="https://*/*" />
<allow-navigation href="data:*" />
```

You can also add an Intent whitelist, where you can specify the list of links that are allowed to be browsed on the device. For instance, open the SMS app from our custom app:

```
<allow-intent href="sms:*" />
```

Or simple web pages:

```
<allow-intent href="https://*/*" />
```

You can also enforce a **Content Security Policy** (**CSP**) `http://content-security-policy.com/`) on your app as well using this plugin. All you need to do is add a `meta` tag to the `www/index.html` file, as follows:

```
<!-- Allow XHRs via https only -->
<meta http-equiv="Content-Security-Policy" content="default-src
'self' https:">
```

This was a quick tour of the Whitelist plugin, and this plugin is applicable to:

- Android 4.0.0 or above
- iOS 4.0.0 or above

Do remember to add this plugin and configure it, otherwise external links will not work.

In the Bookstore app, we built in *Chapter 6, Building a BookStore App*, make sure that the whitelist plugin is set up; otherwise, when you try to deploy the app on the device, the app will not work as expected.

ngCordova

In the earlier example, we have integrated a couple of plugins and used their JavaScript API methods to interact with them. As you may have noticed, all the plugins reside in the global namespace. Unlike AngularJS's philosophy of dependency injection, Cordova's plugins reside in the global namespace and can be accessed from anywhere. This might be a problem when you are testing your application, built with the concept of dependency injection.

So, the Ionic team came up with a wrapper around the Cordova plugins, whereby you can inject the features as services. In the preceding example, instead of using `device.model`, we will inject a dependency named `$cordovaDevice`, and then access properties using the `$cordovaDevice.getModel` method.

The ngCordova library is not specific to Ionic; this can be used in conjunction with any Cordova app built using AngularJS.

The ngCordova library has 71 plugins at the time of writing this chapter.

For now, let's test-drive a few ngCordova plugins.

Setting up ngCordova

Before we start working with ngCordova, we need to download and add it as a dependency. Let's create a new blank project and test it out. Run this:

```
ionic start -a "Example 29" -i app.example.twentynone example29 blank
```

Next, we will add ngCordova as a dependency to this project. Using the `cd` command go to the `example29` folder and run this:

```
bower install ngCordova --save
```

To validate if ngCordova was properly added to the project, navigate to the `www/lib` folder and you should see a folder named ngCordova; inside the `dist` folder, you should find a file named `ng-cordova.min.js` among others.

Next, we need add a reference to this JavaScript file, and inject ngCordova as a dependency to our project.

Open `www/index.html` and add:

```
<!-- ngCordova -->
<script src="lib/ngCordova/dist/ng-cordova.min.js"></script>
```

The ngCordova script should be included after the `ionic.bundle.js` and before `cordova.js`. If the order is changed, you will see errors in the console.

Next, we need to add ngCordova as a dependency to our module. Open `www/js/app.js` and update the Angular module declaration:

```
angular.module('starter', ['ionic', 'ngCordova'])
```

Since the `cordova-plugin-device` is pre-installed, we can start using the `$cordovaDevice` service.

Update the run method in `www/js/app.js` as follows:

```
.run(function($ionicPlatform, $cordovaDevice) {
    $ionicPlatform.ready(function() {
        // Hide the accessory bar by default (remove this to show
the accessory bar above the keyboard
        // for form inputs)
        if (window.cordova && window.cordova.plugins.Keyboard) {
            cordova.plugins.Keyboard.hideKeyboardAccessoryBar(true);
        }
        if (window.StatusBar) {
            StatusBar.styleDefault();
        }

        alert('Platform : ' + $cordovaDevice.getPlatform() + '\nModel
: ' + $cordovaDevice.getModel());
    });
})
```

We are alerting the platform and model of the device.

Any code that deals with plugins should be inside the `$ionicPlatform.ready` method.

Legend

From now on, when I say, "add a platform to the Ionic app", it means you should run:

```
ionic platform add android
```

You can also use this:

```
ionic platform add ios
```

When I say, "add ngCordova support to the Ionic app", it means you should run:

```
bower install ngCordova --save
```

Next, include the `ng-cordova.min.js` in the `www/index.html` file as we did earlier. And finally add ngCordova as a dependency to the AngularJS module.

When I say, "emulate the Ionic app", it means you should run this:

```
ionic emulate android
```

You can also use this:

```
ionic emulate ios
```

And finally when I say, "run the Ionic app", it means you should run:

```
ionic run android
```

You can also use this:

```
ionic run ios
```

Now, add a platform to the `example29` app and emulate the app. You should see:

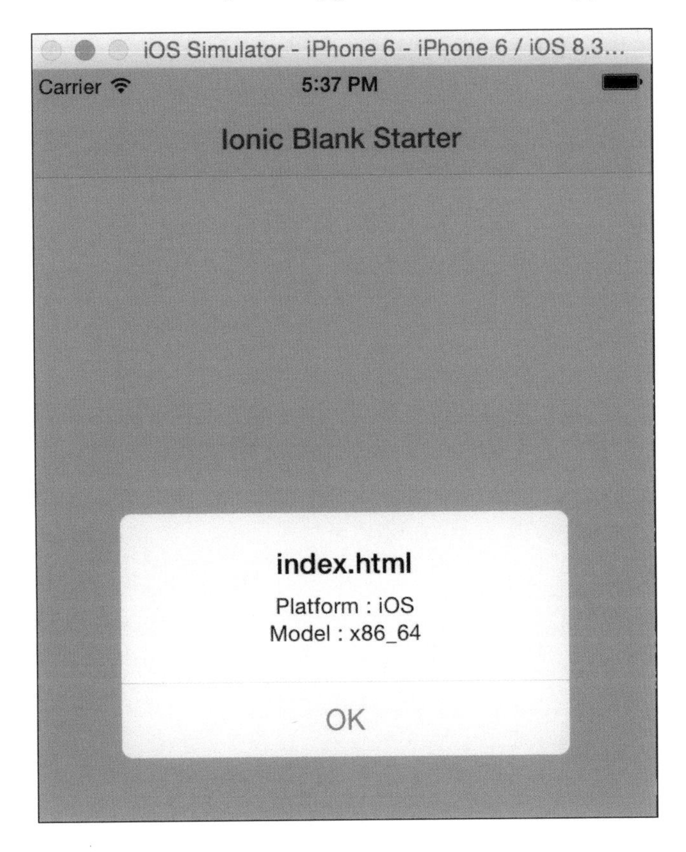

This was an end-to-end example of adding ngCordova and using it. In the next sections, we will work with a few Cordova plugins using the ngCordova service.

I am going to create a new project for each plugin, so you can refer to it easily later. You need not do that if you are planning to practice along with me; you can have all the plugins in one project.

$cordovaToast

The first plugin we are going to work with is the toast plugin. This plugin shows text popups that are not blocking the user's interaction with the app.

We will scaffold a new blank app.

```
ionic start -a "Example 30" -i app.example.thirty example30 blank
```

Next, add ngCordova support to the project. To work with the toast API, we need to add the toast plugin to the project. Run this:

```
ionic plugin add https://github.com/EddyVerbruggen/Toast-PhoneGap-
Plugin.git
```

Now, instead of working with the `run` method, we will create a controller for each plugin we are working with. This way, it will be easy when you refer back.

Open `www/index.html` and add `ng-controller="ToastCtrl"` on the `body` tag. Then we will add the controller definition in the `www/js/app.js` file, below the `run` method:

```
    .controller('ToastCtrl', ['$ionicPlatform', '$cordovaToast',
function($ionicPlatform, $cordovaToast) {

        $ionicPlatform.ready(function() {

            $cordovaToast
                .show('This is a long toast!', 'long', 'center')
                .then(function(success) {
                    // success
                }, function(error) {
                    // error
                });

        });

    }])
```

Next, add a platform to the Ionic App and emulate the app. You should see:

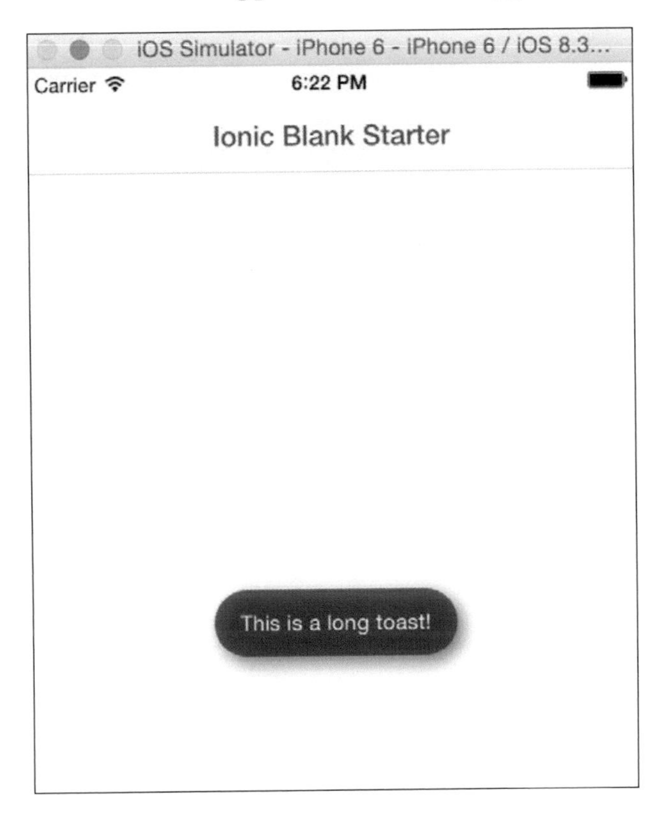

In our examples, we will be working with the bare minimum of API methods. After each plugin, I will provide the link to their API; you can check out the other methods that the plugin supports.

For more information, visit `http://ngcordova.com/docs/plugins/toast/`.

$cordovaDialogs

The next plugin we are going to work with is the dialogs plugin. This triggers the alert, confirm, and prompt windows.

Scaffolding a new blank app for dialogs plugin:

```
ionic start example31 blank
```

Next, add ngCordova support to the project. To work with the dialogs API, we need to add the dialogs plugin to the project. Run this:

```
ionic plugin add cordova-plugin-dialogs
```

We will create a dialog controller. Open `www/index.html` and add `ng-controller="DialogsCtrl"` to the `body` tag.

In this example, we are going to show a prompt and let the user enter text. Once the user enters the text, we will print that on the screen. To do that, we will update our body section in `www/index.html` as follows:

```
<body ng-app="starter" ng-controller="DialogsCtrl">

  <ion-pane>
    <ion-header-bar class="bar-stable">
      <h1 class="title">Ionic Blank Starter</h1>
    </ion-header-bar>
    <ion-content>
      <span class="padding">Hello {{name}}!!</span>
    </ion-content>
  </ion-pane>
</body>
```

We will add `DialogsCtrl` to `www/js/app.js`:

```
.controller('DialogsCtrl', ['$ionicPlatform', '$scope',
'$cordovaDialogs', function ($ionicPlatform, $scope,
$cordovaDialogs) {
    $ionicPlatform.ready(function () {

        $cordovaDialogs.prompt('Name please?', 'Identity',
['Cancel', 'OK'], 'Harry Potter')
            .then(function (result) {
                if (result.buttonIndex == 2) {
                    $scope.name = result.input1;
                }
            });

    });
}])
```

Next, add a platform to the Ionic App and emulate the app. You should see:

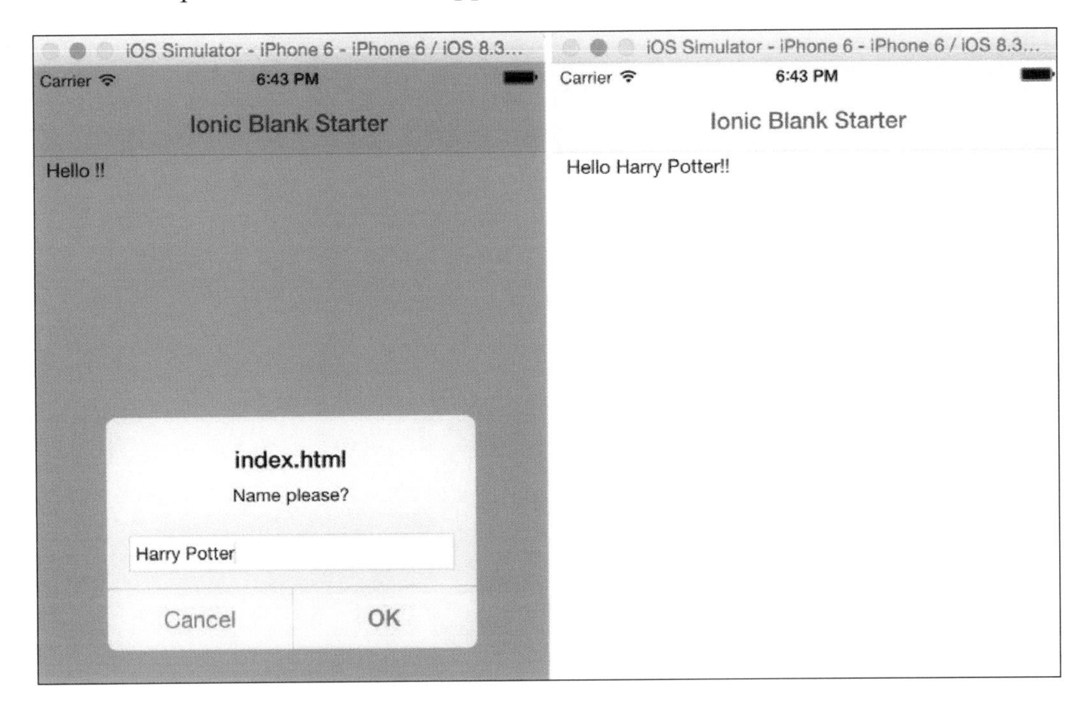

For more information, visit http://ngcordova.com/docs/plugins/dialogs/.

$cordovaFlashlight

The next plugin we are going to work with is a utility plugin. This plugin will help users toggle their flashlight on and off. This plugin cannot be tested on an emulator. So, you need a device to test this plugin.

Scaffolding a new blank app for the flashlight plugin:

```
ionic start -a "Example 32" -i app.example.thirtytwo example32 blank
```

Next, add ngCordova support to the project. To work with the flashlight API, we need to add the flashlight plugin to the project. Run this:

```
ionic plugin add https://github.com/EddyVerbruggen/Flashlight-PhoneGap-Plugin.git
```

We will create a flashlight controller. Open `www/index.html` and add `ng-controller="FlashlightCtrl"` to the `body` tag.

In this example, we are going to show a toggle switch to the user using the `ion-toggle` directive and then, based on its state, we are going switch the flashlight on or off. To do that, we will update our body section in `www/index.html` as follows:

```
<body ng-app="starter" ng-controller="FlashlightCtrl">
    <ion-pane>
        <ion-header-bar class="bar-stable">
            <h1 class="title">Ionic Blank Starter</h1>
        </ion-header-bar>
        <ion-content>
            <ion-list>
                <ion-item>
                    <ion-toggle
                    ng-disabled="notSupported"
                    ng-model="torch"
                    ng-change="toggleTorch()">
                        Torch
                    </ion-toggle>
                </ion-item>
            </ion-list>
        </ion-content>
    </ion-pane>
</body>
```

We will add the `FlashlightCtrl` to `www/js/app.js` after the `run` method.

```
.controller('FlashlightCtrl', ['$scope', '$ionicPlatform',
'$cordovaFlashlight', function($scope, $ionicPlatform,
$cordovaFlashlight) {

    $scope.notSupported = true;

    $ionicPlatform.ready(function() {

        $cordovaFlashlight.available().then(function(availability)
{
            // availability = true || false
            $scope.notSupported = !availability;
        });

        $scope.toggleTorch = function() {
```

```
            if ($scope.notSupported) return;

            $cordovaFlashlight.toggle()
                .then(function(success) { /* success */ },
                    function(error) { /* error */ });
        }


    });

}])
```

We first check if the plugin is available. If it is, only then do we enable the toggle; otherwise, we leave the toggle disabled.

And when the user toggles the switch, we call the `toggleTorch` method, which will toggle the state of the flashlight.

If you run the app on a device, you should see the following:

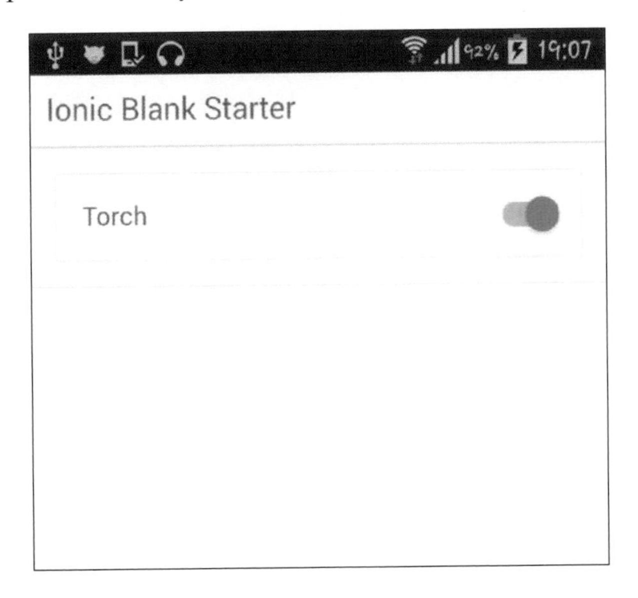

If you want to validate if the toggle is really disabled, you can emulate the app.

For more information, visit `http://ngcordova.com/docs/plugins/flashlight/`.

$cordovaLocalNotification

The next plugin we are going to take a look at is the Notification plugin. This plugin is primarily used to notify or remind users about an activity related to an App. Sometimes notifications are also shown when a background activity is going on—for instance, a large file upload.

We will start off by scaffolding a new blank app. Run this:

```
ionic start -a "Example 33" -i app.example.thirtythree example33
blank
```

Next, add ngCordova support to the project. To work with the notification API, we need to add the notification plugin to the project. Run this:

```
ionic plugin add de.appplant.cordova.plugin.local-notification
```

In this example, we will trigger a notification on a button press, and display the text that the user has entered in the textbox we provided. For that we will be adding a controller named `NotifCtrl` and a textbox and button.

The updated `www/index.html` body section with the relevant code would look like:

```
<body ng-app="starter" ng-controller="NotifCtrl">

  <ion-pane>
    <ion-header-bar class="bar-stable">
      <h1 class="title">Ionic Blank Starter</h1>
    </ion-header-bar>
    <ion-content>

      <div class="list">
        <label class="item item-input">
          <span class="input-label">Enter Notification text</span>
          <input type="text" ng-model="notifText">
        </label>
        <label class="item item-input">
         <button class="button button-dark" ng-
click="triggerNotification()">
            Notify
         </button>
        </label>
      </div>

    </ion-content>
  </ion-pane>
</body>
```

The `NotifCtrl` in `www/js/app.js` would look like:

```
.controller('NotifCtrl', ['$scope', '$ionicPlatform',
'$cordovaLocalNotification', function($scope, $ionicPlatform,
$cordovaLocalNotification) {
    $ionicPlatform.ready(function() {

        $scope.notifText = 'Hello World!';

        $scope.triggerNotification = function() {

            $cordovaLocalNotification.schedule({
                id: 1,
                title: 'Dynamic Notification',
                text: $scope.notifText
            }).then(function(result) {
                console.log(result);
            });
        }
    });
}])
```

If you emulate the Ionic app, you may be asked for permission to allow notification. And once that is done, you can dispatch notifications as needed.

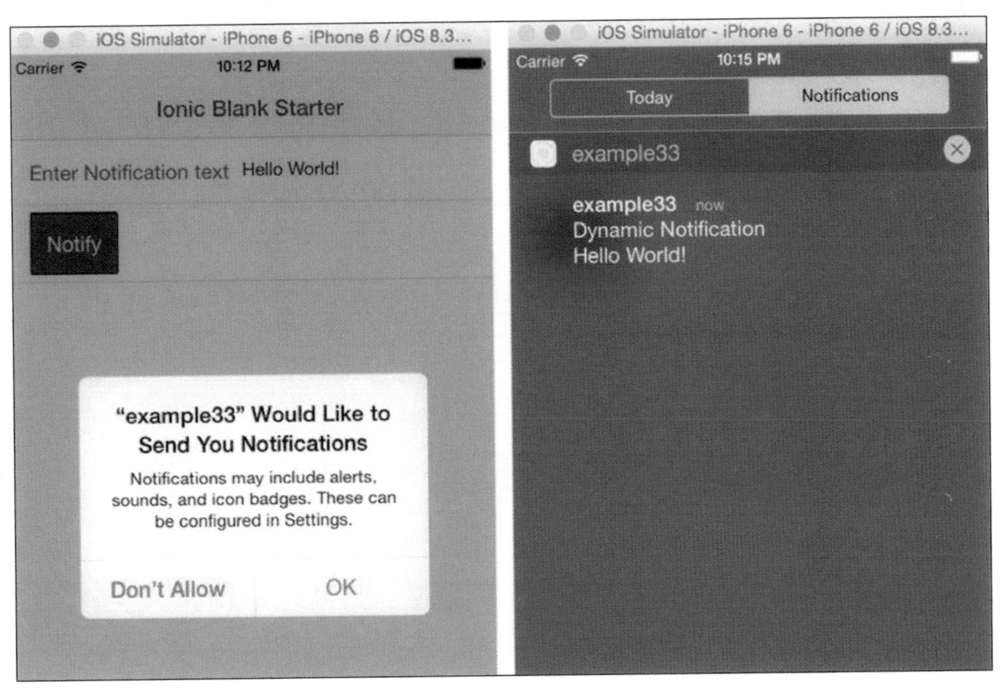

For more information, visit http://ngcordova.com/docs/plugins/localNotification/.

$cordovaGeolocation

The final plugin we are going to take a look at is the Geolocation plugin, which helps to fetch the coordinates of the device.

We will start off by scaffolding a new blank app. Run this:

```
ionic start -a "Example 34" -i app.example.thirtyfour example34 blank
```

Next, add ngCordova support to the project. To work with the Geolocation API, we need to add the Geolocation plugin to the project. Run this:

```
ionic plugin add cordova-plugin-geolocation
```

When the app launches, we are going to fetch the Geolocation of the device. Till we get the Geolocation, we show a loading content message. Once we get the response back, we show the latitude, longitude, and accuracy on the page.

First, we will update the www/index.html body section as follows:

```
<body ng-app="starter" ng-controller="GeoCtrl">

  <ion-pane>
    <ion-header-bar class="bar-stable">
      <h1 class="title">Ionic Blank Starter</h1>
    </ion-header-bar>
    <ion-content>

      <ul class="list" ng-show="dataReceived">
        <li class="item">
          Latitude : {{latitude}}
        </li>

        <li class="item">
          Longitude : {{longitude}}
        </li>

        <li class="item">
          Accuracy : {{accuracy}}
        </li>
```

```
        </ul>

      </ion-content>
    </ion-pane>
  </body>
```

Next, we will add the `GeoCtrl` below the `run` method in `www/js/app.js`:

```
.controller('GeoCtrl', ['$scope', '$ionicPlatform',
'$cordovaGeolocation', '$ionicLoading', '$timeout', function($scope,
$ionicPlatform, $cordovaGeolocation, $ionicLoading, $timeout) {
    $ionicPlatform.ready(function() {

        $scope.modal = $ionicLoading.show({
            content: 'Fetching Current Location...',
            showBackdrop: false
        });

        var posOptions = {
            timeout: 10000,
            enableHighAccuracy: false
        };
        $cordovaGeolocation
            .getCurrentPosition(posOptions)
            .then(function(position) {
                $scope.latitude = position.coords.latitude;
                $scope.longitude = position.coords.longitude;
                $scope.accuracy = position.coords.accuracy;
                $scope.dataReceived = true;
                $scope.modal.hide();
            }, function(err) {
                // error
                $scope.modal.hide();
                $scope.modal = $ionicLoading.show({
                    content: 'Oops!! ' + err,
                    showBackdrop: false
                });

                $timeout(function() {
                    $scope.modal.hide();
                }, 3000);
            });
    });
}])
```

If you emulate the app, you should see a permission request to access Geolocation. Once that is accepted, you can see the details.

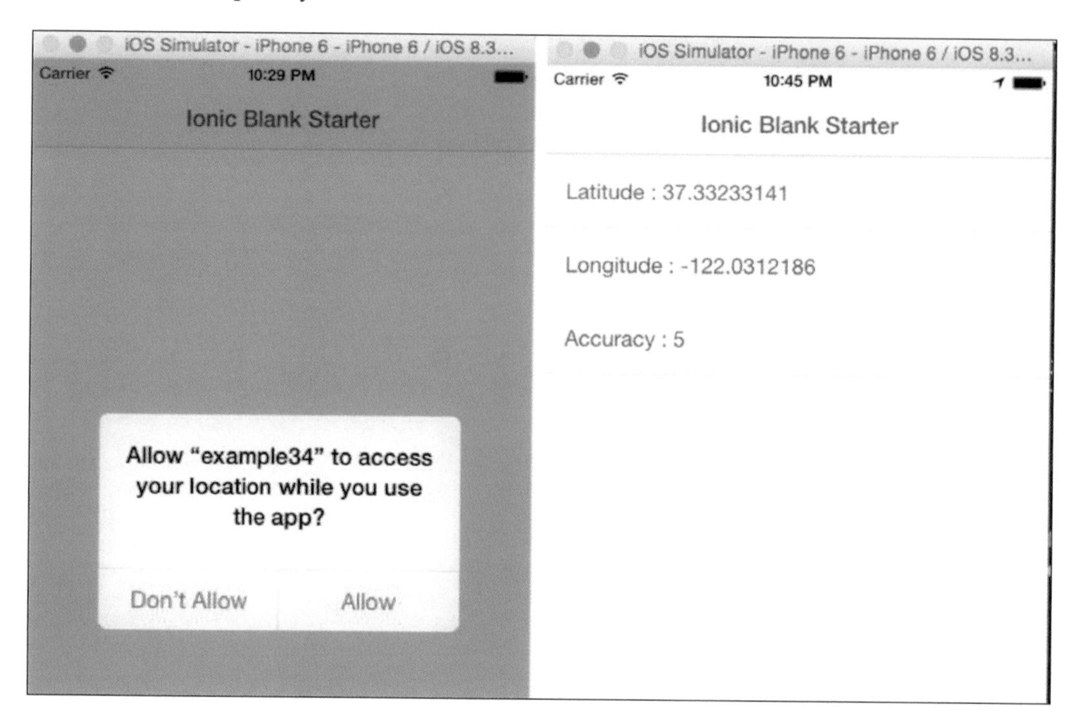

For more information, visit http://ngcordova.com/docs/plugins/geolocation/.

The preceding examples should have provided a good insight into how you can use ngCordova.

You can also check out my other post http://thejackalofjavascript.com/getting-started-with-ngcordova on ngCordova, where I have explored a few more plugins. You can find a complete list of plugins here http://ngcordova.com/docs/plugins/.

When working with ngCordova, you can include only the plugins you will be working with. To customize ngCordova refer to http://ngcordova.com/build/. Remember that, after the customizations, you cannot use bower install to download ngCordova.

Summary

In this chapter, we have seen what Cordova plugins are, and how they can be used in an existing Ionic application. We started off by setting up a local development environment for Android/iOS, and then we learned how to emulate/run the app. Next, we explored how to add Cordova plugins to an Ionic project and use them. Finally, with the aid of ngCordova, we injected plugins as dependencies to our Ionic/Angular app and worked with them in a more Angular way.

In the next chapter, we are going to build another app that uses Ionic, ngCordova, and Firebase.

The application we are going to build is a Chat app, where a user logs in into the app and sees all the users who are online. Once the user selects another user to chat with, they can exchange texts, photos, and Geolocation details.

The aim of the Chat app is to integrate Ionic with a real-time data store, such as Firebase and, at the same time, access device features to make communication richer.

8

Building a Messaging App

As we have gone through almost all the topics needed to build a mobile hybrid app, we will be building one in this chapter. The application we are going to build is a messaging app named *Ionic Chat*. The app we have developed in *Chapter 6, The Bookstore App,* deals with integrating REST API, while the Ionic Chat app we are going to build in this chapter will be more concerned with integrating device features such as camera and Geolocation with Ionic as well as talking to a real-time data store such as Firebase.

We will be going through the following topics:

- Getting an idea about Firebase and setting up a Firebase account
- Understanding AngularFire
- Understanding the application architecture
- Scaffolding the Ionic app and building it
- Installing the required plugins and integrating them with the Ionic App
- Testing the app on the device

For this chapter, you can also access the code, raise issues, and chat with the author at GitHub (`https://github.com/learning-ionic/Chapter-8`).

The Ionic Chat app

The application we are going to build in this chapter is named Ionic Chat. This app aims to get you familiar with a chat application that is built using AngularFire and Ionic, at the same time integrating Cordova plugins with Ionic using ngCordova.

We will first take a look at Firebase, then talk a bit about AngularFire, and finally see how we can integrate AngularFire with the Ionic Chat application. We will be using Firebase as our real-time data store to manage data in our application. Firebase will take care of syncing data in real-time. We will also be using a combination of the oAuth Cordova plugin and Firebase Auth to manage user authentication in our app.

Once the user is logged in, he/she will see all the users online in the first of the three tabs on our home page. The second tab will consist of the chat history, a list of users the current user has engaged in conversation with. And finally, the third tab will consist of settings and logout.

When the user clicks on a person's name in the chat list, a chat page will open where the user can see the past conversation as well as send new messages, photos, and Geolocation to the other user.

For simplicity in the app, we are showing all the users who are online. If you want, you can implement an "Add to Friends" (feature) from the list of online users.

Firebase

Firebase is a **Backend As A Service** (**BAAS**) that provides cloud-based backed services, with a real-time data store, user authentication, and static hosting.

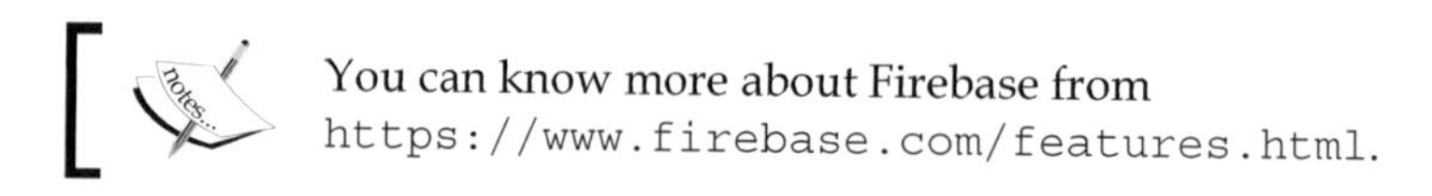

You can know more about Firebase from `https://www.firebase.com/features.html`.

To quickly demonstrate how Firebase works, we will take a look at a code snippet:

```
var ref = new Firebase("https://<YOUR-FIREBASE-
APP>.firebaseio.com");
ref.set({ name: "Arvind Ravulavaru" });
ref.on("value", function(data) {
  var name = data.val().name;
  alert("My name is " + name);
});
```

On line 1, we refer to our instance of Firebase (that we will be creating in the next section). Once we have the reference, we will set/save a JSON document in the default end-point. Firebase, being a real-time data store, has an event-driven approach to managing and syncing data. That can be seen on line 3, where we subscribe to a value event that gets invoked when there is a new piece of data inserted at the default end-point.

To understand line 3 better, imagine user 1 has already set the value in the data store and has registered for the value event. Now, when user 2 loads this script in their browser, he/she will first set the value; this will trigger the callback on line 3 for user 1, alerting the value of user 2 to user 1.

The value callback will be invoked, passing in the snapshot of the newly added data. And the `data.val` method will return the newly added record.

You need to include this Firebase code in your page for the earlier code to execute as expected:

```
<script
src="https://cdn.firebase.com/js/client/2.2.2/firebase.
js"></script>
```

Setting up a Firebase account

You can create a new Firebase account by filling the form `https://www.firebase.com/signup/`, or you can also use your GitHub account to login to Firebase from here: `https://www.firebase.com/login/`.

Once you have registered/logged in, you will be taken to a page (`https://www.firebase.com/account/#/`), where you can add a new project. You can enter the app name and Firebase will let you know if that name is already available. For instance you can type "ionic-chat-app", and you should see that it is already taken (by me, for building this app).

You can give a name that you think is appropriate and available and click on **Create New App**. This will create a new app, and along with this comes the Firebase URL. This URL in simple terms is the API KEY for your account. This is a very elegant solution for letting users add API keys without the fuzz of random alphanumeric characters.

To test if everything is set up as expected, we will implement the earlier code snippet. Create a new folder named `chapter8`, and inside that another folder named `example35`. Inside this folder create a new file named `index.html`. Update the file as follows:

```
<!DOCTYPE html>
<html>

<head>
    <title>Firebase Test Page</title>
    <script src="https://cdn.firebase.com/js/client/2.2.2/firebase.
js"></
script>
```

```
</head>

<body>
    <input type="button" onclick="addNewName()" value="Add New
Name">
    <br>
    <ul id="namesList"></ul>
    <script type="text/javascript">
    var ref = new Firebase("https://<YOUR-FIREBASE-
APP>.firebaseio.com");

    ref.on('value', function(data) {
        var names = data.val();
        clearList();
        for (var n in names) {
            setName(names[n].name);
        }
    });

    function clearList() {
        document.querySelector('#namesList').innerHTML = '';
    }

    function setName(name) {
        var newName = document.createElement('li');
        newName.innerHTML = 'Name : <b>' + name + '</b>';
        document.querySelector('#namesList').appendChild(newName);
    }

    function addNewName() {
        var name = prompt('Enter Name');
        if (name) {
            // the below statement will save data to the Firebase
data store and will invoke the ref.on('value') callback. This will
the call the saveName to setdata
            ref.push({
                'name': name
            });
        }
    }
    </script>
</body>

</html>
```

In the earlier example, we referenced the Firebase source file in the head. In the body section, we have added a button that, when clicked, will show a prompt and the user can enter his/her name. Once the user enters his/her name, this data is saved to the Firebase default collection as an array. Once the data is saved, the `ref.on('value')` event will be triggered. Once this callback is triggered, we clear the HTML on the page, and add the list of names again, using the `setName` method.

You can also open a new tab and then open the same page. By default, the earlier added values will be populated. You need not do anything from your side. You can add some more data and see that both the pages are in sync.

The preceding example shows how a real-time data store works. Now you can see how apt Firebase is for our chat application.

> When the user enters the name, we do not show the value directly. We wait for it to be saved in the data store, and then we wait for Firebase to invoke the value event. Inside the value callback, we display the value to the user.
>
> You can navigate to `https://<your-firebase-url>.firebaseio.com` to see the data update in real-time.

If you navigate to your app on Firebase, you should see this:

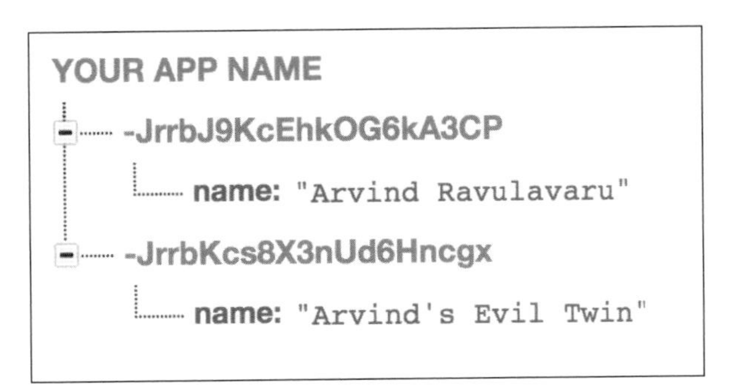

All the names added will be directly under your app name.

AngularFire

Since Ionic uses AngularJS as its client side JavaScript framework, we will be using a flavor of Firebase named AngularFire, to interact with Firebase in the Angular way.

We will quickly go through AngularFire using the following code snippet:

```
var app = angular.module("nameApp", ["firebase"]);
app.controller("NamesCtrl", function($scope, $firebaseArray) {
    var ref = new Firebase("https://<YOUR-FIREBASE-
APP>.firebaseio.com/names");
    // create a synchronized array
    $scope.names = $firebaseArray(ref);

    $scope.addName = function() {
        $scope.names.$add({
            text: $scope.newName
        });
    };
});
```

First we will create a new AngularJS app, then add firebase as a dependency. Then we create a controller and inject `$firebaseArray` as a dependency. Once the controller is invoked, we will be creating a reference to the Firebase App. This time, instead of saving the data to the root collection, we will create a subcollection/nested collection with the name names and then save the data to it.

Assigning the output of `$firebaseArray(ref)` to `$scope.names` makes this a synchronized collection. In simple terms, if the data changes in the data store, our scope variable gets automatically updated, which will also trigger an update in the view/template. Sweet, isn't it? This phenomenon is also called Three-Way Data binding.

> You can read more about Three-Way Data binding at `https://www.firebase.com/blog/2013-10-04-firebase-angular-data-binding.html`.
>
> You need to include Firebase, AngularJS, and AngularFire script files in your page for the earlier code to execute as expected.

We will implement a quick example to see how AngularFire works. Create a folder named `example36`, and create a file named `index.html` inside it. Update it as follows:

```
<!DOCTYPE html>
<html>

<head>
    <title>AngularFire Test Page</title>
    <script src="https://cdn.firebase.com/js/client/2.2.2/firebase.
js">
</script>
    <script src="https://ajax.googleapis.com/ajax/libs/
angularjs/1.3.15/
angular.min.js"></script>
    <script src="https://cdn.firebase.com/libs/angularfire/1.1.1/
angularfire.
min.js"></script>
</head>

<body ng-app="NamesApp" ng-controller="NamesCtrl">
    <input type="button" ng-click="addNewName()" value="Add New
Name">
    <br>
    <ul>
        <li ng-repeat="n in names">
            Name : <b> {{n.name}} </b>
        </li>
    </ul>
    <script type="text/javascript">
    var app = angular.module("NamesApp", ["firebase"]);

    app.controller("NamesCtrl", function($scope, $firebaseArray) {
        var ref = new Firebase("https://<YOUR-FIREBASE-APP>.
firebaseio.com/names");
        // create a synchronized array
        $scope.names = $firebaseArray(ref);

        $scope.addNewName = function() {
            var name = prompt('Enter Name');
            if (name) {
                $scope.names.$add({
                    name: name
                });
            };
        }
```

```
    });
    </script>
</body>

</html>
```

In the preceding example, we reference Firebase, AngularJS, and AngularFire source files.

Do remember to load AngularFire only after Firebase and AngularJS are loaded.

We create a new module named `NamesApp`, and add a controller named `NamesCtrl`. Our HTML consists of an ng-repeat that repeats over the names array from scope. The names variable is a synchronized array.

When a user clicks on **Add New Name** button, we show a prompt where the user enters a name. Once the name is entered, we will use the `$add` method on our name-synchronized array to push the new object to the data store. Then Firebase takes care of synchronizing the data across.

Now, if you open `https://<your-firebase-url>.firebaseio.com` you should see this:

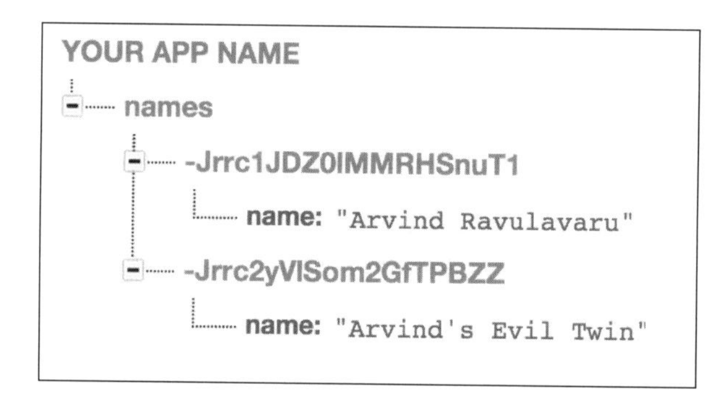

This time, the data is added inside a subobject/nested object named names.

I have deleted the old data before I ran the earlier example.

If you want to build a **Create, Read, Update, and Delete (CRUD)** application using Firebase, check out: `http://thejackalofjavascript.com/getting-started-with-firebase/`.

The application architecture

Now that we are acquainted with Firebase and AngularFire, we will take a look at how the app will be designed:

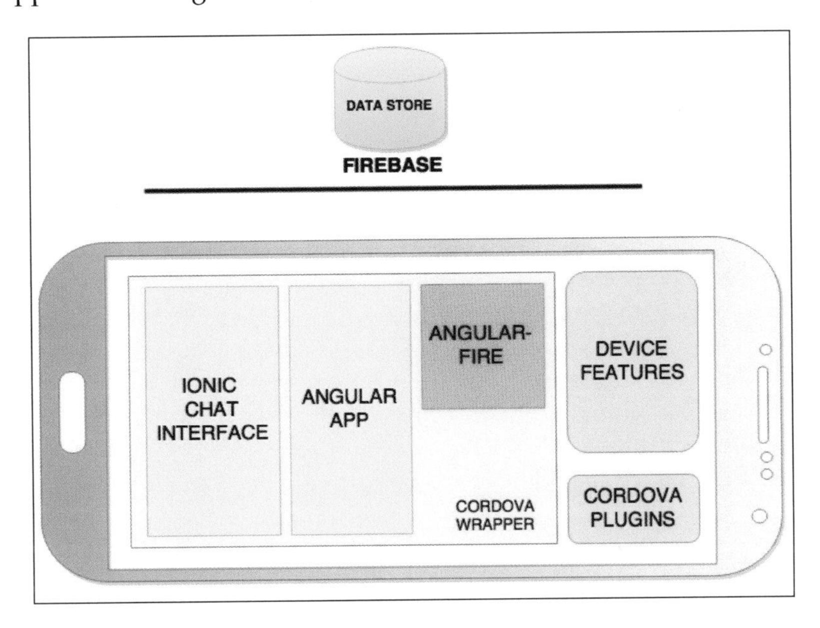

As shown in the preceding diagram, we will be using Firebase as our data store. We will be using AngularFire in our Ionic application to interact with Firebase. The Ionic application will also be interacting with Cordova plugins to implement device features via ngCordova.

In the chat application we are building, the role of Firebase is to manage the chat data. There are two endpoints we will be creating in our Firebase collection:

- **Online users**: This end point will store all the users who are online
- **Chats**: This end point will store the chat between two users

As part of the chat application, we will allow users to:

- Send text messages
- Share photos from the gallery
- Take a picture and share it
- Share the user's location

We will be saving all this data in Firebase. Are you wondering how we save images in Firebase? Well, this is the smart part; we will be converting the image to a base64 format and then saving the `base64-encoded` string to Firebase. Then, to share the user's location, we will be saving only the coordinates of the user and replicating these on the other user's interface.

To share the Geolocation, you can also consider the Google Static Maps API at `https://developers.google.com/maps/documentation/staticmaps/`.

Authentication

We will be using Google Open ID authentication to authenticate users. We will also be using a combination of a Cordova plugin named `ng-cordova-oauth` and Firebase oAuth for authentication. The Cordova plugin is used to manage the pop-up authentication using the in-browser plugin and retrieve the token. This token will then be passed to the Firebase authentication to establish a session. This will get clearer as we start developing the app.

The application flow

When the user launches the app, we will show the application home page that will consist of a slide box and a **Login** button.

As of now the application supports login with Google only. Once the user clicks on the **Login** button, he/she will be redirected to the Google login page. Once logged in and after the access is provided to the app, the user will be redirected to the first page, where the token from Google oAuth will be sent to Firebase to establish a session. Then the user is redirected to the page, which has three tabs.

Tab 1 consists of all the users who are online. Tab 2 consists of a list of users the current user had conversations with and finally tab 3 consists of a settings screen and a **Logout** option.

When the current logged in user taps on a user displayed in either tab 1 to 2, he/she will be taken to the chat detail page, where a chat history between the users will be displayed (if any).

I have designed the app in this way to keep things simple as well as to cover a few topics, which will help you understand the complete ecosystem of mobile hybrid application development better.

Previewing the app

Before we continue, we will quickly take a look at the final output, since we are not going to see any output till we finish the code.

The **Login** screen of the application will be as shown on the left-hand side in the following image. The **Home** screen with the three tabs is as shown on the right-hand side:

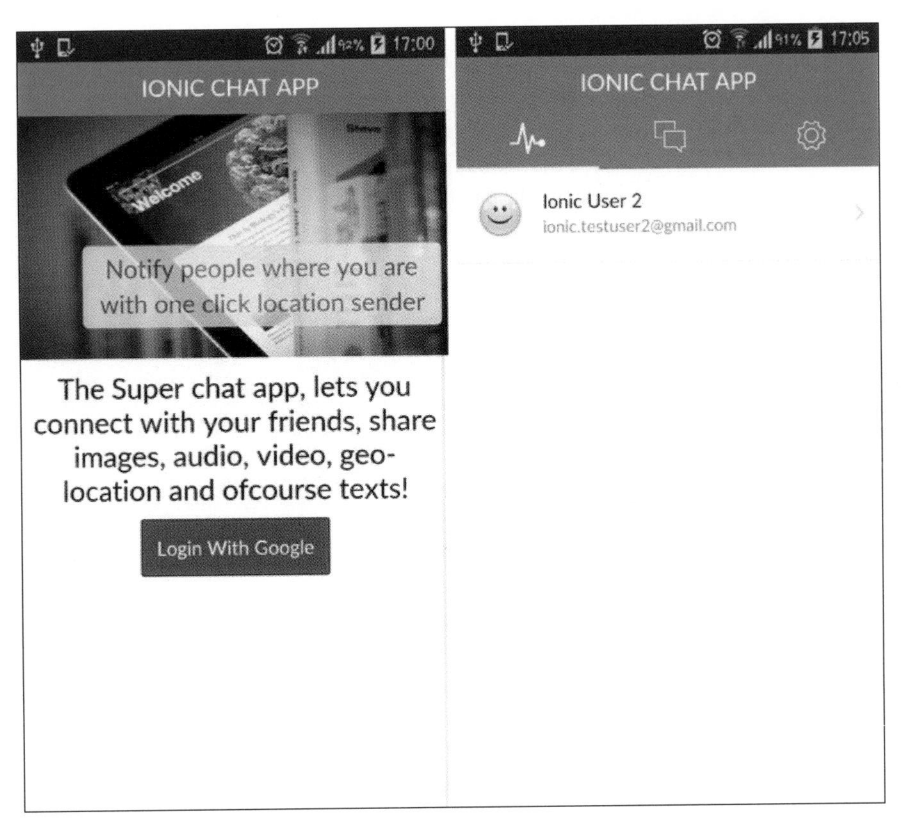

The chat interface will be as shown in the image on the left-hand side and the maps screen from which the user shares their Geolocation will be as shown on the right-hand side:

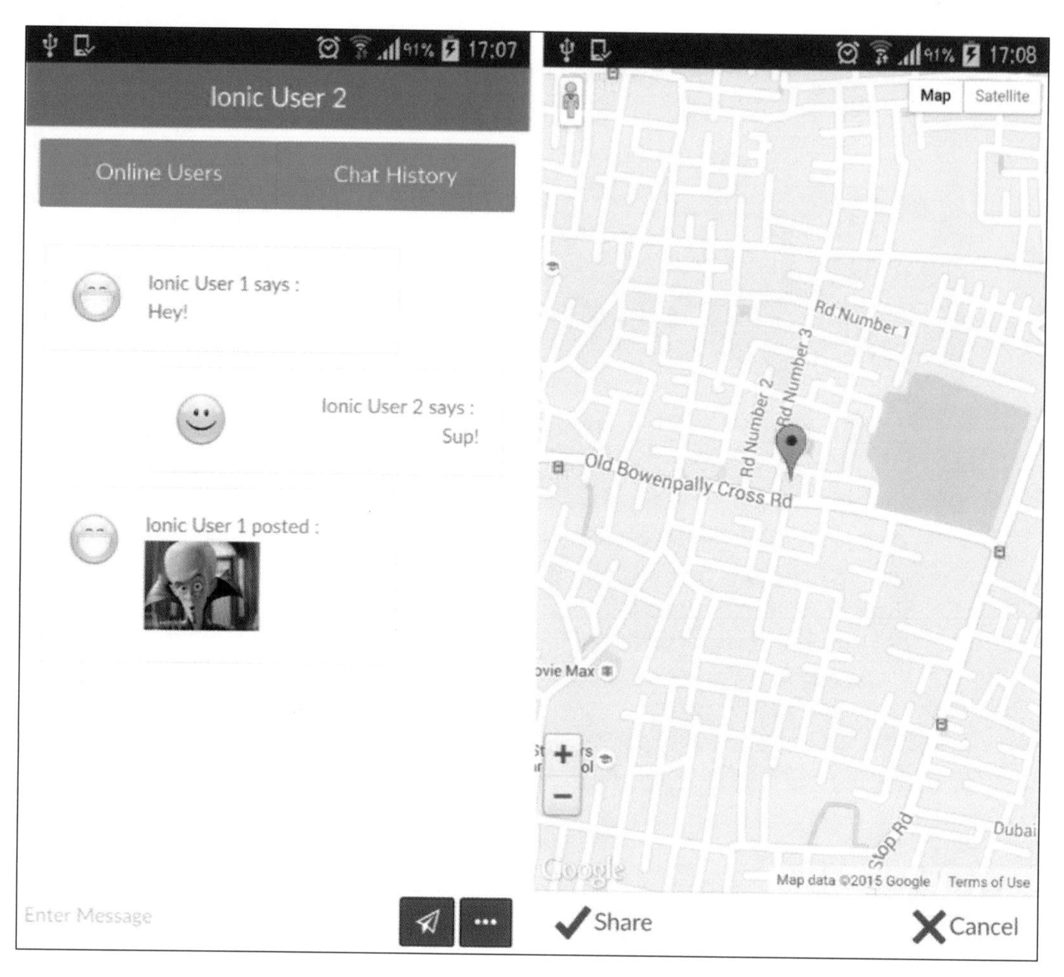

Data structure

By default Firebase notifies all of its clients when a new data set is added to a collection. If we are building a common chat room, where all users who are connected to the app will be notified, we need not to do anything extra.

But since we are looking at a one-to-one chat application, we need to have some kind of logic that will help us manage the communication between the intended users.

When the user logs in, we will update the "Online Users" collection with the current user's details. This will be broadcasted to all the other users who are already logged in the app. Once any user goes offline, we remove the user object from the "Online Users" collection.

We are using Firebase Authentication to store the login information. You will not see the registered user's details in the Forge.

Now that the user is logged in, he/she will appear in the list of users online. If User B wants to chat with User A, we need to create a new endpoint, where only User A and User B can communicate.

The logic to create a new dynamic endpoint is a bit complex. The steps are as follows:

1. Identify User A's email address and User B's e-mail address.
2. Execute a hashing function on User A's e-mail address and User B's e-mail address. This hashing function will return the same string when we pass in two e-mail address, in any order.
3. Using the preceding-hashed string, we build a new endpoint inside the chats collection.
4. If User B has initiated a chat with User A, the dynamic endpoint will be created by User B and, upon the first message from User B to User A, a listener running on the chat collection will be triggered. This listener will check if the chat message is intended for the current logged in user. If it is, it will notify User A.

A bit complicated, but it works fine.

I have implemented the same logic in a node-webkit desktop chat application. You can read more at `http://thejackalofjavascript.com/one-to-one-chat-client/`.

Now that we have an idea as to how the data is structured, we will take a look at what Cordova plugins we are going to use.

Cordova plugins

We are going to include the following plugins (apart from the ones that are downloaded as part of the template):

- `cordova-plugin-inappbrowser`: This is used to manage Google authentication
- `cordova-plugin-media-capture`: This is used to take a picture and share it with the user
- `com.synconset.imagepicker`: This is used to pick an image from the gallery
- `cordova-plugin-file`: This is used to interact with filesystem while converting images to base64 strings
- `cordova-plugin-geolocation`: This is used to get the user's Geo coordinates

We will look into each plugin when we work with it.

Code on GitHub

I have hosted the code for this chapter on GitHub as well. You can check out the repository at `https://github.com/learning-ionic`. If you are facing any trouble, you can raise an issue in this repository and I will try my best to answer it. Also I will be fixing any bugs reported by the readers here.

Developing the application

First, we will scaffold and set up the app.

Scaffolding and setting up the app

We will start off by scaffolding a tabs application. Run this:

```
ionic start -a "Ionic Chat App" -i app.ionic.chat ionic-chat-app tabs
```

Using the `cd` command, go to the `ionic-chat-app` folder and run this:

```
ionic server
```

To view the sample tabs app.

Before we proceed, we are going to install dependencies needed for this application via Bower. From the root of the project, run this:

```
bower install ngCordova ng-cordova-oauth firebase angularfire lato --
save
```

The gist of what these bower components are used for is as follows:

- `ngCordova`: The ngCordova library.
- `ng-cordova-oauth`: At the time of writing, there is an issue with the `ng-cordova-oauth` module that is bundled with ngCordova, so we are installing it separately and using it. The issue I am facing now might have been fixed by the time you are executing this code.
- `firebase`: This is the firebase source.
- `angularfire`: This is the AngularFire source.
- `lato`: This is the Lato font (`https://www.google.com/fonts/specimen/Lato`).

I have installed the Lato font locally, instead of loading it from Google fonts. This is to make sure that the fonts are available when the device does not have the network. You can also take a look at `localFont` to implement local storage Web font caching in seconds (`https://github.com/jaicab/localFont`) to achieve the same.

Next, we will add SCSS support to the project; run this:

```
ionic setup sass
```

Now, we will add references to the dependencies we have downloaded. We will make the following changes in the `index.html` file.

First, let's turn our attention to `ng-cordova` and `ng-cordova-oauth`. The following two `script` tags after the Ionic bundle is loaded and before `cordova.js`:

```
<script src="lib/ngCordova/dist/ng-cordova.js"></script>
<script src="lib/ng-cordova-oauth/dist/ng-cordova-
oauth.js"></script>
```

Next, after the `cordova.js`, we will add reference to Firebase and then AngularFire in that order:

```
<script src="lib/firebase/firebase.js"></script>
<script src="lib/angularfire/dist/angularfire.min.js"></script>
```

We will be adding a directive to manage the maps in our app. So, we will be creating a directive later, but to complete the `index.html` we will add the reference now.

Add the following `script` tag after the `services.js` file reference:

```
<script src="js/directives.js"></script>
```

Next, we will also need reference to the maps APIs from Google. Add the following script just before the closing of the `head` tag:

```
<script src="https://maps.googleapis.com/maps/api/
js?key=AIzaSyDgE3k3per7m
f0qjZLWwlbMXQL1OhH-x44&sensor=true"></script>
```

I will show how to obtain your own Google API key (used in the preceding script tag) when we are dealing with Google authentication setup.

Finally, we will add the Lato font. Above the reference to `ionic.app.css`, add this:

```
<link href="lib/lato/css/lato.min.css" rel="stylesheet">
```

As time passes, the afore-referenced assets may not be in the same path as they are today. So, if you see a "not found (404)" error on any of the assets, recheck the path inside the `lib` folder.

We will rename the module from `starter` to `IonicChatApp`, present on the `body` tag. Next, we will rename the `nav bar` class from `bar-stable` to `bar-positive`.

With this, we wrap up the `index.html` setup.

Next, open `www/js/app.js`. Since we have renamed the module on the index page, we need to rename the module in `app.js` as well. The updated AngularJS module declaration is as follows:

```
angular.module('IonicChatApp', ['ionic', 'chatapp.controllers',
'chatapp.services', 'chatapp.directives', 'ngCordova',
'ngCordovaOauth', 'firebase'])
```

We have also renamed controllers and services namespace and added reference to the directives module, `ngCordova`, `ngCordovaOauth`, and `Firebase`.

Do note that we have explicitly added the `ngCordovaOauth` module as a dependency to our main module. This is because the bundled version (`ng-cordova.js`) has an issue, at the time of writing this chapter. If you are consuming the Cordova oAuth plugin from the bundled version as it is; you do not need to include this dependency as well as its source file.

Installing the required Cordova plugins

We will install the required Cordova plugins. Run the following commands to set them up:

```
ionic plugin add https://github.com/wymsee/cordova-imagePicker.git
ionic plugin add cordova-plugin-file
ionic plugin add cordova-plugin-geolocation
ionic plugin add cordova-plugin-inappbrowser
ionic plugin add cordova-plugin-media-capture
```

Getting the Google API key

Since our app uses Google's OAuth, we need a Client ID. To acquire a Client ID, you can follow these steps:

1. Navigate to `https://console.developers.google.com`.
2. Click on **Create project** and enter a project name.
3. Once the project is created, click on the project to open it.
4. From the left-hand side menu, click on **APIs and auth** and then click on **Consent** screen. Fill in the required details here. The product name is mandatory.
5. From the left-hand side menu, click on **APIs and auth** and then click on **Credentials**.
6. Click on **Create new Client ID** under the OAuth section.
7. Select the following:
   - Application type as web application
   - Authorized JavaScript origins as `http://localhost`
   - Authorized redirect URIs as `http://localhost/callback`
8. Once the preceding information is filled, click on **Create Client ID** and you should see the Client ID for the web application.

Once you have the Client ID, we need to update it in our Firebase Forge as well. Navigate to the Firebase app page (where you see the live data updates). On the left-hand side of the page, you will find a menu item named **Login and Auth**; click on it. When the right-hand side of the page refreshes, click on the Google tab and fill in your Google Client ID and Secret, which we generated earlier.

The preceding step is important for the authentication to work.

If you want to create an API key for accessing the Google maps API, you can do so by carrying out the following steps:

1. From the left-hand side menu, click on **APIs and auth** and then click on **Credentials**.
2. Click on **Create new Key** under the **Public API Access** section.
3. Select browser key from the popup.
4. Leave the **Accept requests from these HTTP referrers** text area blank.
5. Click on **Create**. This will generate the API key, which you can replace in `index.html`.
6. From the left-hand side menu, click on **APIs and auth** and then click on **APIs**.
7. Search for **Google Maps JavaScript API v3** from the search box and click on the link.
8. Enable the API by clicking on the **Enable API** button.

Now that we have the Client ID, we will set up a few constants. Inside `www/js/app.js`, after the `run` method and before the `config` method, we will add three constants:

```
.constant('FBURL', 'https://ionic-chat-app.firebaseio.com/')
.constant('GOOGLEKEY', '1002599169952-
4uchnlc7ahm6ng4696p9tgr1adhsiqv5.apps.googleusercontent.com')
.constant('GOOGLEAUTHSCOPE', ['email'])
```

Replace the FBURL with your Firebase application URL. Replace the Google key with the Client ID we generated earlier. As part of the OAuth request, we need to send a scope to Google, so that we get the required information back. For our application, we need only the basic information of the user; hence we have used e-mail as a scope.

Setting up routes and route authentication

Since we have scaffolded the tabs application, we almost have all the routes we need. We will be making a couple of changes to the existing routes and adding authentication to each route. This way, the view will not be shown if the authentication fails. We will be using the `resolve` property on the route to achieve this.

Before proceeding further, I recommend going through the `resolve` attribute of the AngularJS state router. This property takes care of resolving any promises you specify before loading the controller. This will be helpful for us in validating the user authentication state before loading the controller.

You can find more information at `https://github.com/angular-ui/ui-router/wiki#resolve`.

Firebase has two methods on the `$firebaseAuth` function. They are as follows:

- `$waitForAuth`: This returns a promise that will be resolved with the current authentication state. This will be used only on the home route.
- `$requireAuth`: This returns a promise that will be resolved with the current authentication state; otherwise, it rejects the promise. This will be used on all the routes that need authentication.

We will be leveraging these two methods to control what an unauthenticated user can see and cannot see.

We will be adding one more route to the existing routes named `main`. This route will be the default route and will act as the home page for our application. On each route, we will add a `resolve` property that will be resolved with Firebase Auth. Also, we will modify the chat-detail route to not to be a child route of chats.

The updated routes section looks like this:

```
$stateProvider.state('main', {
            url: '/',
            templateUrl: 'templates/main.html',
            controller: 'MainCtrl',
            cache: false,
            resolve: {
                'currentAuth': ['FBFactory', 'Loader',
function(FBFactory, Loader) {
                    Loader.show('Checking Auth..');
                    return FBFactory.auth().$waitForAuth();
                }]
            }
        })
        .state('tab', {
            url: "/tab",
            abstract: true,
            cache: false,
            templateUrl: "templates/tabs.html"
```

```
            })
            .state('tab.dash', {
                url: '/dash',
                cache: false,
                views: {
                    'tab-dash': {
                        templateUrl: 'templates/tab-dash.html',
                        controller: 'DashCtrl'
                    }
                },
                resolve: {
                    'currentAuth': ['FBFactory', function(FBFactory) {
                        return FBFactory.auth().$requireAuth();
                    }]
                }
            })
            .state('tab.chats', {
                url: '/chats',
                cache: false,
                views: {
                    'tab-chats': {
                        templateUrl: 'templates/tab-chats.html',
                        controller: 'ChatsCtrl'
                    }
                },
                resolve: {
                    'currentAuth': ['FBFactory', function(FBFactory) {
                        return FBFactory.auth().$requireAuth();
                    }]
                }
            })
            .state('tab.account', {
                url: '/account',
                cache: false,
                views: {
                    'tab-account': {
                        templateUrl: 'templates/tab-account.html',
                        controller: 'AccountCtrl'
                    }
                },
                resolve: {
                    'currentAuth': ['FBFactory', function(FBFactory) {
                        return FBFactory.auth().$requireAuth();
                    }]
```

```
            }
        })
        .state('chat-detail', {
            url: '/chats/:otherUser',
            templateUrl: 'templates/chat-detail.html',
            controller: 'ChatDetailCtrl',
            cache: false,
            resolve: {
                'currentAuth': ['FBFactory', 'Loader',
  function(FBFactory, Loader) {
                    Loader.show('Checking Auth..');
                    return FBFactory.auth().$requireAuth();
                }]
            }
        });

    $urlRouterProvider.otherwise('/');
```

We will set up `FBFactory` and `Loader` shown in the preceding snippet while working with the factory.

Do notice that we have updated the otherwise route to `'/'`.

Now, if `$requireAuth` rejects the promise, that means the user is in a page that needs authentication, and he/she does not have it. So, we need to add a listener when this happens and redirect the user to the login page. When Firebase Auth rejects the promise, it fires a `stateChangeError` event. We will be listening to this event in our `run` method and then redirect the user to the home page.

Add the following `stateChangeError` event to the `run` method, inside the `$ionicPlatform.ready` method:

```
$rootScope.$on('$stateChangeError', function(event, toState,
toParams, fromState, fromParams, error) {
if (error === 'AUTH_REQUIRED') {
    $state.go('main');
}
});
```

Do not forget to inject `$rootScope` and `$state` as a dependency to the `run` method.

Next, we will use `$ionicConfigProvider` to set up a few defaults.

Add `$ionicConfigProvider` as a dependency to the `config` method. Add the following snippet inside the `config` method, before we start initializing the routes:

```
$ionicConfigProvider.backButton.previousTitleText(false);
$ionicConfigProvider.views.transition('platform');
$ionicConfigProvider.navBar.alignTitle('center');
```

The preceding configuration is really not necessary. It is just an example of how you can use `$ionicConfigProvider` in a real-time app.

Setting up services/factories

Now that we have the main app set up, we will be working with the factories that are needed. We will be adding the factories in `www/js/services.js` file. You can open that file and clear its contents.

First, we will add the `chatapp.services` module and a factory to interact with the `localStorage`:

```
angular.module('chatapp.services', [])

.factory('LocalStorage', [function() {
    return {
        set: function(key, value) {
            return localStorage.setItem(key,
JSON.stringify(value));
        },

        get: function(key) {
            return JSON.parse(localStorage.getItem(key));
        },

        remove: function(key) {
            return localStorage.removeItem(key);
        },
    };
}])
```

Next, we will add another factory that manages the Ionic loading service for us:

```
.factory('Loader', ['$ionicLoading', '$timeout',
    function($ionicLoading, $timeout) {

        return {
            show: function(text) {
                //console.log('show', text);
                $ionicLoading.show({
                    content: (text || 'Loading...'),
                    noBackdrop: true
                });
            },

            hide: function() {
                //console.log('hide');
                $ionicLoading.hide();
            },

            toggle: function(text, timeout) {
                var that = this;
                that.show(text);

                $timeout(function() {
                    that.hide();
                }, timeout || 3000);
            }
        };
    }
])
```

We will also create a factory to interact with Firebase:

```
.factory('FBFactory', ['$firebaseAuth', '$firebaseArray', 'FBURL',
'Utils',
    function($firebaseAuth, $firebaseArray, FBURL, Utils) {
        return {
            auth: function() {
                var FBRef = new Firebase(FBURL);
                return $firebaseAuth(FBRef);
            },
            olUsers: function() {
                var olUsersRef = new Firebase(FBURL +
'onlineUsers');
                return $firebaseArray(olUsersRef);
```

```
            },
            chatBase: function() {
                var chatRef = new Firebase(FBURL + 'chats');
                return $firebaseArray(chatRef);
            },
            chatRef: function(loggedInUser, OtherUser) {
                var chatRef = new Firebase(FBURL + 'chats/chat_' +
Utils.getHash(OtherUser, loggedInUser));
                return $firebaseArray(chatRef);
            }
        };
    }
])
```

In the preceding snippet, `olUsers` points the Firebase reference to `https://ionic-chat-app.firebaseio.com/onlineUsers`, `chatBase` to `https://ionic-chat-app.firebaseio.com/chats`, and `chatRef` to the dynamically created end points between two users.

We will also have a user factory that stores the user information, online users, and a presence ID. Presence ID is the object ID of the entry made in to `https://ionic-chat-app.firebaseio.com/onlineUsers`. This presence ID will be used to delete the object from the `onlineUsers` collection, when the user goes offline:

```
.factory('UserFactory', ['LocalStorage', function(LocalStorage) {

    var userKey = 'user',
        presenceKey = 'presence',
        olUsersKey = 'onlineusers';

    return {
        onlineUsers: {},
        setUser: function(user) {
            return LocalStorage.set(userKey, user);
        },
        getUser: function() {
            return LocalStorage.get(userKey);
        },
        cleanUser: function() {
            return LocalStorage.remove(userKey);
        },
        setOLUsers: function(users) {
            // >> we need to store users as pure object.
```

```
            // else we lose the $ method of FB.

            // >> sometime, onlineUsers becomes null while
            // navigating between tabs, so we save a copy in LS
            LocalStorage.set(olUsersKey, users);
            return this.onlineUsers = users;
        },
        getOLUsers: function() {
            if (this.onlineUsers && this.onlineUsers.length > 0) {
                return this.onlineUsers
            } else {
                return LocalStorage.get(olUsersKey);
            }
        },
        cleanOLUsers: function() {
            LocalStorage.remove(olUsersKey);
            return onlineUsers = null;
        },
        setPresenceId: function(presenceId) {
            return LocalStorage.set(presenceKey, presenceId);
        },
        getPresenceId: function() {
            return LocalStorage.get(presenceKey);
        },
        cleanPresenceId: function() {
            return LocalStorage.remove(presenceKey);
        },
    };
}])
```

Finally a few utility methods:

```
.factory('Utils', [function() {
    return {
        escapeEmailAddress: function(email) {
            if (!email) return false
                // Replace '.' (not allowed in a Firebase key)
with ','
            email = email.toLowerCase();
            email = email.replace(/\./g, ',');
            return email.trim();
        },
        unescapeEmailAddress: function(email) {
            if (!email) return false
            email = email.toLowerCase();
```

```
            email = email.replace(/,/g, '.');
            return email.trim();
        },
        getHash: function(chatToUser, loggedInUser) {
            var hash = '';
            if (chatToUser > loggedInUser) {
                hash = this.escapeEmailAddress(chatToUser) + '_' +
this.escapeEmailAddress(loggedInUser);
            } else {
                hash = this.escapeEmailAddress(loggedInUser) + '_'
+ this.escapeEmailAddress(chatToUser);
            }
            return hash;
        },
        getBase64ImageFromInput: function(input, callback) {
            window.resolveLocalFileSystemURL(input,
function(fileEntry) {
                    fileEntry.file(function(file) {
                            var reader = new FileReader();
                            reader.onloadend = function(evt) {
                                callback(null, evt.target.result);
                            };
                            reader.readAsDataURL(file);
                        },
                        function() {
                            callback('failed', null);
                        });
                },
                function() {
                    callback('failed', null);
                });
        }
    };
}])
```

The `getHash` is the method that takes in two e-mail addresses and returns a hash. This will be used to construct the dynamic endpoint. The `getBase64ImageFromInput` is used to convert an image to a base64-encoded string, to be saved in Firebase.

With this, we complete the setup of our factories.

Setting up a map directive

Since we are letting users share their current location, we need a map directive to display the coordinates in a presentable manner. To do that, I have borrowed the `map` directive from the maps template (`https://github.com/driftyco/ionic-starter-maps/blob/master/js/directives.js`) and modified it as necessary.

Create a new file named `directives.js` inside the `www/js` folder. Update the `www/js/directives` as follows:

```
angular.module('chatapp.directives', [])

.directive('map', function() {
    return {
        restrict: 'E',
        scope: {
            onCreate: '&'
        },
        link: function($scope, $element, $attr) {
            function initialize() {
                var lat = $attr.lat || 43.07493;
                var lon = $attr.lon || -89.381388;

                var myLatlng = new google.maps.LatLng(lat, lon);
                var mapOptions = {
                    center: myLatlng,
                    zoom: 16,
                    mapTypeId: google.maps.MapTypeId.ROADMAP
                };

                if ($attr.inline) {
                    mapOptions.disableDefaultUI = true;
                    mapOptions.disableDoubleClickZoom = true;
                    mapOptions.draggable = true;
                    mapOptions.mapMaker = true;
                    mapOptions.mapTypeControl = false;
                    mapOptions.panControl = false;
                    mapOptions.rotateControl = false;
                }

                var map = new google.maps.Map($element[0],
mapOptions);

                // custom function to manage markers
                map.__setMarker = function(map, lat, lon) {
```

```
                    var marker = new google.maps.Marker({
                        map: map,
                        position: new google.maps.LatLng(lat, lon)
                    });
                }

                $scope.onCreate({
                    map: map
                });

                map.__setMarker(map, lat, lon);
            }

            if (document.readyState === 'complete') {
                initialize();
            } else {
                google.maps.event.addDomListener(window, 'load',
initialize);
            }
        }
    }
});
```

The modification I have made is to adapt the `map` directive to work with the inline display of the map in chat messages using the inline attribute as well as in the modal popup. I have also added support for displaying a marker.

Setting up controllers

Now, we will work on controllers for each route. Open `www/js/controller.js` and clear all the code inside it. We will add a new module named `chatapp.controllers`:

```
angular.module('chatapp.controllers', [])
```

We will set up a `run` method on the `chatapp.controllers` module. The `run` method will consist of the logic needed for monitoring incoming chats. We make a connection with the chats base URL and keep listening for changes on it. If there is a new chat added or chat content is changed, we will identify whether the new chat message is for the current user. If it is, we broadcast a `newChatHistory` event that we will use in the history tab, to show new chats:

```
.run(['FBFactory', '$rootScope', 'UserFactory', 'Utils',
    function(FBFactory, $rootScope, UserFactory, Utils) {

        $rootScope.chatHistory = [];
```

```
        var baseChatMonitor = FBFactory.chatBase();
        var unwatch = baseChatMonitor.$watch(function(snapshot) {
            var user = UserFactory.getUser();

            if (!user) return;

            if (snapshot.event == 'child_added' || snapshot.event
== 'child_changed') {
                var key = snapshot.key;
                if (key.indexOf(Utils.escapeEmailAddress(user.email))
>= 0) {
                    var otherUser = snapshot.key.replace(/_/g,
'').replace('chat', '').replace(Utils.escapeEmailAddress(user.email),
'');
                    if ($rootScope.chatHistory.join('_').
indexOf(otherUser) === -1) {
                        $rootScope.chatHistory.push(otherUser);
                    }
                    $rootScope.$broadcast('newChatHistory');
                    /*
                    *  TODO: PRACTICE
                    *  Fire a local notification when a new chat
comes in.
                    */
                }
            }
        });
    }
])
```

To get a good idea of all the pieces, I have left the local notification section un-implemented. Your mission, if you choose to accept it, is to implement local notification whenever there is an incoming chat to the current user. The notification should consist of the message and the user it is from. When tapped on the notification, it will take the current user to the chat screen between the two users.

Next, we will be working with `MainCtrl`. The `MainCtrl` is linked with the main view of our application. Add the following `MainCtrl` definition to the `www/js/controllers.js` file after the `run` method:

```
.controller('MainCtrl', ['$scope', 'Loader', '$ionicPlatform',
'$cordovaOauth', 'FBFactory', 'GOOGLEKEY', 'GOOGLEAUTHSCOPE',
'UserFactory', 'currentAuth', '$state',
```

```
    function($scope, Loader, $ionicPlatform, $cordovaOauth,
FBFactory, GOOGLEKEY, GOOGLEAUTHSCOPE, UserFactory, currentAuth,
$state) {
        $ionicPlatform.ready(function() {
            Loader.hide();
            $scope.$on('showChatInterface', function($event,
authData) {
                if (authData.google) {
                    authData = authData.google;
                }
                UserFactory.setUser(authData);
                Loader.toggle('Redirecting..');
                $scope.onlineusers = FBFactory.olUsers();

                $scope.onlineusers.$loaded().then(function() {
                    $scope
                        .onlineusers
                        .$add({
                            picture:
authData.cachedUserProfile.picture,
                            name: authData.displayName,
                            email: authData.email,
                            login: Date.now()
                        })
                        .then(function(ref) {
                            UserFactory.setPresenceId(ref.key());
UserFactory.setOLUsers($scope.onlineusers);
                            $state.go('tab.dash');
                        });
                });
                return;
            });

            if (currentAuth) {
                $scope.$broadcast('showChatInterface',
currentAuth.google);
            }

            $scope.loginWithGoogle = function() {
                Loader.show('Authenticating..');
                $cordovaOauth.google(GOOGLEKEY, GOOGLEAUTHSCOPE).
then(function(result) {
                    FBFactory.auth()
                        .$authWithOAuthToken('google',
result.access_token)
```

```
                        .then(function(authData) {
                            $scope.$broadcast('showChatInterface',
authData);
                        }, function(error) {
                            Loader.toggle(error);
                        });
                    }, function(error) {
                        Loader.toggle(error);
                    });
                }

            });
        }
])
```

As soon as the promise is resolved in the route's resolve method, `MainCtrl` will be invoked, passing `currentAuth` as one of the dependencies. The `currentAuth` will be equal to the `auth` object, if the user is already logged in; otherwise, it will be `null`.

We register a `showChatInterface` event on the `$scope`. This method is invoked when the user is already logged in (that is, `currentAuth` is not `null`) or when the user explicitly logs in. When this event is fired, we save the user data to `localStorage` using the `UserFactory.setUser` method. Once that is done, we make a request to get all the users who are online. Once we get the list, we add the current user's details to the `onlineUsers` collection. Once that is also done, we `setPresenceId` and `setOLUsers` in `localStorage` and redirect the user to the chat interface page.

The `$scope.loginWithGoogle` method will be invoked when the user clicks on the **Login with Google** button. I have included both Firebase Auth as well as the `cordovaOauth` plugin to show how you can work with both of them together. If you feel this is complicated, you can directly use Firebase Auth to login the user, instead of fetching the token from `cordovaOauth` and authenticating the user with the Firebase `$authWithOAuthToken`.

Once the authentication is successful, we will broadcast a `showChatInterface`, which will take care of saving data and redirecting the user.

As part of this example, I have implemented only Google OAuth. For practice, you can integrate other oAuth providers.

Once the user is successfully logged in, he/she will be redirected to the tabbed interface page. The default tab is the dashboard tab, which is linked with `DashCtrl`.

The purpose of `DashCtrl` is to get a list of users who are online and display them. The required code for `DashCtrl` will be:

```
.controller('DashCtrl', ['$scope', 'UserFactory',
'$ionicPlatform', '$state', '$ionicHistory',
    function($scope, UserFactory, $ionicPlatform, $state,
$ionicHistory) {
        $ionicPlatform.ready(function() {
            $ionicHistory.clearHistory();

            $scope.users = UserFactory.getOLUsers();
            $scope.currUser = UserFactory.getUser();
            var presenceId = UserFactory.getPresenceId();

            $scope.redir = function(user) {
                $state.go('chat-detail', {
                    otherUser: user
                });
            }

        });
    }
])
```

I have added the `$ionicHistory.clearHistory` method in the preceding controller. This is to make sure that, when the user has successfully logged in and is on the tabs page, pressing the hardware back button should not take the user to the login page but rather should exit the app. So, using the `$ionicHistory.clearHistory` method we clear the history and the hardware back button action will close the app.

Next we will work with the middle tab, where the chat history is displayed. Since this is an example app, we are not explicitly maintaining any profile of the user. We are picking the values from the auth object and building the UI. We will be using the same logic to show the user information in the history tab. This user object data is retrieved from the list of online users.

The code for `ChatsCtrl` looks as follows. Add the following code after `DashCtrl`:

```
.controller('ChatsCtrl', ['$scope', '$rootScope', 'UserFactory',
'Utils', '$ionicPlatform', '$state', function($scope, $rootScope,
UserFactory, Utils, $ionicPlatform, $state) {
    $ionicPlatform.ready(function() {
        $scope.$on('$ionicView.enter', function(scopes, states) {
            var olUsers = UserFactory.getOLUsers();
```

```
            $scope.chatHistory = [];
            $scope.$on('AddNewChatHistory', function() {
                var ch = $rootScope.chatHistory,
                    matchedUser;
                for (var i = 0; i < ch.length; i++) {
                    for (var j = 0; j < olUsers.length; j++) {
                        if (Utils.escapeEmailAddress(olUsers[j].email)
== ch[i]) {
                            matchedUser = olUsers[j];
                        }
                    };
                    if (matchedUser) {
                        $scope.chatHistory.push(matchedUser);
                    } else {
                        $scope.chatHistory.push({
                            email: Utils.unescapeEmailAddress(ch[i]),
                            name: 'User Offline'
                        })
                    }
                };

            });
            $scope.redir = function(user) {
                $state.go('chat-detail', {
                    otherUser: user
                });
            }
            $rootScope.$on('newChatHistory', function($event) {
                $scope.$broadcast('AddNewChatHistory');
            });
            $scope.$broadcast('AddNewChatHistory');
        })
    });
}])
```

> Do notice the `matchedUser` object. This will be set to an offline value when the user is not present in the online users list but the current user has already had an interaction with the other user, for the same reasons mentioned earlier.

Here, we keep listening to the `newChatHistory` event that we are broadcasting in the `run` method. Finally, if the current logged in user taps on a username, we redirect the app to the `chat-detail` view.

Next is the most active page of the application, the page where the users interact with each other. This controller is too big to be shown all at once. Hence, I will split the controller into logical chunks and explain it.

First, we add the controller definition and its dependencies:

```
 .controller('ChatDetailCtrl', ['$scope', 'Loader',
'$ionicPlatform', '$stateParams', 'UserFactory', 'FBFactory',
'$ionicScrollDelegate', '$cordovaImagePicker', 'Utils',
'$timeout', '$ionicActionSheet', '$cordovaCapture',
'$cordovaGeolocation', '$ionicModal',
    function($scope, Loader, $ionicPlatform, $stateParams,
UserFactory, FBFactory, $ionicScrollDelegate, $cordovaImagePicker,
Utils, $timeout, $ionicActionSheet, $cordovaCapture,
$cordovaGeolocation, $ionicModal) {
$ionicPlatform.ready(function() {
Loader.show('Establishing Connection...');
          // controller code here..
});
}])
```

That is quite a lot of dependencies!

Next, we fetch `chatToUser` and add it to the scope. Once that is done, we connect to the dynamic Firebase endpoint. The following code (till we end this controller) will go inside `ChatDetailCtrl`:

```
$scope.chatToUser = $stateParams.otherUser;
$scope.chatToUser = JSON.parse($scope.chatToUser);
$scope.user = UserFactory.getUser();

$scope.messages = FBFactory.chatRef($scope.user.email,
$scope.chatToUser.email);
$scope.messages.$loaded().then(function() {
   Loader.hide();
   $ionicScrollDelegate.scrollBottom(true);
});
```

We use the `$ionicScrollDelegate` service to scroll the viewing pane to the bottom/last message. Next, we add a method that will add a new chat message to Firebase:

```
function postMessage(msg, type, map) {
                var d = new Date();
                d = d.toLocaleTimeString().replace(/:\d+ /, ' ');
                map = map || null;
                $scope.messages.$add({
```

```
                content: msg,
                time: d,
                type: type,
                from: $scope.user.email,
                map: map
            });

            $scope.chatMsg = '';
            $ionicScrollDelegate.scrollBottom(true);
        }
```

When the user enters a text and clicks on **Send**, we call the `sendMessage` method:

```
$scope.sendMessage = function() {
            if (!$scope.chatMsg) return;
            var msg = '<p>' + $scope.user.cachedUserProfile.name
+ ' says : <br/>' + $scope.chatMsg + '</p>';
            var type = 'text';
            postMessage(msg, type);
        }
```

To show the list of options such as **Share Picture**, `Take Picture`, and `Share My Location`, we will be using the Action Sheet service:

```
$scope.showActionSheet = function() {
            var hideSheet = $ionicActionSheet.show({
                buttons: [{
                    text: 'Share Picture'
                }, {
                    text: 'Take Picture'
                }, {
                    text: 'Share My Location'
                }],
                cancelText: 'Cancel',
                cancel: function() {
                    // add cancel code..
                    Loader.hide();
                },
                buttonClicked: function(index) {
                  // Clicked on Share Picture
                    if (index === 0) {
                        Loader.show('Processing...');
                        var options = {
                            maximumImagesCount: 1
                        };
                        $cordovaImagePicker.getPictures(options)
```

```
                                        .then(function(results) {
                                            if (results.length > 0) {
                                                var imageData = results[0];
                                                Utils.getBase64ImageFromInput(
imageData, function(err, base64Img)
{

                                                    //Process the image
string.

                                                    postMessage('<p>' +
$scope.user.cachedUserProfile.name + ' posted : <br/><img
class="chat-img" src="' + base64Img + '">', 'img');
                                                    Loader.hide();
                                                });
                                            }
                                        }, function(error) {
                                            // error getting photos
                                            console.log('error', error);
                                            Loader.hide();
                                        });
                                }
// Clicked on Take Picture
else if (index === 1) {
                                    Loader.show('Processing...');
                                    var options = {
                                        limit: 1
                                    };


$cordovaCapture.captureImage(options).then(function(imageData) {



                                        Utils.getBase64ImageFromInput(imageDa
ta[0].fullPath, function(err,
base64Img) {
                                            //Process the image string.
                                            postMessage('<p>' + $scope.user.
cachedUserProfile.name + ' posted : <br/><img class="chat-img" src="'
+ base64Img + '">', 'img');
                                            Loader.hide();
                                        });
                                    }, function(err) {
                                        console.log(err);
                                        Loader.hide();
                                    });
                                }
```

```
// clicked on Share my location
else if (index === 2) {
                            $ionicModal.fromTemplateUrl('templates/
map-modal.html', {
                                scope: $scope,
                                animation: 'slide-in-up'
                            }).then(function(modal) {
                                $scope.modal = modal;
                                $scope.modal.show();
                                $timeout(function() {
                                    $scope.centerOnMe();
                                }, 2000);
                            });
                        }
                        return true;
                    }
                });
            }
```

When an option is selected from the Action Sheet and if the:

- `index = 0`: We invoke `$cordovaImagePicker` service and let the user choose one image. Once the user chooses an image, we invoke the `Utils.getBase64ImageFromInput` method passing in the image, to get the base64 string back. Then we send this message to Firebase using the `postMessage` method.
- `index = 1`: We invoke the `$cordovaCapture` service `captureImage` method to take a picture, convert it to a base64 string, and save it to Firebase.
- `index = 2`: We invoke an Ionic Modal that will consist of the map, pointing to the current location of the user.

To work with the map in the popup, we will need a few methods to be defined on the scope:

```
$scope.mapCreated = function(map) {
                $scope.map = map;
            };

            $scope.closeModal = function() {
                $scope.modal.hide();
            };

            $scope.centerOnMe = function() {
                if (!$scope.map) {
```

```
                    return;
                }

                Loader.show('Getting current location...');
                var posOptions = {
                    timeout: 10000,
                    enableHighAccuracy: false
                };
                $cordovaGeolocation.getCurrentPosition(posOptions).
then(function
(pos) {
                    $scope.user.pos = {
                        lat: pos.coords.latitude,
                        lon: pos.coords.longitude
                    };
                    $scope.map.setCenter(new google.maps.
LatLng($scope.user.pos.lat, $scope.user.pos.lon));
                    $scope.map.__setMarker($scope.map,
$scope.user.pos.lat, $scope.user.pos.lon);
                    Loader.hide();

                }, function(error) {
                    alert('Unable to get location, please enable
GPS to continue');
                    Loader.hide();
                    $scope.modal.hide();
                });
            };

            $scope.selectLocation = function() {
                var pos = $scope.user.pos;

                var map = {
                    lat: pos.lat,
                    lon: pos.lon
                };
                var type = 'geo';

                postMessage('<p>' + $scope.user.cachedUserProfile.name
+ ' shared : <br/>', type,
map);
                $scope.modal.hide();
            }
```

The `mapCreated` method will be called when the map is created. The `closeModal` method will be used to close the pop-up modal. The `centerOnMe` method will be automatically called once the map is initialized. This method uses the `$cordovaGeolocation.getCurrentPosition` method to fetch the user's current position. Once it gets the position, it will place a marker at that point. If the `$cordovaGeolocation.getCurrentPosition` method is not able to get the location, we ask the user to enable GPS.

When you see the preceding functionality in action, you will get a better idea as to what is happening.

Finally, `AccountCtrl`, which is linked with `Tab3`. This controller has a method to manage user logout:

```
.controller('AccountCtrl', ['$scope', 'FBFactory', 'UserFactory',
'$state',
    function($scope, FBFactory, UserFactory, $state) {

        $scope.logout = function() {
            FBFactory.auth().$unauth();
            UserFactory.cleanUser();
            UserFactory.cleanOLUsers();
            // remove presence
            var onlineUsers = UserFactory.getOLUsers();
            if (onlineUsers && onlineUsers.$getRecord) {
                var presenceId = UserFactory.getPresenceId();
                var user = onlineUsers.$getRecord();
                onlineUsers.$remove(user);
            }
            UserFactory.cleanPresenceId();
            $state.go('main');
        }

    }
]);
```

Here, you can implement preferences such as **Show notification when the app is open**, **Play sound**, and so on.

Setting up templates

Now that we are done with all the JavaScript code, we will implement the templates for each view. All the views are very logically implemented, and quite simple to understand.

First we will create a file named `main.html` in the `www/templates` folder. The contents of `www/templates/main.html` will be:

```
<ion-view view-title="IONIC CHAT APP" cache-view="false">
    <ion-content>
        <ion-slide-box does-continue="true" auto-play="true" show-
pager="false">
            <ion-slide>
                <label class="t-r">Share Photos seamlessly between
family & Friends</label>
                <img
src="http://placeimg.com/640/480/tech/grayscale" />
            </ion-slide>
            <ion-slide>
                <label class="c-c">Simple One click login to start
the fun!!</label>
                <img
src="http://placeimg.com/640/480/people/sepia" />
            </ion-slide>
            <ion-slide>
                <label class="b-r">Notify people where you are
with one click location sender</label>
                <img src="http://placeimg.com/640/480/tech/sepia"
/>
            </ion-slide>
        </ion-slide-box>
        <div class="text-center padding">
            <h3>The Super chat app, lets you connect with your
friends, share images, audio, video, geo-location and ofcourse
texts!</h3>
            <button class="button button-dark" ng-
click="loginWithGoogle()">
                Login With Google
            </button>
        </div>
    </ion-content>
</ion-view>
```

Next, the `www/templates/tabs.html` file. Replace the content inside this file with the following content:

```
<ion-tabs class="tabs-striped tabs-top tabs-background-positive
tabs-color-light">
  <!-- Dashboard Tab -->
  <ion-tab title="IONIC CHAT APP" icon-off="ion-ios-pulse" icon-
on="ion-ios-pulse-strong" href="#/tab/dash">
    <ion-nav-view name="tab-dash"></ion-nav-view>
  </ion-tab>

  <!-- Chats Tab -->
  <ion-tab title="IONIC CHAT APP" icon-off="ion-ios-chatboxes-
outline" icon-on="ion-ios-chatboxes" href="#/tab/chats">
    <ion-nav-view name="tab-chats"></ion-nav-view>
  </ion-tab>

  <!-- Account Tab -->
  <ion-tab title="IONIC CHAT APP" icon-off="ion-ios-gear-outline"
icon-on="ion-ios-gear" href="#/tab/account">
    <ion-nav-view name="tab-account"></ion-nav-view>
  </ion-tab>
</ion-tabs>
```

Next, `www/templates/tab-dash.html`; replace the content inside this file with the following content:

```
<ion-view view-title="IONIC CHAT APP">
    <ion-content>
        <ion-list>
            <ion-item ng-show="users.length == 1">
                <h3 class="text-center padding">Looks like no one
is online</h3>
            </ion-item>
            <ion-item class="item-avatar item-icon-right" ng-
repeat="user in users | filter:search:user" ng-if="user.email !=
currUser.email" ng-click="redir('{{user}}')">
                <img ng-src="{{user.picture}}">
                <h2>{{user.name}}</h2>
                <p>{{user.email}}</p>
                <i class="icon ion-chevron-right icon-
accessory"></i>
            </ion-item>
        </ion-list>
    </ion-content>
</ion-view>
```

Next, the second tab, `www/templates/tab-chats.html`; replace the content inside this file with the following content:

```
<ion-view view-title="IONIC CHAT APP">
    <ion-content>
        <ion-list>
            <ion-item ng-show="chatHistory.length == 0">
                <h3 class="text-center padding">Looks like there
is no chat history</h3>
            </ion-item>
            <ion-item class="item-icon-right item-icon-left" ng-
class="{'item-avatar' : user.picture}" ng-repeat="user in
chatHistory | filter:search:user" ng-if="user.email !=
currUser.email" ng-click="redir('{{user}}')">
                <img ng-src="{{user.picture}}" ng-
show="user.picture">
                <h2>{{user.name}}</h2>
                <p>{{user.email}}</p>
                <i class="icon ion-chevron-right icon-
accessory"></i>
            </ion-item>
        </ion-list>
    </ion-content>
</ion-view>
```

Now the third tab, `www/templates/tab-account.html`; replace the content inside this file with the following content:

```
<ion-view view-title="IONIC CHAT APP">
    <ion-content has-header="true">
        <ion-list>
             <!-- Uncomment below if you would like to add
preferences to the app -->
            <!-- <ion-item>
                <ion-toggle ng-change="updatePreference()" ng-
model="preference.notification" toggle-class="toggle-positive">Show
Notifications</ion-toggle>
            </ion-item> -->
            <ion-item>
                <button class="button button-dark button-block"
ng-click="logout()">
                    Logout
                </button>
            </ion-item>
        </ion-list>
    </ion-content>
</ion-view>
```

The page where all the action happens, `www/templates/chat-detail.html`:

```
<ion-view view-title="{{chatToUser.name}}">
    <ion-pane>
        <ion-content class="has-header padding">
            <div class="button-bar">
                <a class="button button-calm" ui-
sref="tab.dash">Online Users</a>
                <a class="button button-calm" ui-
sref="tab.chats">Chat History</a>
            </div>
            <br>
            <ion-list>
                <ion-item ng-show="messages.length == 0">
                    <h3 class="text-center">No messages yet!</h3>
                </ion-item>
                <ion-item class="item-avatar" ng-repeat="message
in messages" ng-class="{left : message.from == user.email, right :
message.from != user.email}">
                    <img ng-src="{{user.cachedUserProfile.picture}}"
ng-if="message.from ==
user.email">
                    <img ng-src="{{chatToUser.picture}}" ng-
if="message.from != user.email">
                    <p ng-bind-html="message.content"></p>
                    <map inline="true" class="inline-map"
lat="{{message.map.lat}}" lon="{{message.map.lon}}" ng-
if="message.map.lat && message.map.lon">
                </ion-item>
                <div class="padding-bottom"></div>
            </ion-list>
        </ion-content>
        <ion-footer-bar class="bar-footer">
            <input class="footerInput" type="text"
placeholder="Enter Message" ng-model="chatMsg">
            <button class="button button-dark  icon-left ion-
paper-airplane" ng-click="sendMessage();"></button>
            <button class="button button-dark  icon-left ion-more"
ng-click="showActionSheet();"></button>
        </ion-footer-bar>
    </ion-pane>
</ion-view>
```

Do notice that we have used the map directive here, with the inline attribute set to `true`.

When the user selects the share location option from the action sheet, we show a modal with a map. Now, we will create that modal.

Create a new file named `map-modal.html` inside the `www/templates` folder and update it as follows:

```
<ion-modal-view>
    <ion-content scroll="false">
        <map on-create="mapCreated(map)"></map>
    </ion-content>
    <ion-footer-bar class="bar-stable">
        <a ng-click="selectLocation()" class="button button-icon
icon ion-checkmark">Share</a>
        <a ng-click="closeModal()" class="button button-icon icon
ion-close">Cancel</a>
    </ion-footer-bar>
</ion-modal-view>
```

Setting up SCSS

To complete the app, we will update `scss/ionic.app.scss` as follows with a few overrides and a few new styles.

First, we override four Ionic SCSS variables and then include the Ionic SCSS framework:

```
$positive: #1976D2 !default;
$font-family-base: 'Lato',
sans-serif !default;
$tabs-striped-off-opacity: 1 !default;

// The path for our ionicons font files, relative to the built CSS
in www/css
$ionicons-font-path: "../lib/ionic/fonts" !default;

// Include all of Ionic
@import "www/lib/ionic/scss/ionic";
```

Next, we will override styles related to the bar title and the slide box:

```
.bar .title {
    font-size: 21px;
}

.slider {
    background-color: #eee;
    min-height: 200px;
    max-height: 400px;
}

ion-slide img {
    width: 100%;
    height: 50%;
    margin: 0 auto;
    display: block;
    max-height: 350px;
    max-width: 500px;
}

.t-r {
    position: absolute;
    top: 5px;
    right: 0;
    margin: 20px;
    margin-right: 5px;
    margin-left: 25px;
    text-align: center;
    width: 84%;
}

.b-r {
    position: absolute;
    bottom: 5px;
    margin: 20px;
    right: 0px;
    margin-right: 5px;
    margin-left: 25px;
    text-align: center;
    width: 84%;
}

.c-c {
```

```
    position: absolute;
    top: 25%;
    margin: 20px;
    left: 0px;
    margin-right: 5px;
    margin-left: 25px;
    text-align: center;
    width: 84%;
}

ion-slide label {
    font-size: 21px;
    color: #333;
    padding: 5px;
    border-radius: 5px;
    background: linear-gradient(to right, #e2e2e2 0%, #dbdbdb 50%,
#d1d1d1 51%, #fefefe 100%);
    opacity: 0.8;
}
```

We add styles for the chat interface:

```
.footerInput {
    width: 77%;
}

.chat-img {
    width: 50%;
}

.left,
.right {
    width: 75%;
    clear: both;
    margin: 5px;
}

.left {
    float: left;
    text-align: left;
}

.right {
    float: right;
    text-align: right;
```

```
}

.usr-img {
    width: 48px;
}

map {
    display: block;
    width: 100%;
    height: 100%;
}

.inline-map {
    height: 200px;
    border: 1px solid #787878;
}

.scroll {
    height: 100%;
}
```

Testing the application

Now that we are done with building the application, we will add the iOS and Android platforms, to test the application. Run this:

```
ionic platform add ios
ionic platform add android
```

Next, we will emulate/run the app. I have a Samsung Galaxy Note 3 mobile as one device and an iOS emulator as another device.

I have tested the app by running it on the Android device and emulating it on the iOS emulator. You can do so the same way or you can use an Android emulator and an iOS emulator for test purposes as well. To launch/emulate the application, run this:

```
ionic run android -l -c
```

You can also use this:

```
ionic emulate ios -l -c
```

The `-l` flag sets up the live reload option when emulating/running on an emulator/device and the `-c` flag enables JavaScript console logs to be printed in a command prompt/terminal. These are the two of the most helpful flags while debugging Ionic apps on emulators/devices.

Once the app is launched in both the devices, you should see the main page of the app:

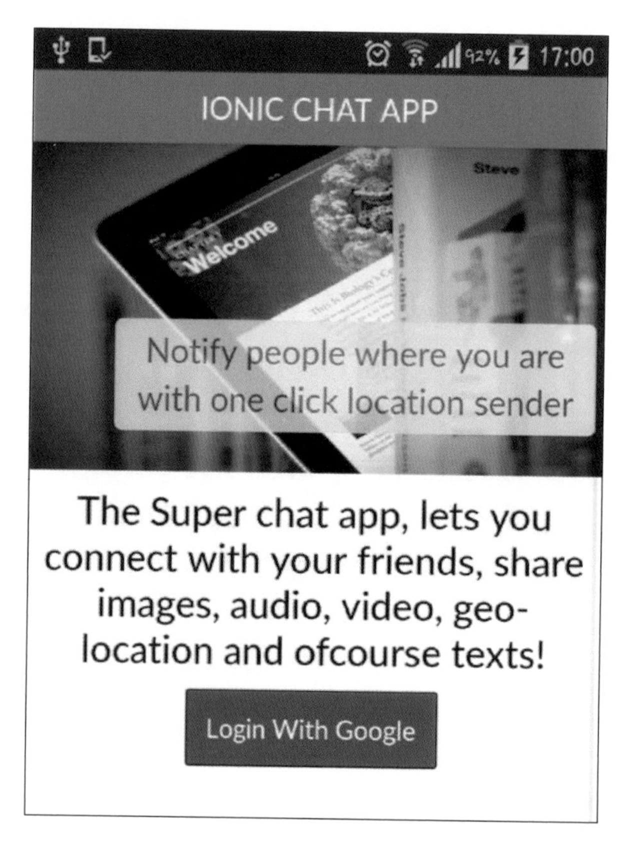

Once you click on **Login With Google**, you should see the Google authentication page:

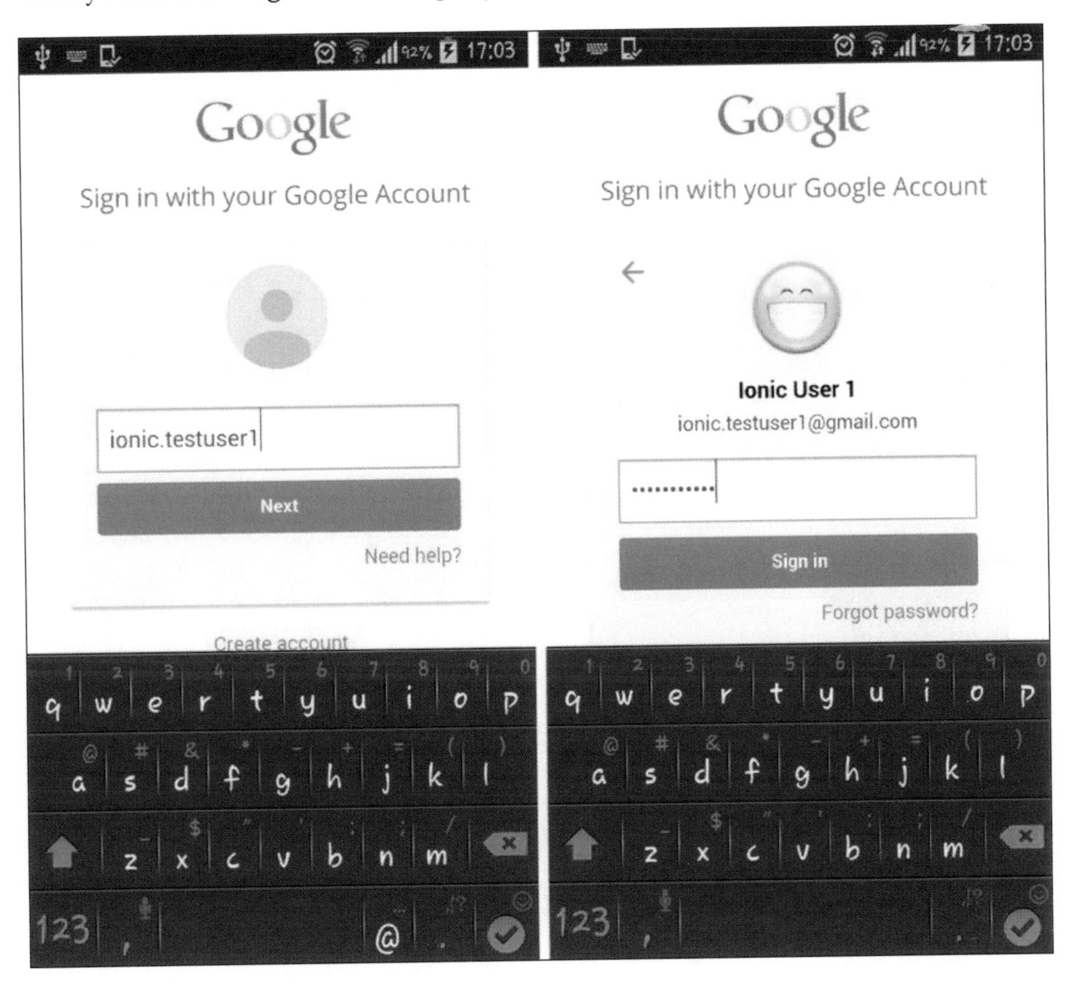

Once you are authenticated, you will be shown the consent screen (in the following screenshot, the one on the left-hand side) and, if you are a returning user, you will be asked for offline access (in the following screenshot, the one on the right-hand side):

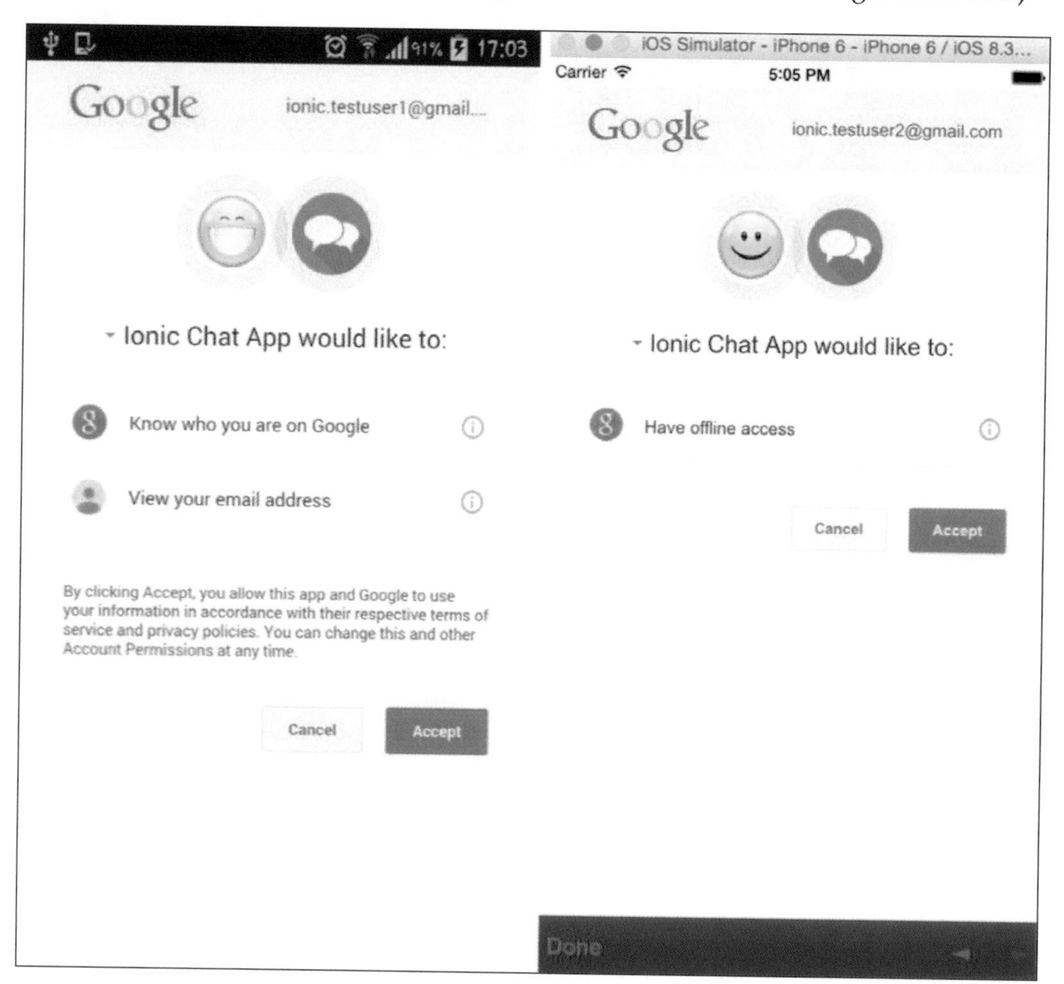

I have logged in with `ionic.testuser1@gmail.com` from my Android device and `ionic.testuser2@gmail.com` from the iOS emulator.

Once you have successfully logged in, you will be shown the dashboard tab with the list of online users as shown in the left-hand side screenshot in the following image. When you tap on the user, you will be taken to the chat screen shown in the right of the two following screenshots:

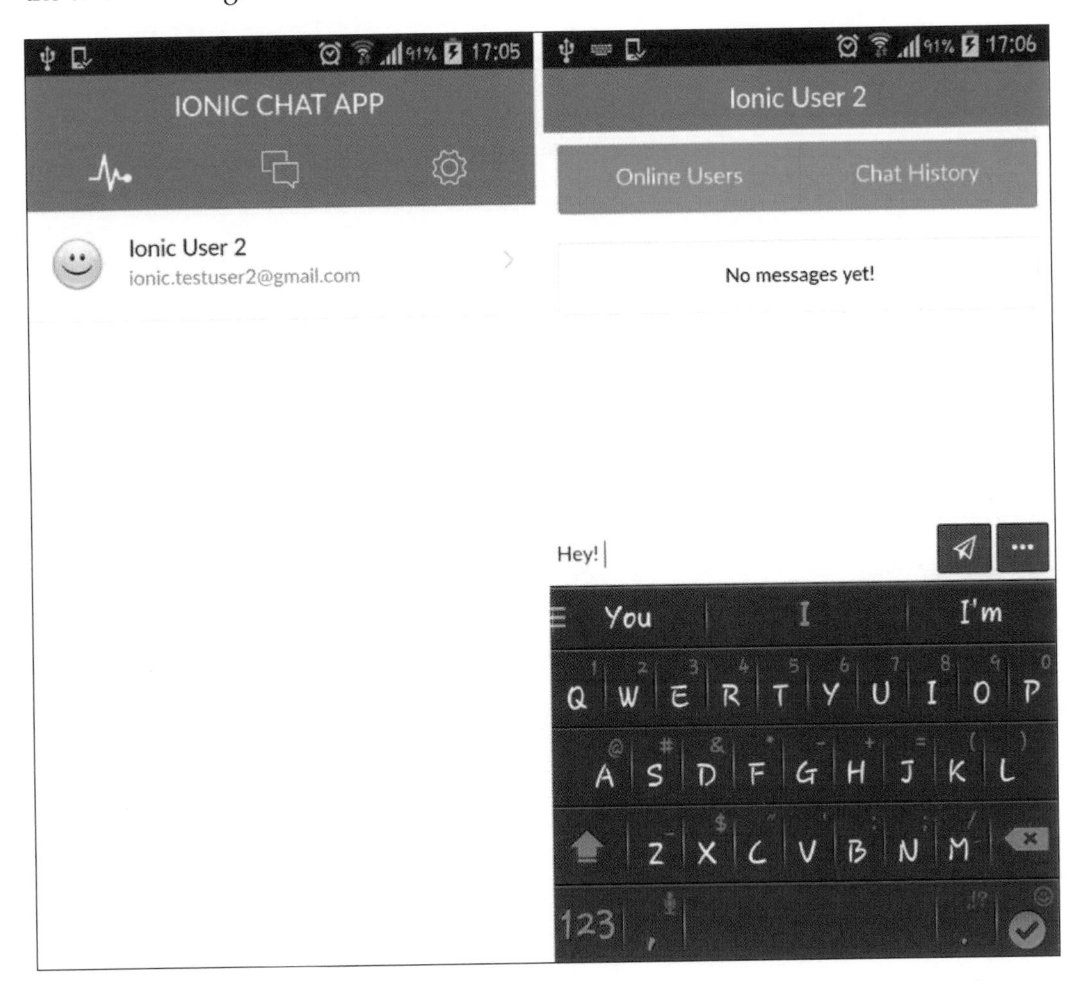

Users can chat with each other by typing in the text area and clicking on the (airplane) icon-button to send the message. Then, by clicking on (more) icon-button, the user can see an action sheet as shown in the left-hand side of the two following screenshots. Using the Action Sheet options, a user can share a picture with the other user, as shown in the right of the two screenshots:

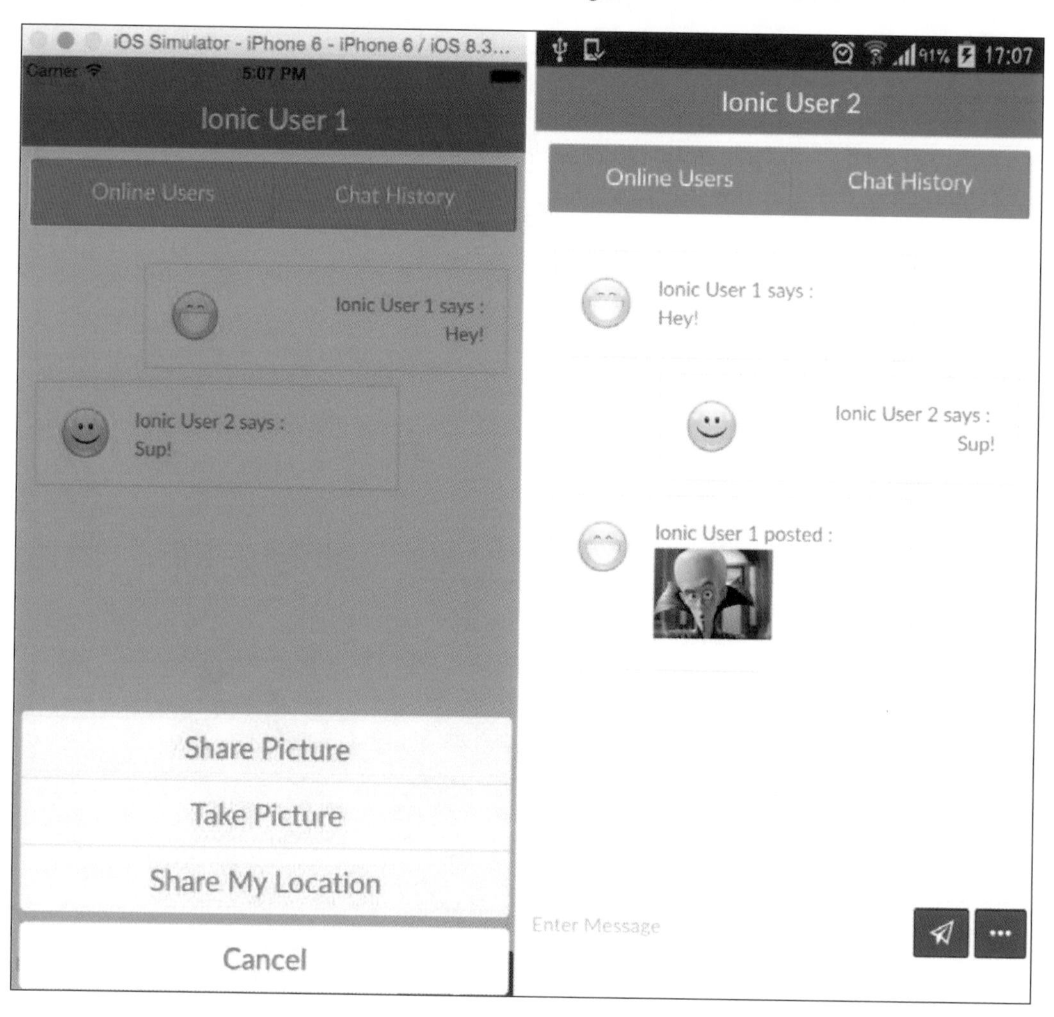

Users can also share their location by selecting the **Share My Location** option (the left-hand side of the two following screenshots). And the other user can see the same inline in the chat interface (the right-hand side screenshot):

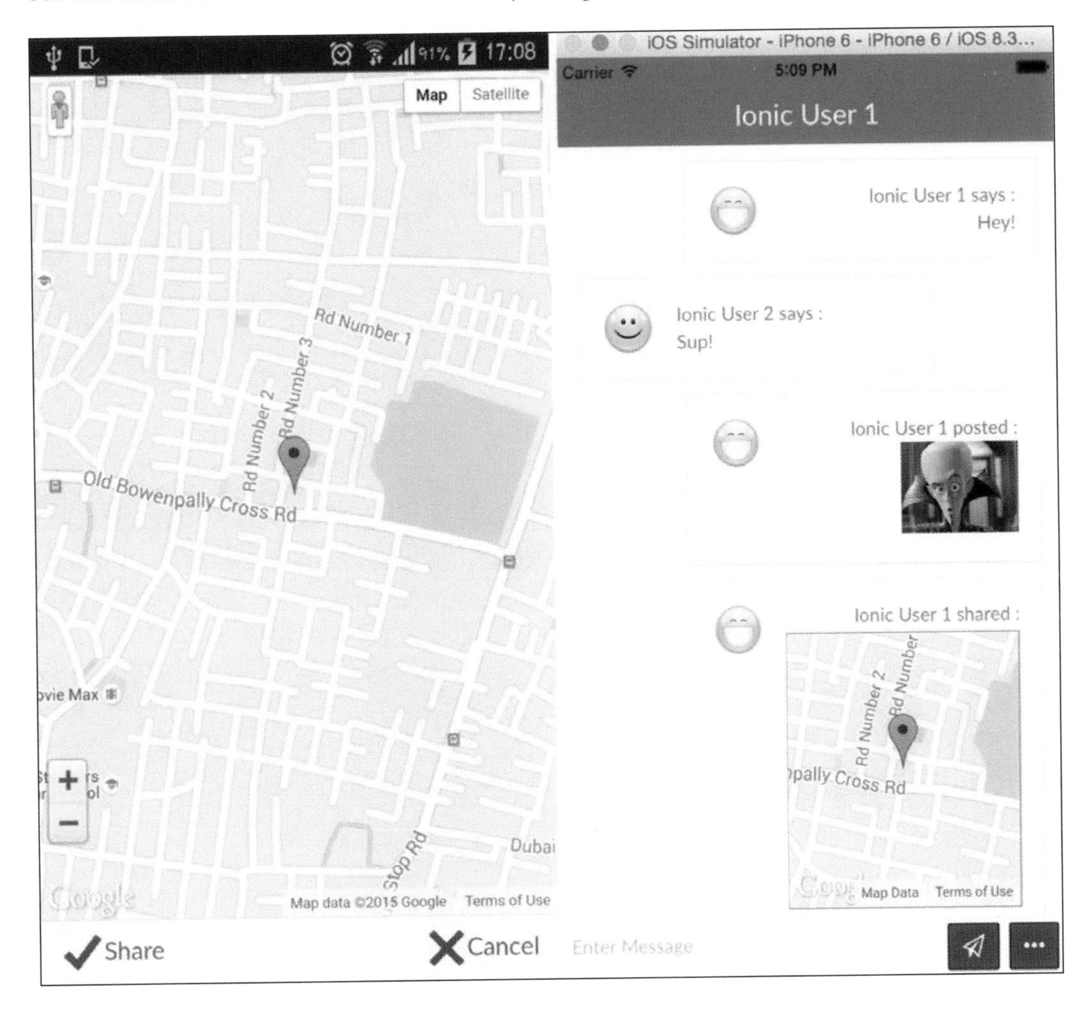

This is our simple Ionic chat application!

At any point, you can visit the Firebase forge to see how the data is stored. A quick snapshot of this looks like this:

Summary

In this chapter, we saw how to build a simple chat application using Ionic, Cordova, and Firebase. We started off by understanding the architecture, learned about Firebase and AngularFire, and then we integrated these in the Ionic app. We also saw the implementation of key concepts such as integrating Cordova plugins in an Ionic app and triggering various features on demand.

In the next chapter, the final one, we will see how to generate device-specific installers for an app like this and share it with the world.

9

Releasing the Ionic App

In this chapter, we will take a look at three ways of generating the installer for your Ionic app: one using the PhoneGap build service, the second using the Cordova CLI, and the third using the Ionic package service. We will be generating installers for both Android as well as iOS operating systems. The topics that we are going to look at in this chapter are as follows:

- Generating icons and splash screens
- Validating `config.xml`
- Using the PhoneGap build service to generate the installer
- Using Cordova CLI to generate the installer
- Using the Ionic package to generate the installer

Preparing the app for distribution

Now that we have successfully built our Ionic application, we want to distribute it. The best way to reach a wider audience is with the help of App Stores. But before we start distributing the app, we need our app-specific icons and splash screens integrated with the app. Splash screens are totally optional and depend on the product idea.

Setting up icons and splash screens

By default, when you run:

```
ionic platform add android
```

You can also run this:

```
ionic platform add ios
```

The CLI automatically adds a new folder named `resources`. You can check this out in the `ionic-chat-app` we created in *Chapter 8, Building a Messaging App*. The `resources` folder consists of Ionic, Android, or both subfolders, depending on the platforms you have added. In each of these folders, you will see two subfolders named icon and splash.

> If your app uses splash screens, you can keep the `splash` folder; if not, delete the folder to save a few bytes of your final app installer.

To generate icons, you can get a copy of your icon in a size greater than 1024 x 1024 and use any service such as:

- `http://icon.angrymarmot.org/`
- `http://makeappicon.com/`
- `http://www.appiconsizes.com/`

This is used to generate icons and splash screens for both Android and iOS.

> I have no association with any of the preceding services. You use these services at your own risk.

Alternatively, the best part is that you can place files named `icon.png` and `splash.png` in the `resources` folder and run this:

```
ionic resources
```

Ionic will take care of uploading your images to the cloud, then resizing them as required, and saving them back to the `resources` folder.

If you want to convert only icons, you can use this:

```
ionic resources --icon
```

If you just want to convert splash screens, you can use this:

```
ionic resources --splash
```

> You can use this PSD `http://code.ionicframework.com/resources/icon.psd` to design your icon and this PSD `http://code.ionicframework.com/resources/splash.psd` to design your splash screens.
>
> You can place an `icon.png` image, an `icon.psd` file, or an `icon.ai` file at the root of the resources folder and the ionic resources task will do its magic!

Updating the config.xml file

As we already know, `config.xml` is the single source of truth that the Cordova API trusts while generating the OS-specific installers. So, this file needs to be validated thoroughly before you start the deployment process. You can carry out the following checklist to make sure that everything is in place:

- Widget ID is defined and valid
- The widget version is defined and valid
- In the case of an app update, the widget version is updated and valid
- The name tag is defined and valid
- The description is defined and valid
- Author information is defined and valid
- Access tag is defined and is limited to the required domains (`https://github.com/apache/cordova-plugin-whitelist#network-request-whitelist`)
- Allow navigation is defined and is limited to the required domains (`https://github.com/apache/cordova-plugin-whitelist#navigation-whitelist`)
- Allow intent is defined and is limited to the required domains (`https://github.com/apache/cordova-plugin-whitelist#intent-whitelist`)
- Cross-check preferences
- Cross-check icons and the splash image path
- Cross-check permissions if any
- Update `index.html` with content security policy meta tag (`https://github.com/apache/cordova-plugin-whitelist#content-security-policy`)

Once the preceding points are verified, we will get started with the installer generation process.

For this chapter, you can chat with the author and clear your queries at GitHub (`https://github.com/learning-ionic/Chapter-9`).

The PhoneGap service

The first approach we are going to explore is generating app installers using the PhoneGap build service. This is perhaps the simplest way to generate installers for Android and iOS.

The process is quite simple. We upload the entire project to the PhoneGap build service and it takes care of building the installer.

If you think that uploading the complete project is not practical, you can upload the `www` folder only; but, you need to make the following changes:

Firstly, move the `config.xml` inside the `www` folder. Next, move the resources folder inside the `www` folder and, finally, update the path of the `resources` folder in `config.xml`.

If you find yourself doing this often, I would recommend using a build script to generate a `PhoneGap deployable` folder, with the preceding changes made to the project.

If you are planning to release your app only for Android, you do not need to do anything more. But if you are planning to generate iOS installers, you need to get an Apple Developer Account and follow the steps at `http://docs.build.phonegap.com/en_US/signing_signing-ios.md.html` to generate the required certificates.

You can also sign your Android app using the steps mentioned at `http://docs.build.phonegap.com/en_US/signing_signing-android.md.html`.

Once you have the required certificates and keys, you are good to start generating the installer. You can follow these steps to continue:

1. Create a PhoneGap account and login (`https://build.phonegap.com/plans`).
2. Next, navigate to `https://build.phonegap.com/people/edit`, select the Signing Keys tab, and upload iOS and Android certificates.

3. Next, navigate to `https://build.phonegap.com/apps` and click on **New App**. As part of the free plan, you can have as many apps as you want as long as they are pulled from Public Git repositories. You can also create one private app from a Private repo or by uploading a ZIP file.
4. To test the service, you can create a `.zip` file (not `.rar` or `.7z`) with the following folder structure:
    - `App` (root folder)

      `config.xml`

      `resources` (folder)

      `www` (folder)

      Then, update the path of resources in `config.xml`. This is all you need for the PhoneGap build to work.
5. Upload the ZIP file to `https://build.phonegap.com/apps` and click on Create app.

This process generally takes up to a minute to do its magic.

Sometimes, you may see unexpected errors from the build service. Wait for some time and try again. Depending on the load on the build servers, sometimes the build process may take a bit longer than expected.

Generating installers using the Cordova CLI

Now we are going to generate installers for Android and iOS using the Cordova CLI.

Android installer

First we are going to take a look at generating an installer for Android using the Cordova CLI. You can perform the following steps:

1. Open a new terminal/prompt at the root of the project.
2. Remove unwanted plugins:

```
ionic plugin rm cordova-plugin-console
```

3. Build the app in release mode:

```
cordova build --release android
```

This will generate an unsigned installer in release mode and place it at `/platforms/android/build/outputs/apk/android-release-unsigned.apk`.

4. Next, we need to create a signing key. If you already have a signing key or you are updating an existing app, you can continue to *Step 6*.
5. The private key is generated using the key tool. We will create a folder named `deploy-keys` and then save all these keys there. Once the folder is created, using the cd command, go to the folder and run this:

```
keytool -genkey -v -keystore app-name-release-key.keystore -
alias alias_name -keyalg RSA -keysize 2048 -validity 10000
```

You will be asked the following questions and you can respond as shown here:

```
→ deploy-keys keytool -genkey -v -keystore app-name-release-key.keystore -alias my-ionic-app -keyalg RSA -
keysize 2048 -validity 10000
Enter keystore password:
Re-enter new password:
What is your first and last name?
  [Unknown]:  Arvind Ravulavaru
What is the name of your organizational unit?
  [Unknown]:  Stack Engineering
What is the name of your organization?
  [Unknown]:  JackalStack Technologies Pvt. Ltd.
What is the name of your City or Locality?
  [Unknown]:  Hyderabad, India
What is the name of your State or Province?
  [Unknown]:  Andhra Pradesh
What is the two-letter country code for this unit?
  [Unknown]:  IN
Is CN=Arvind Ravulavaru, OU=Stack Engineering, O=JackalStack Technologies Pvt. Ltd., L="Hyderabad, India", S
T=Andhra Pradesh, C=IN correct?
  [no]:  YES

Generating 2,048 bit RSA key pair and self-signed certificate (SHA256withRSA) with a validity of 10,000 days
        for: CN=Arvind Ravulavaru, OU=Stack Engineering, O=JackalStack Technologies Pvt. Ltd., L="Hyderabad,
 India", ST=Andhra Pradesh, C=IN
Enter key password for <my-ionic-app>
        (RETURN if same as keystore password):
[Storing app-name-release-key.keystore]
```

If you lose this file or forget the alias or the password, you cannot submit updates to the app store, ever.

6. Optional step: You can copy `android-release-unsigned.apk` to the `deploy-keys` folder and run the following commands from there too. I am going to leave the files where they are.
7. Next, we sign the unsigned APK using the `jarsigner` tool:

```
jarsigner -verbose -sigalg SHA1withRSA -digestalg SHA1 -
keystore app-name-release-key.keystore
../platforms/android/build/outputs/apk/android-release-
unsigned.apk my-ionic-app
```

You will be asked for the passphrase, which you entered as the first step while creating the keystore. Once the signing process is completed, the existing `android-release-unsigned.apk` will be replaced with the signed version with the same name.

We run the preceding command from inside the `deploy-keys` folder.

8. Finally, we run the `zipalign` tool to optimize the APK.

```
zipalign -v 4 ../platforms/android/build/outputs/apk/android-
release-unsigned.apk my-ionic-app.apk
```

The preceding command will create `my-ionic-app.apk` in the `deploy-keys` folder.

Now, you can put this APK in the app store.

iOS installer

Next, we are going to generate an installer for iOS using Xcode. You can perform the following steps:

1. Open a new terminal/prompt at the root of the project.
2. Remove unwanted plugins:

```
ionic plugin rm cordova-plugin-console
```

3. Now, run this:

```
ionic build -release ios
```

4. Navigate to the `platforms/ios` folder and launch `projectname.xcodeproj` using Xcode.
5. Once the project is inside Xcode and you have selected **iOS Device** option, from the navigation menu select **Product** and then **Archive**.

If you do not see the **Archive** option enabled, refer to `http://stackoverflow.com/a/18791703`.

6. Next, from the navigation menu select **Window** and select **Organizer**. You will be shown a list of archives created.

7. Click on the archive snapshot you have created now, and click on **Submit to App Store**. The validation of your account is performed and then the app will be uploaded to Apple Store.
8. Finally, you need to log into the Apple Store to set up screenshots, description, and so on.

The Ionic package

At the time of writing, the Ionic package task is still in beta. Hence, I have included it last.

Uploading the project to Ionic cloud

Using Ionic cloud services to generate an installer is quite simple. First we upload our app to our Ionic account by running:

```
ionic upload
```

> Log in to your Ionic account before executing the preceding command.
> If your project has sensitive information, cross-check with the Ionic license before uploading the app to the cloud.

Once the app is uploaded, an app ID will be generated for your app. You can find the app ID in the `ionic.project` file located at the root of the project.

Generating the required keys

You need to follow *Step 5* of the *Android Installer* section, to get the `keystore` file.

Next, we use the `ionic package` command to generate the installer, as shown here:

```
ionic package <options> [debug | release] [ios | android]
```

Then options will consist of the following:

```
package [options] <MODE> <PLATFORM> .......  Package an app using the Ionic Build service (beta)
                                             <MODE> "debug" or "release"
                                             <PLATFORM> "ios" or "android"
      [--android-keystore-file|-k]  .....    Android keystore file
      [--android-keystore-alias|-a]  ....    Android keystore alias
      [--android-keystore-password|-w]  .    Android keystore password
      [--android-key-password|-r]  ......    Android key password
      [--ios-certificate-file|-c]  ......    iOS certificate file
      [--ios-certificate-password|-d]  ..    iOS certificate password
      [--ios-profile-file|-f]  ..........    iOS profile file
      [--output|-o]  ....................    Path to save the packaged app
      [--no-email|-n]  ..................    Do not send a build package email
      [--clear-signing|-l]  .............    Clear out all signing data from Ionic server
      [--email|-e]  .....................    Ionic account email
      [--password|-p]  ..................    Ionic account password
```

For instance, if you would like to generate an installer for Android in release mode, it will be as follows:

```
ionic package release android -k app-name-release-key.keystore -a my-
ionic-app -w 12345678 -r 12345678 -o ./ -e
arvind.ravulavaru@gmail.com -p 12345678
```

We are running the preceding command from inside the `deploy-keys` folder.

Similarly, the preceding command for iOS will be:

```
ionic package release ios -c certificate-file -d password -f
profilefile -o ./ -e arvind.ravulavaru@gmail.com -p 12345678
```

The `ionic package` command is removed as of Ionic CLI 1.5.2. You can read about this at `https://github.com/driftyco/ionic-cli/issues/214#issuecomment-109349399`.

Summary

With this, we conclude our Ionic journey. To quickly summarize, we started understanding why we should use AngularJS. Then, we saw how Mobile Hybrid apps work and where Cordova and Ionic fit in. Next, we looked at various Ionic templates and went through Ionic CSS components, and Ionic directives and services. Using this knowledge, we built an Ionic client for a secure REST API. Next, we went through Cordova and ngCordova and saw how to work with them. We built a chat application using the best of Ionic and Cordova. Finally, we saw how to generate installers for the apps we have built and put them in the app store.

Additional Topics and Tips

The main aim of this book is to get you (the readers) acquainted with as much of Ionic as possible. So, I have followed an incremental approach from *Chapter 1-9*, from the basics of Cordova to building an app with AngularJS, Ionic, and Cordova. We were pretty much focused on learning Ionic with the bare minimums.

In this appendix, we will explore a few more options of the Ionic CLI: Ionic.io, ionic-box and Sublime Text plugins that you can explore.

For this appendix, you can chat with the author and clear up your queries at GitHub (`https://github.com/learning-ionic/Appendix`).

Ionic CLI

Ionic CLI is growing more powerful day-by-day. At the time of writing, the latest version of Ionic CLI is 1.5.5. Since we have been using Ionic CLI 1.5.0 throughout the book, I will be talking about the options from this.

Ionic login

You can log in to your Ionic cloud account in any one of three ways.

First, using a prompt:

```
ionic login
```

Second, without a prompt:

```
ionic login --email arvind.ravulavaru@gmail.com --password 12345678
```

Finally, using environment variables. You can set `IONIC_EMAIL` and `IONIC_PASSWORD` as environment variables and Ionic CLI will pick them up, without prompting. This could be considered a rather unsafe option, as the password would be stored in plain text.

You need to have an Ionic.io account for the authentication to succeed.

Ionic start task

First we are going to take a look at the **No Cordova** flag option.

No Cordova flag

The `Ionic start` task is one of the simplest ways to scaffold a new Ionic application. In this book, we have used `Ionic start` to always create a new Cordova/Ionic project. But we know that Ionic can be used without Cordova as well.

To scaffold an Ionic project without Cordova, you need to run the `Ionic start` with a `-w` flag or `–no-cordova` flag:

```
ionic start -a "My Mobile Web App" -i app.web.mymobile -w
myMobileWebApp maps
```

The generated project would look like this:

```
.
└── myMobileWebApp
    ├── bower.json
    ├── gulpfile.js
    ├── ionic.project
    ├── package.json
    ├── scss
    │   └── ionic.app.scss
    └── www
        ├── css
        ├── img
        ├── index.html
        ├── js
        ├── lib
        └── templates
```

Now, as usual, you can use the `cd` command to go to the `myMobileWebApp` folder and run `ionic serve`.

Initialize a project with SCSS support

To initialize a project with SCSS enabled by default, you can run the `ionic start` task with a `-s` or a `–sass` flag:

```
ionic start -a "Example 1" -i app.one.example --sass example1 blank
```

Listing all Ionic templates

To view the list of all templates up for grabs, run `ionic start` with a `-l` or a `--list` flag:

```
ionic start -l
```

As of today, these are the available templates:

```
blank ................ A blank starter project for Ionic
complex-list ......... A complex list starter template
maps ................. An Ionic starter project using Google Maps and a
side menu
salesforce ........... A starter project for Ionic and Salesforce
sidemenu ............. A starting project for Ionic using a side menu
with navigation in the content area
tabs ................. A starting project for Ionic using a simple tabbed
interface
tests ................ A test of different kinds of page navigation
```

At the time of writing this chapter, the `complex-list` template is still a blank template and the `tests` template is used internally by the core team for testing purposes.

App ID

If you are using the Ionic cloud services, you will be assigned an app ID for every project you create on the cloud (refer to the *Ionic.io apps* section further down for more information). This app id will reside in the `ionic.project` file, present at the root of the project.

When you scaffold a new project, the app ID is empty. If you would like to associate the currently scaffolding project to an existing app in the cloud, you can run the `ionic start` task with the `--io-app-id` flag and pass it the cloud-generated app ID:

```
ionic start -a "Example 2" -i app.two.example --io-app-id "b82348b5"
example2 blank
```

Now, the `ionic.project` looks like this:

```
{
  "name": "Example 2",
  "app_id": "b82348b5"
}
```

Ionic link

The locally scaffolded project can be linked to a cloud project (refer to the *Ionic.io apps* section for more information) at any time by running this:

```
ionic link b82348b5
```

You can also remove the existing app ID by running this:

```
ionic link --reset
```

Ionic info

To view the installed libraries and their versions, run this:

```
ionic info
```

The information looks like this:

```
Cordova CLI: 5.0.0

Gulp version:  CLI version 3.8.11

Gulp local:

Ionic Version: 1.0.0

Ionic CLI Version: 1.5.0

Ionic App Lib Version: 0.1.0

ios-deploy version: 1.7.0

ios-sim version: 3.1.1

OS: Mac OS X Yosemite

Node Version: v0.12.2

Xcode version: Xcode 6.3.2 Build version 6D2105
```

Ionic templates

To view the list of available templates, you can either use the start task or the templates task.

```
ionic templates
```

Ionic browsers

By default, Ionic uses the OS-specific browser to render the contents in web view. You can replace this default browser with Crosswalk (`https://crosswalk-project.org/`) or Crosswalk lite (`https://github.com/crosswalk-project/crosswalk-website/wiki/Crosswalk-Project-Lite`) to get a better user experience and support for modern features. As of today, you can only add these two browsers. You can view the list of supported browsers by running this:

```
ionic browser list
```

Then, you should see:

```
iOS - Browsers Listing:
Not Available Yet - WKWebView
Not Available Yet - UIWebView



Android - Browsers Listing:
Available - Crosswalk - ionic browser add crosswalk
        Version 8.37.189.14
        Version 9.38.208.10
        Version 10.39.235.15
        Version 11.40.277.7
        Version 12.41.296.5
 (beta)  Version 13.42.319.6
 (canary) Version 14.42.334.0

Available - Crosswalk-lite - ionic browser add crosswalk-lite
 (canary) Version 10.39.234.
 (canary) Version 10.39.236.1

Available - Browser (default) - ionic browser revert android
Not Available Yet - GeckoView
```

As you can see, there is no support for `WKWebView` and `UIWebView` yet. But for Android-specific apps, you can use Crosswalk. To add Crosswalk to an existing project (Example 3), run:

```
ionic browser add crosswalk
```

Once the browser is successfully added, you can verify it in the `ionic.project` file.

To revert to the default browser, run this:

```
ionic browser revert android
```

Ionic lib

You can upgrade to the latest version of Ionic library by running this:

```
ionic lib update
```

You can also pass in a version to which the library needs to be updated:

```
ionic lib update -v 1.0.0-rc.1
```

Ionic state

Using the Ionic state task, you can manage the state of your Ionic project. Let's say that you are adding a couple of plugins and platforms to test something in your Ionic app; but you would not like to use these if they fail. In that case, you would use the save and restore task.

You can avoid saving the plugins or platforms to the `package.json` file by running them with a `--nosave` flag:

```
ionic plugin add cordova-plugin-console --nosave
```

You have tested your app with a couple of new plugins (adding them using a `--nosave` flag) and things seem to work fine. Now, you want to add them to your `package.json`. For that, run this:

```
ionic state save
```

This task looks up your installed plugins and platforms and then adds the required information to the `package.json` file. Optionally, you can save only plugins or platforms by running the preceding task with a `--plugins` or `--platforms` flag respectively.

If you have added a bunch of plugins and things are not working as expected, you can reset to the previous state by running this:

```
ionic state reset
```

If you would like to restore your application to a list of Cordova plugins and platforms, you can update these in `package.json` and run this:

```
ionic state restore
```

The reset task deletes the platforms and plugins folders and installs them again, whereas restore only restores the missing platforms and plugins in the platforms and plugins folders.

Ionic ions

According to the ions CLI:

> *"Ionic ions are a curated collection of useful addons, components, and ux interactions for extending ionic."*

As of today, there are four ions. You can view the list of ions by running this:

```
ionic ions
```

The options will be:

```
Header Shrink ........ 'ionic add ionic-ion-header-shrink'
A shrinking header effect like Facebook's


Android Drawer ....... 'ionic add ionic-ion-drawer'
Android-style drawer menu


iOS Rounded Buttons .. 'ionic add ionic-ion-ios-buttons'
iOS "Squircle" style icons


Swipeable Cards ...... 'ionic add ionic-ion-swipe-cards'
Swiping interaction as seen in Jelly


Tinder Cards ......... 'ionic add ionic-ion-tinder-cards'
Tinder style card swiping interaction
```

You can add an ion using `Add task` as shown in the response. Once an ion is added, you can navigate to the `www/lib/` folder and into the `ion` folder and check out the components.

For instance, if we have scaffolded a blank project (`example4`), you can add the Swipe Cards ion by running:

```
ionic add ionic-ion-swipe-cards
```

Now, if you navigate to the `www/lib/ionic-ion-swipe-cards` folder, you will find the bower component. And in the `example4` folder, you can find more information on how to set it up.

You can remove an added ion by running this:

```
ionic rm ionic-ion-swipe-cards
```

The `ionic add` and `ionic rm` tasks can be used to add and remove bower packages as well.

Ionic resources

When you add a new platform, by default the `resources` folder is created with icons and splash screens for the given platform. These icons and splash screens are default images. If you would like to use your logo/icon for the project, all you need to do is run the Ionic resources task.

This task will look for an image named `icon.png` inside the `resources` folder to create icons for all devices for that OS, and `splash.png` inside the `resources` folder to create splash screens for all the devices for that OS.

You can replace these two images with your brand images and run this:

```
ionic resources
```

If you only want to convert icons, you can pass in an `-i` flag; to only convert splash screens, use the `-s` flag.

> You can also use `.png`, `.psd` (sample template: `http://code.ionicframework.com/resources/icon.psd` and `http://code.ionicframework.com/resources/splash.psd`), or `.ai` files as well to generate icons from. You can find more information at `http://blog.ionic.io/automating-icons-and-splash-screens/`.

Ionic server, emulate, and run

Ionic provides an easy way to run your Ionic apps in browsers, emulators, and devices. Each of these three tasks comes with a bunch of useful options.

If you want live reload to be running on an emulator as well as the actual device, while debugging, use the `-l` flag for live reload and `-c` to enable printing JavaScript console errors in the prompt. This is by far the best and most used utility in the Ionic CLI. This task saves a lot of your debugging time:

```
ionic serve -l -c
ionic emulate -l -c
ionic run -l -c
```

You can use the following flags while working with `ionic serve`:

```
serve [options] ............................ Start a local development server for app dev/testing
      [--consolelogs|-c] .................. Print app console logs to Ionic CLI
      [--serverlogs|-s] ................... Print dev server logs to Ionic CLI
      [--port|-p] ......................... Dev server HTTP port (8100 default)
      [--livereload-port|-r] .............. Live Reload port (35729 default)
      [--nobrowser|-b] .................... Disable launching a browser
      [--nolivereload|-d] ................. Do not start live reload
      [--noproxy|-x] ...................... Do not add proxies
      [--address] ......................... Use specific address or return with failure
      [--all|-a] .......................... Have the server listen on all addresses (0.0.0.0)
      [--browser|-w] ...................... Specifies the browser to use (safari, firefox, chrome)
      [--browseroption|-o] ................ Specifies a path to open to (/#/tab/dash)
      [--lab|-l] .......................... Test your apps on multiple screen sizes and platform types
      [--nogulp] .......................... Disable running gulp during serve
      [--platform|-t] ..................... Start serve with a specific platform (ios/android)
```

If your app has a different look and feel for Android and iOS, you can test both the apps at once by running this:

```
ionic serve -l
```

You can explore other options listed earlier according to your requirements. While working with ionic run and emulate, you can use the following options:

```
run [options] <PLATFORM> ..................  Run an Ionic project on a connected device
    [--livereload|-l] ....................  Live reload app dev files from the device (beta)
    [--port|-p] ..........................  Dev server HTTP port (8100 default, livereload req.)
    [--livereload-port|-r] ...............  Live Reload port (35729 default, livereload req.)
    [--consolelogs|-c] ...................  Print app console logs to Ionic CLI (livereload req.)
    [--serverlogs|-s] ....................  Print dev server logs to Ionic CLI (livereload req.)
    [--debug|--release]
    [--device|--emulator|--target=FOO]

emulate [options] <PLATFORM> ..............  Emulate an Ionic project on a simulator or emulator
        [--livereload|-l] ................  Live reload app dev files from the device (beta)
        [--port|-p] ......................  Dev server HTTP port (8100 default, livereload req.)
        [--livereload-port|-r] ...........  Live Reload port (35729 default, livereload req.)
        [--consolelogs|-c] ...............  Print app console logs to Ionic CLI (livereload req.)
        [--serverlogs|-s] ................  Print dev server logs to Ionic CLI (livereload req.)
        [--nohooks|-n] ...................  Do not add default Ionic hooks for Cordova
        [--debug|--release]
        [--device|--emulator|--target=FOO]
```

Quite self-explanatory!

Ionic upload and share

You can upload the current Ionic project to your Ionic.io account by running this:

```
ionic upload
```

You need to have an Ionic.io account to work with this feature.

Once the app is uploaded, you can head to `https://apps.ionic.io/apps` to view the newly updated app. You can share this app with anyone using the share task and passing in the e-mail address of the intended person; for example:

```
ionic share arvind.ravulavaru@gmail.com
```

Ionic view

You can use Ionic view to preview your app on a device. Once your app is uploaded to your Ionic.io account, you can download the Ionic View app for Android or iOS and you can preview the app on the device.

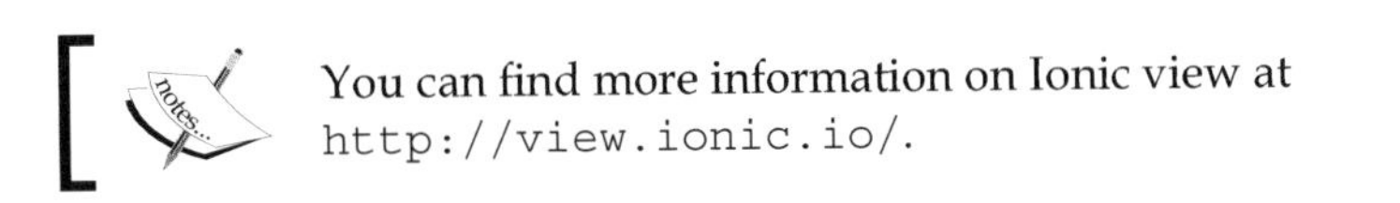

You can find more information on Ionic view at `http://view.ionic.io/`.

Ionic help and docs

At any point in time, you can view the list of all Ionic CLI tasks by running this:

```
ionic -h
```

You can open the docs page by running this:

```
ionic docs
```

To view the list of available docs, you can run this:

```
ionic docs ls
```

Also, to open a specific doc (in this case, `ionicBody`), you can run this:

```
ionic docs ionicBody
```

Ionic Creator

Ionic Creator is another handy tool that you can use to quickly build Ionic UI. You can head to `http://creator.ionic.io/` and start using the tool. You will need an Ionic.io account to work with this tool.

Using Ionic Creator, you can quickly drag-and-drop Ionic components and start building a prototype for your app. This app is persisted in the cloud and you can access this at any time and make modifications.

Ionic Creator (in the process of designing an app) will look like this:

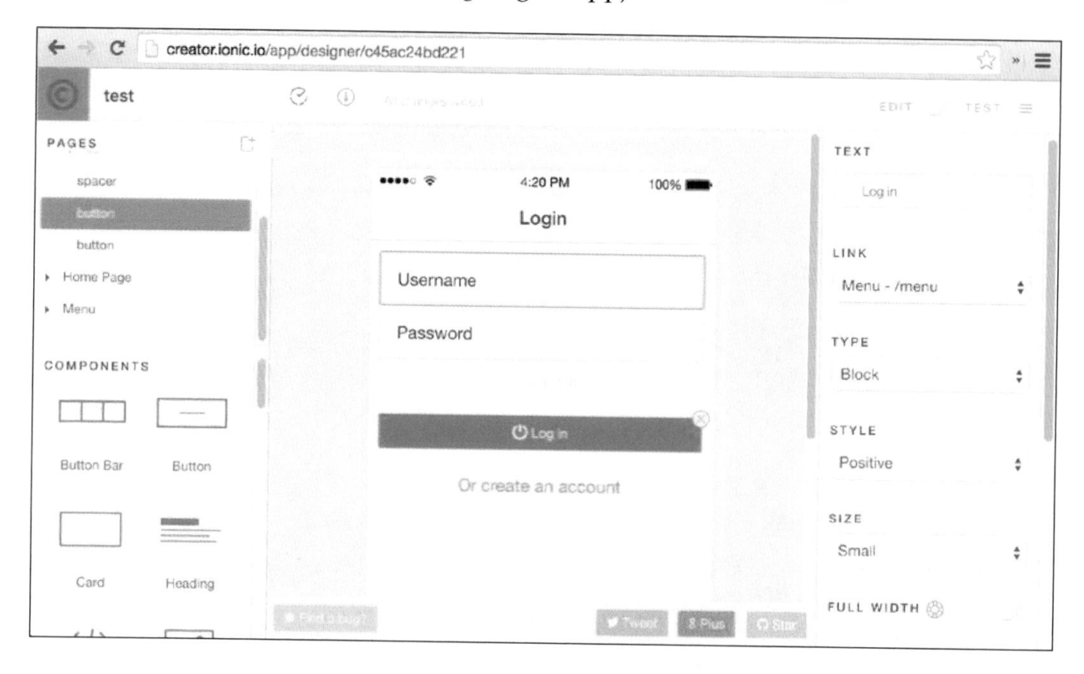

Once you are done designing your app, you can download the app using any of these three ways:

- First, using Ionic CLI:

```
ionic start [appName] creator:c45ac24bd221
```

- Second, downloading the ZIP file of the project
- Finally, downloading the pure HTML

You can find these options when you click on the (export) icon, present at the top left of the page.

You can read more about Ionic Creator at http://thejackalofjavascript.com/ionic-creator-beta/.

Ionic.io apps

You can create and manage your Ionic apps at `https://apps.ionic.io/apps`. In the preceding tasks, the app ID we were referring to is the app ID that gets generated when we create a new app using the `https://apps.ionic.io/apps` interface.

You can create a new app by clicking on the **New App** button inside the `https://apps.ionic.io/apps` page. Once the app is created, you can click on the app name and then you will be taken to the app details page.

You can update the app settings by clicking on the **Settings** link on the app details page.

You can read more about setting up Ionic apps at `http://docs.ionic.io/v1.0/docs/io-quick-start`.

As of today, apps created with Ionic Creator do not appear in `https://apps.ionic.io/apps`.

Ionic Push

You can add push notifications to your Ionic app by adding the Push plugin (`https://github.com/phonegap-build/PushPlugin`) and configuring it. Or you can use the push template from Ionic to do so:

```
ionic add ionic-service-core
ionic add ionic-service-push
ionic start myPushApp push
cd myPushApp
ionic plugin add https://github.com/phonegap-build/PushPlugin.git
ionic upload
```

Now, you can head back to the `app.ionic.io` page and click on the setting for the preceding app. In `www/js/app.js`, you will find the `config` section, which you can update with the values from the app settings page:

```
.config(['$ionicAppProvider', function($ionicAppProvider) {
  // Identify app
  $ionicAppProvider.identify({
    // The App ID for the server
    app_id: 'YOUR_APP_ID',
    // The API key all services will use for this app
    api_key: 'YOUR_PUBLIC_API_KEY'
  });
}])
```

Then, you can follow the Android Push setup guide (`http://docs.ionic.io/v1.0/docs/push-android-setup`) or the iOS push setup guide (`http://docs.ionic.io/v1.0/docs/push-ios-setup`) to implement the Push notifications.

You can find more information about integrating push notifications to your app at `http://docs.ionic.io/v1.0/docs/push-from-scratch`.

Ionic Deploy

Ionic Deploy is one of the Ionic.io services. Ionic Deploy lets you deploy the new changes to your app without submitting the app to App stores. This saves a lot of time for the developers to push new changes to their users.

Changes that do not need a binary update can only be pushed—for example, assets such as HTML, CSS, JavaScript, and images.

As of today, Ionic Deploy is in Alpha.

You can read more about Ionic deploy at `http://blog.ionic.io/announcing-ionic-deploy-alpha-update-your-app-without-waiting/` and `http://docs.ionic.io/v1.0/docs/deploy-from-scratch`.

Ionic Vagrant box

If your team has multiple developers and each of them uses a different environment to develop Ionic apps, you can use Ionic Vagrant box to have a unified development environment.

If you are new to Vagrant, check out: `http://vagrantup.com` and you can find more information on ionic-box at `https://github.com/driftyco/ionic-box`.

Ionic Sublime Text plugins

If you are a Sublime Text user and would like to have Ionic autocomplete/snippets, you can install the following packages:

- Ionic snippets: `https://packagecontrol.io/packages/Ionic%20Snippets`
- Ionic Framework Snippets: `https://packagecontrol.io/packages/Ionic%20Framework%20Snippets`
- Ionic Framework Extended Autocomplete: `https://packagecontrol.io/packages/Ionic%20Framework%20Extended%20Autocomplete`

Summary

With this, we conclude the *Learning Ionic* book. I hope you enjoyed learning Ionic as much as I have enjoyed explaining it.

Feel free to follow me on Twitter: `https://twitter.com/arvindr21` and on GitHub: `https://github.com/arvindr21` (shameless publicity :D).

Thanks!

Index

Symbols

A

B

C

D

E

F

G

J

L

M

N

O

P

R

S

T

U

V

W

X

Y

Thank you for buying
Learning Ionic

About Packt Publishing

Packt, pronounced 'packed', published its first book, *Mastering phpMyAdmin for Effective MySQL Management*, in April 2004, and subsequently continued to specialize in publishing highly focused books on specific technologies and solutions.

Our books and publications share the experiences of your fellow IT professionals in adapting and customizing today's systems, applications, and frameworks. Our solution-based books give you the knowledge and power to customize the software and technologies you're using to get the job done. Packt books are more specific and less general than the IT books you have seen in the past. Our unique business model allows us to bring you more focused information, giving you more of what you need to know, and less of what you don't.

Packt is a modern yet unique publishing company that focuses on producing quality, cutting-edge books for communities of developers, administrators, and newbies alike. For more information, please visit our website at `www.packtpub.com`.

About Packt Open Source

In 2010, Packt launched two new brands, Packt Open Source and Packt Enterprise, in order to continue its focus on specialization. This book is part of the Packt Open Source brand, home to books published on software built around open source licenses, and offering information to anybody from advanced developers to budding web designers. The Open Source brand also runs Packt's Open Source Royalty Scheme, by which Packt gives a royalty to each open source project about whose software a book is sold.

Writing for Packt

We welcome all inquiries from people who are interested in authoring. Book proposals should be sent to `author@packtpub.com`. If your book idea is still at an early stage and you would like to discuss it first before writing a formal book proposal, then please contact us; one of our commissioning editors will get in touch with you.

We're not just looking for published authors; if you have strong technical skills but no writing experience, our experienced editors can help you develop a writing career, or simply get some additional reward for your expertise.

Mastering Spring Application Development

ISBN: 978-1-78398-732-0 Paperback: 288 pages

Gain expertise in developing and caching your applications running on the JVM with Spring

1. Build full-featured web applications, such as Spring MVC applications, efficiently that will get you up and running with Spring web development.

2. Reuse working code snippets handy for integration scenarios such as Twitter, e-mail, FTP, databases, and many others.

3. An advanced guide which includes Java programs to integrate Spring with Thymeleaf.

WordPress Web Application Development - Second Edition

ISBN: 978-1-78217-439-4 Paperback: 404 pages

Build rapid web applications with cutting-edge technologies using WordPress

1. Develop rapid web applications using the core features of WordPress.

2. Explore various workaround techniques to prevent maintenance nightmares by identifying the limitations of WordPress.

3. A practical guide filled with real-world scenarios that will guide you through how to build modular and scalar applications.

Please check **www.PacktPub.com** for information on our titles

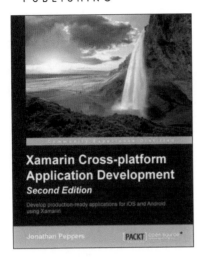

Made in the USA
Lexington, KY
17 October 2016